The Path of Beauty
A Study of Chinese Aesthetics

LI ZEHOU

TRANSLATED BY GONG LIZENG

HONG KONG
OXFORD UNIVERSITY PRESS
OXFORD   NEW YORK
1994

Oxford University Press

Oxford   New York
Athens   Auckland   Bangkok   Bombay
Calcutta   Cape Town   Dar es Salaam Delhi
Florence   Hong Kong   Istanbul   Karachi
Kuala Lumpur   Madras   Madrid Melbourne
Mexico City   Nairobi   Paris   Singapore
Taipei   Tokyo   Toronto

and associated companies in
Berlin   Ibadan

Oxford is a trade mark of Oxford University Press

First published 1994

Published in the United States
by Oxford University Press, New York

British Library Cataloguing in Publication Data
available

Library of Congress Cataloging-in-Publication Data
Li, Tse-hou.
[Mei ti li ch'eng. English]
The path of beauty : a study of Chinese aesthetics /
Li Zehou ; translated by Gong Lizeng.
p.   cm.
Includes bibliographical references and index.
ISBN 0-19-586526-X
1. Aesthetics, Chinese.   I. Title.
BH221.C6L5   1994   93-48191
700′.951—dc20   CIP

Printed in Hong Kong
Published by Oxford University Press (Hong Kong) Ltd
18/F Warwick House, Taikoo Place, 979 King's Road, Quarry Bay,
Hong Kong

Preface

MORE than a decade has passed since the Chinese Edition of *The Path of Beauty* was first published in 1981. Since then some 200,000 copies of the book have been printed and an unknown number of at least three pirated editions are circulating around Taiwan. This is probably the most widely circulated of my books, particularly among the younger generation, and I feel greatly honoured for it.

I am delighted, though still somewhat mystified that this one, of all my books, has met with such enduring popularity. Many of the ideas and concepts in the book represent the culmination of long years of thought and development, recorded in notes I had made over the years. The actual process of writing, however, flew quickly. I did not pay strict homage to the commonly accepted forms, conventional methods, standard styles, or other rules for the treatment of Chinese classical art and literature. Instead, the work exceeds the traditional boundaries of literature and art by teaching on interrelated subjects, such as philosophy and history, at the same time. This sort of interdisciplinary approach was a novel and serious breach of conventions in China at that time. As a result, although the book met with warm welcome, it also encountered harsh criticism from the orthodox ideologists. Nevertheless, I was pleased with the outcome and felt happy about my 'rebellion'.

This book is neither a detailed historical study, nor an in-depth analysis of texts, but rather an impressionistic overview. If it enlightens readers on the ancient Chinese sense of beauty and enables them to acquire an aesthetic appreciation of Chinese literature and art, then I will have achieved my aim.

I would like to express my gratitude to Oxford University Press for publishing the English version in a paperback edition and to thank the Oxford editors for their support.

LI ZEHOU
Colorado Springs, Colorado
28 August 1993

Contents

A Brief Chronology of Chinese History

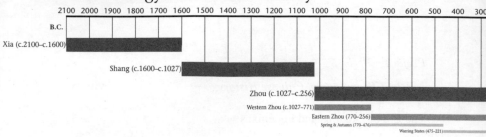

| | 2100 | 2000 | 1900 | 1800 | 1700 | 1600 | 1500 | 1400 | 1300 | 1200 | 1100 | 1000 | 900 | 800 | 700 | 600 | 500 | 400 | 300 |

B.C.

Xia (c.2100–c.1600)

Shang (c.1600–c.1027)

Zhou (c.1027–c.256)

Western Zhou (c.1027–771)

Eastern Zhou (770–256)

Spring & Autumn (770–476)

Warring States (475–221)

Qin (221–2

Han (206 B.C.–220

Western Han (206 B.C.–8

Table of Paleothetic Men and Cultures in China

Years Before the Present				
1,700,000		Yuanmou man	Remains discovered at Yuanmou, Yunnan Province, in 1965
600,000	Lantian culture	Lantian man	Remains first discovered at Lantian, Shaanxi Province, in 1963–4
500,000	Zhoukoudian culture	Peking man	Remains first discovered at Longgushan Mountain, Zhoukoudian, southwest of Beijing, in 1927
		Maba man	Remains discovered at Maba village, Shaoguan, Guangdong Province, in 1958
		Changyang man	Remains discovered at Changyang, Hubei Province, in 1956
100,000	Dingcun culture	Dingcun man	Remains discovered at Dingcun village, Xiangfen, Shanxi Province, in 1954
	Hetao culture	Hetao man	Remains first discovered at the Salawusu River in Inner Mongolia in 1922; belongs to the species *Homo Sapiens*
	Xiaonanhai culture		Remains discovered at Xiaonanhai, Anyang, Henan Province, in 1960
	Upper Cave culture	Upper Cave man	Remains discovered in a cave at Longgushan Mountain, Zhoukoudian, southwest of Beijing, in 1933
		Liujiang man	Remains discovered at Liujiang, Guangxi Province, in 1958
10,000		Ziyang man	Remains discovered at Ziyang, Sichuan Province, in 1951

Table of Neolithic Cultures in China

	B.C. 4000	3500	3000	2500	2000
Yangshao culture Distributed mainly along the upper and middle reaches of the Yellow River. Remains first discovered at Yangshao village, Mianchi, Henan Province, in 1921.	Banpo remains	Hougang remains	Miaodigou remains Dahecun remains	Caojiazui remains (belongs to Majiayao culture)	Majiawan remains (belongs to Ba Qinggangcha remains (belongs to Ba
Longshan culture Distributed mainly along the middle and lower reaches of the Yellow River. Remains first discovered at Chengziya of Longshan town, Zhangqiu, Shandong Province, in 1928.				Dawenkou remains	Miaodigou remains (second stage) Hougang remains
Qingliangang culture Distributed mainly over the lower reaches of the Yangtse and Huai rivers. Remains first discovered at Qingliangang, Huai'an, Jiangsu Province, in 1951.	Dadunzi remains	Caoxieshan remains Songze remains			
Liangzhu culture Distributed mainly along the southeastern coast. Remains first discovered at Liangzhu town, Hangzhou, Zhejiang Province, in 1938.				Qianshanyang remains	Quemuqia
Qujialing culture Distributed mainly on the alluvial plains of the Yangtse and Han rivers. Remains first discovered at Qujialing , Jingshan, Hubei Province, in 1955.				Huanglianshu remains	Qujialing remains
Microlithic culture* Distributed mainly in the northeast, Inner Mongolia, Ningxia, Xinjiang, Tibet.	Jiangjialing remains	Fuhegoumen remains		Hongshan culture	

*In light of recent discoveries, some archaeologists question whether the Microlithic can still be seen as a type or stage of Neolithic culture.

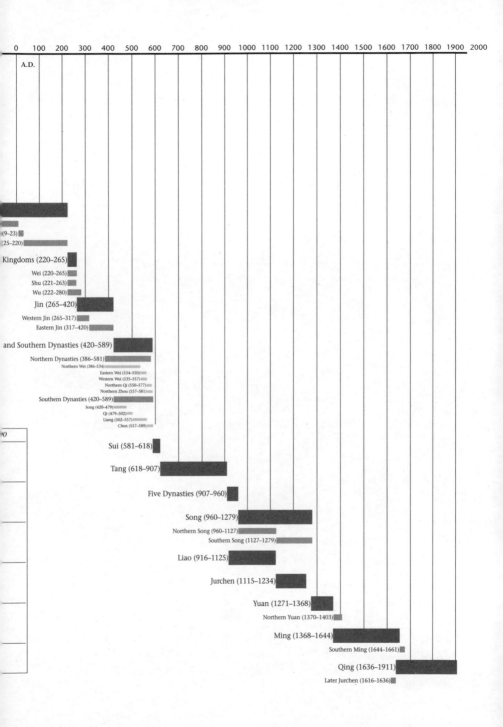

THE PATH OF BEAUTY

1

The Era of Dragons and Phoenixes

Totems of Remote Antiquity

RECENT discoveries have confirmed that China's prehistoric culture is much older and far more complex than has hitherto been assumed. Excavations of Neolithic sites made during the 1970s at Cishan, Hebei Province, and at Xinzheng and Mixian, Henan Province, place the dawn of Chinese civilization at about 6,000 B.C.

The beginnings of Chinese culture can be traced back to the Paleolithic Age, to the days of the Yuanmou man (about 1.7 million years ago) in the south, and Lantian man (600,000 years ago) and Upper Cave man (20,000 to 30,000 years ago) in the north. Although the Chinese equivalent of France's Lascaux cave murals has yet to be discovered, the stone tools found at these sites reveal a rudimentary sense of form and knowledge of the properties of materials. Peking man's tools, 500,000 years old, do not seem to have any fixed form, but those of Shanxi Province's Dingcun man (100,000 years ago) were already somewhat standardized into pointed, round, or oval shapes.

By the time of Upper Cave man, not only had stone tools become uniform and regular in shape, but polished, pierced, and inscribed bone implements and a large number of so-called 'ornamental' objects had appeared.

The ornamental objects included small pebbles and stone beads drilled with holes, pierced canine teeth of the fox, deer, and badger, carved bones, pierced clamshells, and drilled upper eye-socket bones of the black carp. All are of fine workmanship. The pebble ornaments were made of pale green igneous rock with holes drilled from opposite sides. Only regularly shaped pieces were used. The finished products resemble the heart-shaped pendants sometimes worn by women today.

The beads were made of small pieces of ground-down limestone drilled with holes through the centre, while the animal teeth were pierced by boring from opposite sides of the root through the pulp area. Nearly all the holes are stained red on the inside, suggesting that the material used to string them had been dyed with red iron ore.

These archaeological discoveries show that even the earliest humans had a dim understanding of art—that they loved and appreciated smooth and regular forms and clear and distinct colours, and took pleasure in stringing together objects of the same kind or size.

But we must remember that the mere use of tools and the conscious fashioning of ornamental objects were not only separated from each other by hundreds of thousands of years, but are also basically different in nature. Though both can be said to be 'useful,' the usefulness of tools is real while that of ornaments is largely illusory—that is, their purpose is, and always has been, subjective or imaginary. The need for regularity of form in tools is obvious, because it enhances the rhythm, evenness, and smoothness of labour. Tools are the products of material production. But ornamentation is spiritual production, and ornaments are products of ideas and imagination. Useful products like tools are symbols of social life. They are the means of survival, concentrated expressions of human needs. Ornamental objects, however, are symbols and crystallizations of human fantasies and ideas.

The creation and use of tools, along with the evolution of the human body and the proliferation of races, constituted the material basis of primitive society, while the creation of ornamental objects represented the embryonic stirrings of sentiments and ideas that would develop into religion, art, and philosophy. Such primitive activities of the Upper Cave men as scattering red mineral powder beside corpses and making the various kinds of ornaments described above were the beginnings of consciousness and ideas that transcended the material in human society. The rites and magic practiced in primitive society, that is, the ancient worship of totems, was a more matured form of such activities.

Upper Cave men dyed their clothes with red iron ore and scattered red powder beside their dead because that particular colour, red, produced more than just a stimulating effect on the physiological experience of humans, an effect that could also be produced on animals. It possessed or provided a certain conceptual quality which animals could never perceive or share. Primitive humans used and wore red not out of an animal-like physiological reaction to it, but because the actions associated with its use had taken on a socially shared symbolic significance. In other words, human imagination had invested the colour with a unique symbolic, conceptual quality; consequently, what red produced in humans of that period was not just sensory pleasure but an imaginative and conceptual response. It could be said that humanity's ideological activities, as distinguished from the making of tools and the process of labour, began at this point. Though these activities were, like the European cave murals, a primitive form of art, they began as expressions of magic and rites. The use of red by Upper Cave men was not for aesthetic purposes. Aesthetics, or art, was not yet an independent or distinct field of human endeavour; it was still concealed within the totemic activities of various kinds of primitive magic.

The totemic rites and magic of antiquity have been lost for so long that it is hard to say what their forms, content, and patterns were. As a poem says: 'Scenes and sentiments like these are what memories are made of, were they not lost in the dust of time.' Perhaps the only way we can begin to guess at what those ancient rites were like is by referring to the myths, legends, and hearsay that have been handed down to the present. Though these have been reshaped, stretched, and altered from generation to generation, they may still partially reflect the imagination of primitive men and their concept of symbols.

In Chinese mythology, the most popular and copious legends, after the epoch of Suiren, the creature who obtained fire by drilling wood (this may have been Peking man, who knew how to use fire), dealt with Nuwa and Fuxi. Some excerpts from old books are quoted below:

Nuwa was an ancient goddess who transformed the whole universe. (*Shouwen Jiezi*, or *Book of Chinese Characters and Phrases*, one of the earliest Chinese lexicons, c. A.D. 100)

At one point in remote antiquity, the four corners of the earth collapsed, the land split open, the sky no longer covered the earth, and the earth ceased its cycles of production. . . . Nuwa melted coloured rocks, with which she patched up the sky; she cut off the legs of a giant turtle and used them to prop up the corners of the earth. (*Huainanzi*, or *The Works of the Huainan King*, compiled in 139 B.C.)

It is said that when heaven and earth were first formed, there were no people. Nuwa made men out of clay. (*Taiping Yulan*, or the *Taiping Imperial Encyclopedia*, a voluminous work of reference completed in A.D. 983)

Nuwa prayed to the gods for progeny and established the marriage system. (*Complete Book of Customs*, compiled in the third century A.D.)

In the epoch of Fuxi, the world was full of wild animals, so he taught men how to hunt. (Shi Jiao, c.390–330 B.C.: *Monarchy*)

> In ancient times Fuxi was the ruler of the world. . . . He formulated
> the Eight Diagrams . . . knotted ropes to make nets for farming and
> fishing.
> (*Book of Changes*)

From 'making men out of clay' to the establishment of the
marriage system, which may refer to the beginning of marriages outside
the clan, from 'farming and fishing' to the creation of the Eight
Diagrams (abstract symbols of magic and rites?), this story of
humanity's origins, which spanned close to a million years, was
dominated by Nuwa and Fuxi. In ancient records they were often
contemporaneous or belonged to periods that overlapped each other.
This may mean that these two beings symbolized China's earliest
civilization.

Who and what were they? If we remove the human disguise in
which they were cloaked by later generations, we may find that

Silk painting of Fuxi
(right) and Nuwa,
Tang Dynasty,
unearthed from the
remains of Gaochang,
an ancient city in
Turfan, Xinjiang.

primitive peoples saw them as giant reptiles. There are records to support this idea:

> Nuwa, ancient goddess and ruler, had the face of a human and the body of a snake; she changed her form seventy times a day.
> (*Shanhaijing*, or the *Book of Mountains and Seas*, a very ancient geography book)

> Fuxi was born in Suiren's time . . . he had a man's head and a snake's body.
> (Huangfu Shi [215–282]: *Diwang Shiji*, or *Chronicles of Legendary Emperors and Kings*)

> Nuwa . . . who inherited and continued the systems established by Fuxi . . . also had the body of a snake and the head of a human.
> (*Diwang Shiji*)

It is noteworthy that most of the gods, supernaturals, and heroes mentioned in ancient Chinese legends were beings with human heads and snake bodies. Nuwa and Fuxi were like this, and so were many others, such as Gonggong and his subjects, described in the *Book of Mountains and Seas* and other classics. Even Pangu, the fabulous being who separated heaven and earth (which, according to Chinese mythology, were originally one mass) and who appeared much later than many other legendary beings, had the same half-man, half-snake form. Though the *Book of Mountains and Seas* mentions many types of monsters, such as creatures with human heads and horses', hogs', or birds' bodies, the most prominent were the half-man, half-snake creatures:

> Between Danhuzhi and Yuti, a distance of 5,490 *li*,[1] there are twenty-five hills. The gods there all have the faces of human beings and the bodies of snakes.
> (*Beishanjing*, or *Book of the Northern Hills*)

> Between Shoushan and Yubingshan, a distance of 267 *li*, there are nine hills. All the gods there have the bodies of dragons and the faces of human beings.
> (*Zhongshanjing*, or *Book of the Central Hills*)

The gods described here were actually the totems, signs, and symbols of ancient clans. *Zhushu Jinian*, an ancient chronological record written on bamboo slips, tells us that in the epoch of Fuxi there were the so-called Long Dragon, Hidden Dragon, Domiciled Dragon, Subdued Dragon, Upper Dragon, Water Dragon, Green Dragon, Red

---

[1] One *li* equals one-third mile.

Dragon, White Dragon. This corresponds fairly closely with the descriptions in the *Book of Mountains and Seas*; they were a large group of dragons.

This geography book also describes such monsters as the Candle Dragon and Candle Shade:

> Beyond the Northwestern Sea, north of the Red Water, is the Zhangwei Mountain, on which is a god that is half human, half snake, and red all over . . . it is called the Candle Dragon.

> The god of Zhongshan Mountain is called Candle Shade. When it opens its eyes, it is day; when it closes them, it is night; when it blows, it is winter; when it exhales, it is summer. It does not eat or drink or breathe; when it does breathe, its breath is the wind. Its body is a thousand *li* long. . . . It is red and has the face of a man and the body of a snake.

These are highly elaborated images and conceptions of dragons. It may be that these monstrous dragons were the earliest brain creatures of our prehistoric ancestors—they may symbolize a common ideological or conceptual system of many clans, tribes, and tribal alliances in China over an indefinite period of time.

The dragon that has become the symbol of the Chinese nation is a snake[2] to which parts of other animals have been added. It has the body of a snake, the legs of a quadruped, the mane of a horse, the tail of a hyena, the antlers of a deer, the paws of a dog, and the scales and whiskers of a fish. This may indicate that ancient China's clans and tribes, whose totems were mainly snakes, had conquered and assimilated other clans and tribes, in the course of which the snake totem incorporated the features of other totems and gradually evolved into the 'dragon'.

From the fantastic legends of Candle Shade and Nuwa to the horned characters that symbolized dragons and snakes in oracle-bone[3] and bronze inscriptions, from the different types of dragons on ancient bronzes to records in the *Book of Changes* of dragons flying in the air, drinking in gorges, or lurking in the fields, to the images of creatures with human heads and snake bodies in Han Dynasty art, as in the silk paintings and stone carvings at Mawangdui, this fabulous creature that

---

[2] Some scholars have supposed that the origin of the dragon must be a crocodile.

[3] This refers to tortoise shells and animal bones on which are inscribed records of divinations. The earliest oracle-bone inscriptions that have been discovered date back to the Shang Dynasty.

was probably conceived in the human mind in the remote age of hunting and fishing continued to be imagined down to the era of civilization. Possessing such extraordinary vitality, it has been the object of human worship and imagination for eons and has never ceased to change, assuming a thousand-and-one forms.

We know of ancient myths and legends only from what has survived in the documents and archives of later generations. The lid of a pottery vessel in the shape of a human head with a snake body, discovered at a Neolithic site, is perhaps the earliest surviving plastic expression in China of the mythical dragons. This dragon is very primitive: crude, crawling, and sprawled upon the earth. It has not yet learned to fly, and has neither horns nor feet. But maybe its human head suggests that someday it would rise into the sky to fly, and that it would become the chief totemic banner for numerous clans, tribes, and tribal alliances in north, south, and west China.

Simultaneously with the dragons, or maybe a little later, the phoenix appeared as a totemic symbol among various tribal groups in eastern China. Despite differences in the tales of this bird and divergent descriptions of it in later generations, it is certain that the phoenix was an important totem for tribes in the east. Writings about this bird are even richer and more specific than those about the dragon:

> The phoenix is a supernatural bird. Heaven says it has the breast of a wild goose and the rump of a unicorn, the neck of a snake and the tail of a fish, the scales of a dragon and the back of a turtle, the chin of a swallow and the beak of a chicken; it possesses all the colours and comes from the country of gentlemen[4] in the east . . .
> (*Book of Chinese Characters and Phrases*)

> Heaven ordered a fabulous bird to descend on earth and give birth to the Shang Dynasty
> (*Book of Songs: Ode to the Shang*)

> In the great wilderness . . . there were nine gods who had the faces of humans and the bodies of birds. They were called the Nine Phoenixes.
> (*Book of Mountains and Seas*)

Like the description 'face of a human, body of a snake,' descriptions like 'face of a human, body of a bird,' 'a bird of many colours,' 'the male phoenix sings by itself, the phoenix dances alone' are often found in the *Book of Mountains and Seas*. And just as the

---

[4] An ideal country described in some ancient books, where people were kind and courteous and more willing to give than to take.

dragon was an enlarged, exaggerated, and deified form of the snake, so was the phoenix the deification of the bird. Neither was real—both were creatures of the imagination, products of the mind, totems used in magic and ritual. Just as there were dragon clans, so were there bird clans, whose leaders had the names of birds:

> Since the phoenix had just arrived when Shaohao[5] was enthroned, birds were used to mark the epoch; they were venerated as teachers and their names widely used as titles and appellations. The Phoenix was the official chronicler; the Crane was in charge of distribution; the Shrike was the revenue officer; the Bluebird attended to sowing and plowing; the Redbird to harvesting and storage; the Zhujiu (a kind of turtledove) was the Minister of the Land and People; the Fish Hawk was the Minister of War; the Cuckoo, the Minister of Works; the Eagle, the Criminal Judge; the Turtledove, the Minister of Building . . .
> (*Zuo Zhuan*, a commentary on the *Spring and Autumn Annals*, compiled around 400 B.C.)

The two great tribal alliances of the east and west, whose principal totemic symbols were the phoenix and dragon respectively, were gradually amalgamated and unified after a long period of ruthless warfare, slaughter, and pillage. The 'creature with the face of a human and the body of a bird treading on two red snakes' often mentioned in the *Book of Mountains and Seas*, and the saying, 'Fuxi's surname was Phoenix,' may be reflections of this struggle and amalgamation. Historical documents, relics, and studies made in later generations show that the struggle probably ended with the west, represented by the tribes of the Yan Emperor and Yellow Emperor,[6] conquering the east, represented by the Yi tribes. This may be why the snake was given wings and flew into the sky, becoming a dragon, while the phoenix underwent little transformation. But it may also be that the phoenix clans and tribes were too large and numerous to be totally assimilated by the dragon. Therefore, the phoenix, while subordinate to the dragon, retained a relative independence and its totem was preserved in an independent form down to the Warring States period and the kingdom of Chu, in whose silk paintings we still see human beings worshipping the image of the phoenix.

[5] Shaohao was the legendary chief of an ancient tribe called the Eastern Yi.

[6] These are two legendary emperors popularly regarded as the fathers of the Chinese race. Some historians identify the Yan Emperor with Shennong the Exalted Farmer.

'The Dragon Flies,' 'The Phoenix Dances'—these Chinese phrases were probably the two glorious prehistoric totemic banners that flew over the land of China from the Paleolithic Age of hunting and fishing through the Neolithic Age of farming, from matriarchal society through the patriarchal system, to the threshold of the early slave society of the Xia and Shang Dynasties.

Were the dragon and phoenix primitive art—aesthetic expressions? Yes and no. On the one hand, they were merely more developed symbols and more graphic representations than Upper Cave man's rite of scattering red powder. They were merely signs and symbols of conceptual and ideological activities. But on the other hand, the social consciousness—the passions, concepts, and psychology of primitive humans—crystallized and concentrated in these pictorial symbols invested them with a meaning and significance that was beyond pure graphic representation. Primitive humans perceived in them properties and values that transcended pure physiological responses. In other words, these natural forms were sedimented with social values and content, and man's perceptual power and sensibility had acquired a rational quality. This unquestionably was the beginning of an aesthetic awareness and artistic creation.

Primitive Songs and Dances

Primitive aesthetic awareness and artistic creation were not a will-less way of contemplation as latter-day aestheticians discussing the nature of beauty considered them to be. On the contrary, they were processes of activity full of zeal and passion. The expression 'dragons flying, phoenixes dancing' originated precisely because these imaginary creatures, as totems, symbolized and represented fanatical forms of ritual and magical activity. What evolved into the songs, dances, dramas, paintings, myths, and incantations of later generations were, in remote antiquity, an undivided body of ritual and magical activities comparable to a raging fire or drunken madness—devout but savage, serious but passionate. We must not belittle those primitive images that now look rigid and antiquated, the fantastic myths and legends, the positive-negative principles in nature, and the Eight Diagrams for divination that appear so cold and silent today. In their day they were organic components—signs and symbols—of intensely pious rites. They are frozen metaphors of songs, dances, and incantations of old that supposedly possessed magical powers. In them are crystallized the fiery passions, ideas, faith, and hopes of primitive humanity.

Primitive songs and dances are recorded in many ancient documents:

> A hundred beasts dance to the beating and clapping of stones.
> (*Book of History: Canons of Yao*)

> When there was a great drought over the land, they followed the advice of sorcerers and danced to pray for rain.
> (*Book of Rites: Administration of Music*)

> The emperor had eight sons, who initiated songs and dances.
> (*Book of Mountains and Seas: Within the Four Seas*)

> In the music of the ancient Getian clan, three people held oxtails, kicked with their feet and sang eight verses.
> (*Lu's Spring and Autumn Annals: Ancient Music*)

> Fuxi played the *qin* and *se*,[7] Shennong played the *qin* and *se*, Nuwa played the reed and bamboo pipes.
> (*Shiben*, an ancient biographical dictionary)

Such primitive songs and dances were also described in writings of later periods, which moreover stressed that music and dancing are inseparable.

> What the ear perceives in music is called sound; what the eye perceives is called countenance. Sound that is receptive to the ear can be heard, but countenance concealed in the heart is hard to perceive. And so the sages used shields, battle-axes, feathers, and banners to represent the countenance, and developed vigorous movements as an expression of feelings. Only when both sound and countenance are present is the great music complete. . . . This is the origin of dancing.
> (Du You: *Tong Dian*, Vol. 145, a Tang Dynasty treatise on Chinese systems and institutions)

Yueji (*Notes on Music*)[8] also mentions that music and dancing were linked to each other, as in the expression 'involuntarily the hands and feet are dancing [to the music].' Like 'shields, battle-axes, feathers, banners' and 'developing vigorous movements,' the expression alludes to totemic dances, to primitive songs and dances in which feathers and masks were worn.

The totemic songs and dances of remote antiquity, as forms of magic and ritual, had an ideological content and meaning, just as

---

[7] *Qin* and *se* are ancient stringed instruments that are somewhat like the zither.

[8] *Yueji* (*Notes on Music*) is a part of the Book of Rites. It consists of eleven chapters on music compiled by Liu Shang of the Western Han Dynasty.

stories, the precursors of drama and literature, did. Music and ritual were directly linked to the ascent and decline of political states. Songs, dances, music, and rites were directly and inseparably tied to the destinies of the clans and tribes which used them. In the passages quoted above, the beginnings of songs and dances and the making of musical instruments were attributed to the mythical Fuxi, Shennong, and Nuwa. This reinforces the idea that these activities originated in the remote past and all served the same totemic purposes. Jumping about (dancing), reciting or shouting (songs, poems, incantations), clapping and beating in unison (music) always occurred simultaneously, as one heterogeneous activity: 'Poetry is speaking the mind; song is expressing the voice; dancing is moving the body. All three, originating in the heart, produce music' (*Yue Xiang*[9]). These activities were the product of primitive people's spiritual production, as compared to their material production; they were not only primitive songs and dances, but also magic and ritual. It was only later that they gradually diverged, with magic and ritual turning into political and social institutions and primitive songs and dances developing into art and literature.

Over time, totemic songs and dances developed into poetry, songs, dances, music, myths, and legends, each acquiring independent characteristics and developing in its own way.

What succeeded the worship of dragon and phoenix totems, in which men and gods were one, was the worship of heroes and ancestors. This came about when society became a patriarchy. For example, the stories of the conception and rearing of Xie and Yi, legendary ancestors of the kings of the Shang and Zhou dynasties respectively, were intended to show the remarkable origins and historic mission of the ancestors of these clans. Similarly, the stories of Shun, who tamed elephants; of Yi, hero in Chinese mythology who shot down nine suns; and of Gun and Yu, who harnessed rivers and controlled floods, all glorified the exploits of clan chieftains, real or unreal. Totemic myths were gradually replaced by heroes; primitive myths, the ideological core of ancient rites and magic, were gradually humanized and rationalized. Elements that were vague and ambiguous and lacked any rational explanation fell away as time passed; rites, magic, and totems gave way to politics and history. This process, however, was not completed until the Spring and Autumn and Warring States periods. Until then, the worship of totems continued.

[9] *Yue*, music; *xiang*, an ancient dance. *Yue Xiang* is one of the chapters on music in *Yueji*.

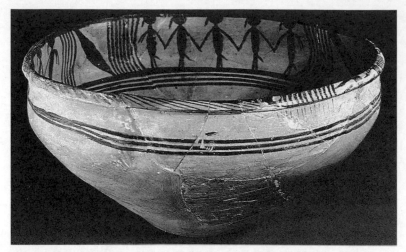

Painted pottery basin with figures of dancers, Majiayao relic.

The dancers depicted on a coloured pottery basin of the New Stone Age, discovered in Qinghai Province in 1973, may be the earliest surviving representation of primitive songs and dances. There were five dancers, holding hands, facing the same direction, each with an oblique line at the side of the head that seems to be a braid of hair. The outer arms of the dancers at the two ends are each represented by two lines, which may suggest that the movements of their free arms were greater and more rapid than those of the other dancers. Of the three lines below the body, the two straight ones that reach to the ground are undoubtedly the legs; the line at one side may be some kind of ornament.

The vivid and lively postures of the dancers, their light, orderly, and harmonious movements, their vitality and charming *naïveté*, all suggest that the basin was made during the legendary epoch of Shennong, a period of relative peace and tranquillity in the heyday of the matriarchal society.

It would be too simplistic, however, to assume that the design on the basin portrayed our ancestors enjoying themselves after work, holding hands while singing and dancing under the trees, near a brook, or on the grass. What it actually portrayed were totemic activities with serious magical intentions or the function of prayers. The braid-like ornament on the head and tail-like ornament below are comparable to 'oxtails' and to 'shields, battleaxes, feathers, and banners.' And holding hands while dancing evidently symbolized the 'development of vigorous movements.' The basin design is therefore a vivid example of the primitive songs and dances described in ancient writings.

The basin design is both realistic and allegorical. Certain similarities can be found between its regular, pattern-like images and the realistic imagery in the later European cave murals—both were accurate depictions of lively movements but crude in outline. However, being a product of the Neolithic, the basin design had to conform to the idea of geometric lines that was predominant at the time; consequently, it possessed a far more abstract form and mystical significance than did the cave murals. It was not, as modern observers might believe, a portrayal of leisurely moments but a realistic expression of solemn and serious rituals.

Dancing was the form of activity in magic and rites; and primitive songs and dances were exercises in the worship of the dragon and phoenix totems.

Significant Form

Primitive society underwent a long and slow process of development in China, passing through many different stages, with alternating periods of relative peace and violent warfare. The matriarchal society of the early Neolithic was probably a period of relative peace and stability, judging by surviving pictorial signs and symbols. This period may be the legendary epoch of Shennong recorded in ancient documents:

> In ancient times people ate the flesh of birds and beasts. By the time of Shennong, however, there were so many people in the world that the supply of birds and beasts was no longer enough to feed them. So Shennong, making use of the benefits of nature and the productivity of the earth, invented tools called *leisi* (an ancient hoe) and taught people how to farm. Farming became an exalted occupation and people liked it, so they called their leader Shennong (Exalted Farmer).
> (Ban Gu, A.D. 32–92: *Baihu Tongyi*, or *A General Discourse at White Tiger Palace*)

> In the epoch of Shennong, people slept peacefully at night and went about freely during the day. They knew only their mothers, not their fathers. They lived with the deer, farmed for food, wove for clothing, and harboured no evil against others.
> (*Philosophy of Zhuangzi*)

To 'live with the deer' implied domestication of this animal. Images of the deer are not infrequently seen on the Neolithic painted

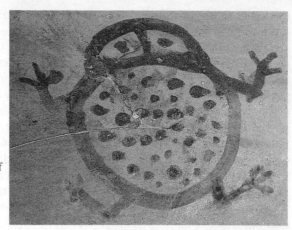

Basin with image of
frog (detail),
Yangshao relic
unearthed at Xi'an,
Shaanxi Province.

pottery of Yangshao discovered at Banpo village, east of Xi'an, and at
Miaodigou in Henan Province. The designs on such pottery, and those
on the later Majiayao-type pottery,[10] are reflections of a relatively
peaceful and stable world. Their depictions of fish, running dogs,
crawling lizards, and clumsy birds and frogs—especially the fish with
human faces on the inside of a basin—while possessing totemic
features, are simple, lively, and innocent-looking. The images
communicate the impression of an era free of violence, terror, and
tension. The atmosphere is reminiscent of a happy and healthy
childhood.

Yangshao painted pottery unearthed at Banpo village is noted for
its abundance of animal designs and images, especially fish designs, of
which more than a dozen varieties have been found. The modern
Chinese scholar Wen Yiduo (1899–1946), in his monograph *On Fish*,
says that the term 'fish' in Chinese implies a wish for prolific
reproduction. He did not search further than the *Book of Songs* and
Book of Changes, written in the Zhou Dynasty, for support for his
statement, but perhaps we can now trace this desire back to the era of
Yangshao culture. It seems likely that the fish and mermaid-like
designs seen so often on the clay vessels of Yangshao were indeed
ritual representations of wishes for a long, unending posterity. Because

[10] Yangshao and Majiayao represent two types of Chinese culture of the
Neolithic Age. Yangshao culture lasted approximately from 5000–3000 B.C.
and Majiayao culture from 3000–2000 B.C. Remains of the former were first
discovered at Yangshao village in Henan Province in 1921, those of the latter
at Majiayao in Gansu Province in 1923.

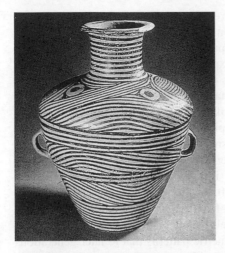

Flask with a wavelike pattern,
Majiayao relic

people's wish to reproduce and perpetuate their race was a decisive factor in the development of primitive societies, blood and clan relations were the basis of social structure.

The *Book of Mountains and Seas* tells us that 'snakes evolved into fish';[11] tombs of the Han Dynasty contain murals of monsters that are half snake and half fish. These raise two questions. First, is there any connection between the fish and mermaids and mermen of Yangshao and the dragons, snakes, and half-snake, half-human creatures mentioned earlier in this chapter? Second, is there a connection between the birds depicted on pottery and the fabulous phoenix?

As society changed, so did the images and designs on pottery. As in the Neolithic cultures of other peoples in the world, pottery designs of the Neolithic Age in China were dominated not by animal images but by geometric patterns—curved, straight, wavy, spiral, triangular, and zigzag lines. How and why such patterns were formed is one of art history's long-standing riddles, one about which there are many theories and a good deal of controversy. Some scholars maintain that the geometric patterns originated in life, nature, and material production—that vein-like patterns were modeled on the veins of leaves, wavy lines were images of waves on water, and spiral patterns were inspired by the eddies in flowing water. These scholars argue that humans wanted their creations to be beautiful as well as practical, so their designs gradually became regularized and patterned, and ornamentation, in time, became the chief need. But this viewpoint is

[11] It seems that the crocodile combines these two.

flawed. In the first place, there is no evidence that 'beauty' and 'ornamentation' were independent needs in primitive society.[12] Moreover, to say that geometric patterns were modeled upon leaves and waves is simplistic: it does not explain why leaves and waves should be chosen as models. Other scholars offer a more profound and convincing explanation. They hold that many of the geometric patterns were associated with the worship of snake totems by the ancient Yue nationality;[13] for example, the spiral pattern resembles a coiled snake and the wavy pattern suggests a snake crawling.

Some of the geometric patterns of Yangshao and Majiayao clearly evolved from realistic animal images into abstract symbols. The direction of development, in form and content, was from simple imitation to stylized abstraction, from realism to symbolism. This was the primary process in the development of the concept of beauty as 'significant form.' Thus the geometric patterns that to later generations seemed to be only ornamentation, with no specific meaning or content, actually possessed much of both in earlier times—they had serious totemic implications. Those seemingly pure forms were far more than mere visually balanced, symmetrical stimuli; they possessed a highly complicated conceptual significance. Though totemic images gradually became simplified and abstracted into pure geometric patterns—turned into symbols—their totemic implications did not disappear. Indeed, these implications could be said to have been enhanced by virtue of the fact that geometric patterns covered the whole surface of a vessel more often than animal images did. Thus abstract geometric patterns were not merely formal beauty, for there was content in the abstract form and concept in what was perceived by the senses. This is a characteristic that beauty and aesthetics have in common.

This common characteristic developed through a process of 'sedimentation' by which content settled into form, and imagination and concept into sense. This process, by which realistic animal images became abstracted into symbols, is a crucial point in the history of art

---

[12] The designs of human heads on painted pottery unearthed at Majiayao appear to be examples of 'cropped hair and tattooing,' but such were not for purposes of beauty or ornamentation. They had primarily an important ritual significance. The desire to beautify material objects appeared even later than the desire to beautify the human body.

[13] An ancient people who inhabited large areas south of the middle and lower reaches of the Yangtse before the Qin and Han era. In the course of time, they were assimilated into the Han, Chuang, Li, and Tai nationalities.

and aesthetic awareness. Archaeologists have described some facts concerning this process:

> There are many clues to show that such geometric patterns evolved from fish-shaped designs . . . a simple law governing the process was that the body of the fish became more stylized as the form of the head became simpler.
> (*Banpo Village, Xian*, Cultural Press, 1963)

> The process of change in bird designs was from realism to impressionism (expression of different movements of birds) to symbolism.
> (*Chinese Journal of Archaeology*, No. 1/65)

> The principal geometric patterns probably evolved from animal designs. Those of a representative nature may be divided into two categories: scroll (spiral) patterns that evolved from bird images, and wavelike, curved, or tapestry patterns that evolved from frog images. . . . That these two categories should be so distinctly different from each other was probably because they were the totemic symbols of different clans and tribes.

> In primitive society, designs on pottery were not pure decorative art. They were an expression of the material culture of the clan community. . . . In the great majority of cases, they existed as clan totems or other symbols of worship.
>   According to our analysis, the geometric patterns on the painted pottery of Banpo village evolved from fish designs, while those on the painted pottery of Miaodigou evolved from bird designs. This explains why the former consisted of simple straight lines and the latter of wavelike curves.

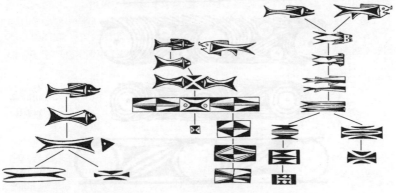

Evolution of the fish design.

> If indeed the designs on painted pottery were the totemic symbols of a clan or symbols with some special significance . . . then the Banpo-type and Miaodigou-type of Yangshao culture must have belonged to clans or tribes that worshipped fish totems and bird totems respectively, and Majiayao culture to two clans or tribes that worshipped bird totems and frog totems respectively.
> (*Chinese Journal of Archaeology*, No. 6/62)

When a comparative study is made of the pottery designs of the successive periods of Banpo, Miaodigou, and Majiayao, one finds an obvious hereditary relationship and evolutionary sequence in them. In the beginning, the designs were vivid and realistic, with much variation in imagery; gradually they became patterned, systematized, and standardized. The bird design began to take the form of spirals during the Majiayao era. The spiral patterns of Banshan and the large

Evolution of the bird design.

disc patterns of Machang,[14] which resemble the sun and may be called simulated sun designs, must be a more developed form of the Majiayao type of spirals.

There are many stories of birds and frogs in Chinese mythology, not a few of which are related to the worship of totems. In due course, the bird image evolved into the 'golden crow' that represented the sun and the frog image into the fabled toad-in-the-moon.[15] This may mean that the bird and frog designs of Banpo and Miaodigou down to Majiayao, the frog designs of the Banshan and Machang periods down to the cultures of Qijia and Siba,[16] and the simulated sun patterns of Banshan and Machang were actually forms of worship to the sun god and moon goddess. The fact that the two parent themes, the bird and the frog, lasted so long is in itself evidence that they were not incidental phenomena but were associated with the faith and traditional concepts of a people.

The evolution of the ancient pottery designs is a complicated and difficult scientific question that still requires much study. For instance,

	Frog Design	Bird Design
Banpo period		
Miaodigou period		
Majiayao period		

[14] Banshan and Machang are sites of late Neolithic culture in Shaanxi Province and Qinghai Province respectively.

[15] See the *Works of the Huainan King*, which says: 'There is a crow in the sun and a toad in the moon.'

[16] Qijia and Siba are types of Chinese culture intermediate between the Stone and Bronze Age. They date back to around 2000 B.C. when the primitive commune system in China disintegrated. Their remains were first discovered in Gansu.

	Simulative Frog Design	Simulative Sun Design
Banshan period		
Machang period		
Qijia culture, Siba culture		
Silk paintings in Han tombs		

could the frog images actually be images of the turtle, and are they related in any way to the 'giant turtle' and 'supernatural turtle' mentioned in ancient writings? But although the evolutionary process is largely speculative, and some conclusions may even be wrong, we can be reasonably sure of two things: The general law or trend was from realistic, vivid, and varied animal images to abstract, symbolic, and standardized patterns; and the pottery designs, whether animal or geometric, were not mere ornaments but possessed the sacred implications of clan totems.

As was stated earlier, humanity's aesthetic experiences differ from animal-like sensory pleasures because they include ideological and imaginative elements. Beauty is not ordinary form but 'significant form'—natural form that has acquired a socially defined content. So while form defines beauty, beauty is not just form. There is no beauty without form, but form by itself is not beauty.

It was Clive Bell[17] who put forward the famous theory that beauty

[17] Clive Bell, English art critic and aesthetician. In his book *Art* (1914) he expounded the theory of 'significant form.' It became a vogue and is still widely accepted. He and Roger Fry (1866–1934) were prominent aestheticians of the formalist school.

is 'significant form'. He repudiated mere reproduction in art and underscored the aesthetic quality of pure forms such as lines, which provided a theoretical basis for post-impressionist painting. His theory holds that 'significant form' is defined by whether an 'aesthetic emotion' different from ordinary feelings is produced, and that 'aesthetic emotion' originates only in 'significant form.' This is a vicious circle. But according to the idea of Bell's book just mentioned, these seemingly pure geometric lines are different from ordinary forms and lines because they evolved from realistic images and incorporated their socially defined content or meaning. They are 'significant form' because human feelings towards them incorporated special conceptual and imaginative elements—feelings so different from ordinary emotions, perceptions, and experience that they are a special kind of 'aesthetic emotion.'

The social feeling in primitive magic and ritual was passionate but vague and confused; it contained many concepts and much imagination that could not be explained through reasoning, logic, or abstraction. When such feeling became sensory experience, it naturally elicited a deep emotional reaction for which no general and definite explanation is possible. Some psychologists, such as C.G. Jung,[18] have linked this reaction to humanity's mysterious 'collective unconscious.' Actually, it is not very mysterious—the reaction was elicited by the special socially defined content and feeling that form and experience had acquired. But it should be noted that, as time passed, what was originally significant form gradually lost its significance through repetition and imitation. It became ordinary, standardized, formal beauty—and aesthetic emotion became a general feeling for form. Thus these geometric patterns became in time the earliest models and specimens of decorative and formal beauty.

The principal 'melody' of the geometric patterns on early Chinese pottery is the composition, flow, and turning of the lines. Line and colour are two basic elements in the visual arts. Aesthetically, colour is more primitive because human feeling for colour is an instinctive animal-like physiological response. Feeling, understanding, and appreciating the significance of lines is more difficult: it is an indirect process that requires the ability to conceptualize, imagine, and comprehend. Aesthetic feeling for colour dates back to the Upper Cave

---

[18] C.G. Jung (1875–1961), Swiss psychologist, author of *Psychology of the Unconscious*, *Types of Psychology*, *Archetypes of the Collective Unconscious*, and many other books.

men of the Paleolithic Age, but real shared aesthetic feeling for line was not apparent until the making of clay vessels began in the Neolithic Age. Through mastery of the fast-developing art of pottery and the production of earthenware of elaborate workmanship—bowls, plates, basins, stemmed cups, cooking tripods of all shapes and sizes—people began to appreciate the beauty of line, which became the core of the aesthetics of this period. The gradual sedimentation or incorporation of content in form was also achieved through material production, through the inherent laws that people grasped in the course of their productive labour and daily life.

To sum up, in the historical process from representation to 'expression,' from realism to symbolism, from figures to lines, humankind unconsciously created and cultivated a relatively pure form of beauty and aesthetic feeling for form. Line is a purer form than colour in labour, life, and natural objects: The various laws of form—rhythm, rhyme, symmetry, balance, continuity, intermission, overlapping, singleness, thickness, density, repetition, intersection, complexity, consistency, change, unity—were gradually understood and expressed in a concentrated way.

In the farming society of the Neolithic Age, life, labour, and objects such as crops that bore regular and patterned relationships to farming were depicted much more prominently, clearly, and precisely than were phenomena related to hunting in the Paleolithic Age. Through magic and rites, these patterns became condensed and concentrated in the seemingly ossified abstract designs and symbols on pottery; those linear forms embodied much that was significant to primitive society. Moreover, those lines appealed to more than the senses; they were not merely direct expressions of objects but often symbols or representations of subjective feelings in motion. Like a melody in music, what one perceives in the lines is not a series of objects in space but rather an epoch in time. And so it may be said that the violent passions first expressed in primitive magic and rites became condensed and sedimented in a special form in those linear ornaments, which seem so commonplace today. Those wavelike, repeating, rhythmic patterns and forms can be regarded as crystallizations of primitive songs and dances into abstract symbols. We have already seen singing and dancing represented by figures holding hands on a clay basin. The social and aesthetic significance of the whole art of pottery, including its geometric patterns, may be understood and interpreted in the same perspective. For example, the practice in later times of sitting and viewing pottery designs will-lessly may have followed the motion of 'holding hands' in primitive singing and dancing. The action of primitive magic and witchcraft may have evolved into the passivity of prayers and meditation.

As important as the designs are the shapes of the clay objects. The cultural relics of Dawenkou and Longshan[19] include a cooking tripod called a *gui*, with a spout that resembles a bird's beak. This may be related to the bird totem of tribes in eastern China. Here we will mention only two other objects that seem to be of special significance to the Chinese: the clay hog of Dawenkou and the tripod. The former is a realistic *object d'art*. The domestication of pigs was an important feature in the life of ancient Chinese tribes in the regions of Hemudu and Dawenkou. It shows that settlements and intensive farming existed in those regions at a very early date. Bones and clay models of hogs have also been discovered at Feiligang, a prehistoric site in Henan Province that dates back 7,500 years, and hog heads are known to have been used as funerary objects during the later stages of Yangshao culture. The hog is not a means of production but a means of subsistence, and pork-eating is an ancient practice in China. Even today, unlike many other countries, pork is still the principal meat choice of the Han nationality who constitute the overwhelming majority of the Chinese people; its consumption far exceeds that of either beef or mutton. Thus the clay images of pigs discovered at Dawenkou were an important ancient symbol of the Han nationality.

The tripod, another treasure of the Chinese nation,[20] is more important than the clay pig in terms of art and aesthetics. The tripod is not imitative or realistic in shape, for most animals have four legs and birds have only two. It was a product of necessity, the need to cook over a fire, because it was more stable and solid than a two-legged vessel, and steadier and easier to make than a four-legged one. Such a feeling for form and the unique image thus created show a high degree of both functional and aesthetic awareness. The tripod eventually developed into the main Chinese ritual vessel, called *ding*.

As soon as form had freed itself of the fetters of imitation and realism, it acquired an independent character and embarked on its own

---

[19] Dawenkou and Longshan represent two types of Chinese culture of the Neolithic and late Neolithic Age respectively. They are so called because the first remains of those cultures were unearthed at Dawenkou and Longshan, both in Shandong Province. Dawenkou culture began around 4500 B.C. and turned into Longshan culture around 2500 B.C.

[20] Although there were also tripods in Greece and other places, they were not so popular as in ancient China.

path of development. Its own laws and requirements assumed an ever more important role, which acted upon people's feelings and concepts, which in turn promoted development that enabled the laws of form to be expressed even more freely and the properties of lines to be more fully utilized. The changes in the shape of the tripod and the designs on pottery all followed this process. In spite of this, however, the evolution and development of pottery designs were still basically governed by changes in social structure and primitive ideology.

From the cultures of Banpo, Miaodigou, and Majiayao to those of Banshan, Machang, and Qijia in the west, to the late Dawenkou and Longshan cultures in the east, one general trend can be noticed in pottery designs in spite of their many and often complex changes: though all were abstract geometric patterns, those of the late Neolithic Age were much more mysterious and awesome in appearance. Early Neolithic designs were vivid, lively, free, easy, smooth, and open, but those of the late Neolithic tended to be rigid, immutable, solemn, obscure, and awe-inspiring. In the later designs, straight lines predominated over curved ones and closed patterns over continuous ones. Arcs and wavy lines were reduced and replaced by straight lines and triangles. Dots, circles, and round corners gave way to square and rectangular boxes. The same saw-toothed and triangular patterns were portrayed differently during different cultural eras: Banpo and Miaodigou patterns differed from those of Longshan, and Majiayao patterns differed from those of Banshan and Machang. The large and sharply pointed triangular outlines, upright or inverted, that rigidly and mechanically occupied large sections and prominent positions on the earthenware of the late Dawenkou or Longshan culture possess a strange and mysterious quality not present in the earlier triangular patterns. And the alternating red and black sawtooth that was a basic feature of Banshan-Machang pottery designs has never been seen on the earlier Majiayao paroducts.

We may infer from this that by the time of the Banshan-Machang culture the relative peace and stability of the Shennong epoch was gone and society had entered a period characterized by ruthless warfare, pillage, and slaughter. Matriarchal society had given way to a patriarchal system that was rapidly developing into a slave society. As exploitation and oppression increased, the earlier realistic and geometric designs, with their exuberance, *naïveté*, gentle curves, and easy style, gradually disappeared. The designs of later periods clearly reflected the oppressive weight of autocratic rule and power. As to the pottery designs unearthed in northeastern China, and the famous adze designs on stones of the late Longshan culture discovered at Rizhao, Shandong Province, both bear obvious resemblances to the bronzes of the Shang Dynasty, signifying that a radical change had begun. They were the forerunners of designs on bronze.

2

The Bronze Art

Ferocious Beauty

THE CASTING of the legendary nine *ding*[1] in the Xia Dynasty was probably the beginning of the Bronze Age in China. Though much remains to be explored and studied in the field of Xia culture, it is quite certain that the discoveries made at Longshan and Erlitou, in Henan Province, belonged to this historical period.

Pottery designs discovered at a number of Neolithic sites, in both north and south China, show obvious indications of the transition to bronze designs. Of course, there is still much controversy over whether these pottery designs appeared before, simultaneously with, or after bronze designs, but the general trend in pottery designs—from lively playfulness to gloom and mystery—is indisputable evidence of the transition to the Bronze Age.

From the epoch of the Yellow Emperor, through the system of dual leadership of Yao, Shun, and Yu, to the Xia Dynasty, China had entered a new stage. Though the clan democracy was still the nucleus of the social structure, an early form of hierarchy system based on slavery gradually evolved. Two distinct classes, the aristocracy and the common people, or countrymen, appeared, with the latter becoming virtual slaves of the aristocracy. There emerged the beginnings of a shamanistic culture with a strong religious character. Its mode of expression was ritual and its essence was ancestor worship. It was during this period that the primitive magic and rites that belonged to the whole people became the laws and regulations of a society ruled by religion and under a hierarchy system monopolized by (tribe-clan) aristocrats. The witch doctors of late primitive society became the powerful religious-political leaders.

As recorded in the oracle-bone inscriptions of the Shang Dynasty, divinations were required to be made every day during that era. Many of the divinations concerned farming, for example crops, seasons,

[1] An ancient vessel made of bronze or clay, used for cooking and other purposes. It was usually a tripod, but there were some with four legs. 'Nine' here actually means many.

rainfall. Others concerned wars, worship, and medicine. These religious activities were basically the same as the activities of witch doctors in primitive society, but as time passed they turned into tools for protecting the interests of the clan's small aristocratic ruling clique. As the practice of divination spread, it became increasingly important to appeal to the gods on all matters, large or small, to find out whether the gods would bring good or bad luck. Divinations for all kinds of activities were recorded on the oracle bones unearthed at the sites of Yin ruins. The practice was also common in the Zhou Dynasty, as we learn from the bronze inscriptions of this period. As a matter of fact, the *Book of Changes* was a book of divinations. And the following passage from the *Book of History*[2] is a typical account of such practices in the societies of the Shang and Zhou:

> When in serious doubt, seek advice from the heart, from officialdom, from the common people, and through divination. . . . Follow it. If the tortoise shell and the alpine yarrow[3] approve, but the officials and common people do not, it is a sign of good luck. If the officials, the tortoise shell, and the alpine yarrow approve, but you and the common people do not, it is also a sign of luck. If the common people, the tortoise shell, and the alpine yarrow approve while you and the officials do not, it is still a sign of luck. If the tortoise shell approves but the alpine yarrow, the officials, and the common people disapprove, the [contemplated] action is good for domestic purposes only. If the tortoise shell and alpine yarrow are both opposed to the wishes of men, it is bad to take any action.

Thus, of all the conditions that governed an action, approval by the tortoise shell and alpine yarrow was the most important. It was more important than even the will of kings and emperors. Since no action should be taken when 'both the tortoise shell and the alpine yarrow are opposed to the wishes of men,' we may sense the power and position of the priests who manipulated the divinatory process. Some of these priests actually held the reins of state:

> I have heard that in ancient times when Tang (the first king of the Shang Dynasty) received his mandate, there were men like Yi Yin who owed their allegiance to High Heaven.
> (*Book of History*)

---

[2] *Book of Changes* and *Book of History* are two classics attributed to Confucian scholars of the Zhou Dynasty.

[3] Tortoise shells and alpine yarrow were materials used in divination. Divination with tortoise shells was called *bu*; with alpine yarrow, *shi*.

> During the reign of Taiwu (a king of the Shang Dynasty), there were
> men like Yi She who assisted the king but owed their allegiance to
> the Supreme Ruler.
> (*Book of History*)

In those days, the tribe-clan aristocracy included officials called
wu (shaman), *yin* (assistant), and *shi* (royal historian); these were
'thinkers' with the ability to command. They were the earliest kind of
priests, and were thought to owe their allegiance to 'High Heaven' and
to the 'Supreme Ruler.' They fostered the illusion that they possessed
superhuman mental abilities, that they could imagine things yet to
come. They put forward 'ideals,' prophesied the future, and concocted
illusions about the society, claiming that the rule of the (tribe-clan)
aristocracy was part of the divine order of things.

> Since ancient times, emperors, kings, and generals, when they have
> established a state, received a mandate, or are about to embark on a
> cause, always resort to divinations to assist them in doing good.
> There is no way of knowing what happened in the Tang and Yu
> periods and further back, but since the rise of the Three Dynasties[4] all
> have relied on divination to decide what is auspicious.
> (*Historical Records: On Tortoise Shells and Alpine Yarrow*)

This passage tells us that the (tribe-clan) aristocracy of the three
dynasties relied in part on the fabrications of the *wu*, *yin*, and *shi* to
buttress their power by spreading illusions about their class and its
'auspiciousness.'

These illusions, the special products of ideology, also found
expression in the realistic images engraved on bronze. The making,
evolution, and standardization of pottery designs were probably the
work of clan leaders who had not yet divorced themselves from
material production and were thus still able to express the concepts and
ideals of their clan or tribe as a whole. The making and standardization
of bronze designs, however, must be attributed to political and religious
personages—the *wu*, *yin*, and *shi* who 'could realistically imagine
things.' Though bronzes were actually cast by manual labourers and
even slaves, and though the origin of some bronze designs can be
traced back to primitive totems and pottery, such designs were
primarily expressions of the will and power of the rulers of early
hierarchical society. They are different in nature from the mystical

---

[4] The Three Dynasties is a popular reference to the Xia, Shang, and Zhou
Dynasties. Tang and Yu are the names of two legendary dynasties that
preceded the Xia. Their rulers were Yao and Shun respectively.

geometric patterns on pottery. Typified by the *taotie*, bronze designs were not mysterious and abstract patterns but images of animals, realistically portrayed. Those images, however, were not of real things, for no such animals as the *taotie* existed in the real world. They were imaginary images that symbolized 'auspiciousness' or other things that served the needs and interests of the ruling clique. The new dominating class used these supernatural, mysterious, and awesome animal images to establish and idealize its rule.

According to historical records, the *taotie* was an auspicious symbol—it asserted itself to protect society, to coordinate the upper and lower classes, and to inherit the fortunes of heaven. In other words, it was a defender of the status quo.

What, then, was the *taotie*? The only thing we are sure of is that it had the head of an animal. But was it an ox, a sheep, a tiger, a deer, or a baboon? I believe it was intended to be the head of an ox, but not an ordinary ox; it was the sacred ox associated with the magic and religious rites of remote antiquity. Studies of southwestern China's national minorities suggest that the ox head was an important symbol in ancient religious rites, during which it was hung high on a treetop. It was extremely important and sacred to a clan or tribe because it was supposed to have the power to protect against evil. Though only a symbolic object used in primitive sacrificial ceremonies, it became a symbol of mystery, terror, and awe because of the extraordinary power it was deemed to possess. In all probability, this was masterminded by the *wu*, *yin*, and *shi*.

Thus, all *taotie* designs and motifs communicate an overwhelming feeling of mystery, power, terror, and ferocity. The beast or perhaps

Square bronze *ding* with sculptured human faces, Shang Dynasty, unearthed in Hunan Province.

human face on the large ancient battleaxe called *yue*; the images of *kui*-dragons and *kui*-phoenixes[5] intertwined with the *taotie*; the terrifying human faces on the *ding* of the Shang and early Zhou; the distorted animal images that are nowhere to be found in the real world, for example the *chixiao*, a mysterious messenger of the night—these are indeed vastly different from the lively, pleasant, and realistic images on Yangshao pottery and the early geometric patterns which, though mysterious, are abstract.

The bronze images are distorted, stylized, imaginary, and fearsome depictions. They emanate an aura of threat and mystery because they represented an all-powerful, transcendent supernatural concept. They are beautiful not because of their ornamental quality, but because their sturdy lines, cast or carved in bold relief, symbolize primitive sentiments and concepts that could not be expressed in words. They and the strong, solid vessels on which they appear aptly reflect the savage epoch of blood and fire that preceded the era of civilization.

The march of history has never been accompanied by gentle, pastoral songs. Rather, its forward path has often been strewn with corpses. War is one of mankind's most ruthless means of progress. Since late primitive society, which saw clans and tribes swallowed up, wars have become increasingly frequent and larger in scale. Mature writings on warfare appeared as early as they did in China[6] because they were summaries of long periods of war and strife. From the epochs of the Yan and Yellow emperors down to the Shang and Zhou, history consisted mainly of extensive clan and tribal wars of conquest accompanied by massacres, captivity, plunder, enslavement, exploitation, and oppression. Violence was the midwife of civilization, and the flaunting of violence and military prowess was the pride and glory of the entire period of early hierarchy society because it brought about the large-scale amalgamation of clans and tribes.

Thus it was that primitive myths and legendary heroes were replaced by eulogies that glorified one's own clan, ancestry, and wars of annexation. Most of the bronze objects of the Shang and Zhou were ritual vessels used in sacrificial ceremonies to make offerings to one's ancestors, or were inscribed with records of military exploits and victories. It was also the custom in those days to slaughter prisoners of war for sacrificial purposes, and to kill and even eat one's enemies. The

[5] The *kui* was a legendary monster with one leg used as a prefix. It denotes something anomalous.

[6] Sun Wu's *Art of War*, China's earliest book on military strategy, was written in the late Spring and Autumn period (770–476 B.C.).

creed then was: 'He who is not of my own clan must be an enemy at heart.' The man-eating *taotie* was therefore a supremely appropriate symbol of those times.

According to *Lu's Spring and Autumn Annals: Prophecy*, 'The *taotie* on Zhou bronzes has a head but no body. When it eats people, it does not swallow them, but harms them.'[7] It is hard to explain what is implied in this, as so many myths concerning the *taotie* have been lost, but the indication that it eats people accords fully with its cruel, fearful countenance. To alien clans and tribes, it symbolized fear and force; to its own clan or tribe, it was a symbol of protection. This religious concept, this dual nature, was crystallized in its strange, hideous features. What appears so savage today had a historical, rational quality in its time. It is for precisely this reason that the savage old myths and legends, the tales of barbarism, and the crude, fierce, and terrifying works of art of ancient clans possessed a remarkable aesthetic appeal. As it was with Homer's epic poems and African masks, so it was with the *taotie*, in whose hideous features was concentrated a deep-seated historic force. It is because of this irresistible historic force that the mystery and terror of the *taotie* became the beautiful—the exalted.

Humans had no place or power in such a society. What held power was this mystic and deformed animal that threatened, devoured, suppressed, and trod upon man's body and soul. But society at that time, to open up its path ahead, had to pass through this savage and terrible ordeal of blood and fire. It is impossible to appreciate the art of the Bronze Age if one takes a sorrowful view of this. The epoch of the slaying of thousands of slaves and captives belongs to a distant past, but the art that expressed or represented the spirit of that epoch is still admired and appreciated today because it symbolizes the mysterious force of history on the march. This irresistible force, expressed in the ferocious beauty of bronze art, is like the fatalism of Greek tragedy, which instilled fear in men yet possessed beauty because it expressed a historical inevitability. Power combined with primitive mysticism gave bronze art an aura of fatalism, which enhanced its mysterious and ferocious qualities.

However, because this society remained closely linked to primitive society, its images, though cruel and forbidding, retained a certain surprising *naïveté*, a charm reminiscent of childhood. This quality is even more obvious to present-day observers. Looking again

---

[7] Some scholars consider that the meaning of *taotie* is not 'eating people' but making a mysterious communication between people and Heaven (gods).

Bronze axe called *yue*
with the image of a human
face, Shang Dynasty,
unearthed in Shandong
Province.

at the battleaxe called *yue*—though it was a gross, deliberate attempt to magnify the fierce and terrible, there was still something in it that is charming, childish, and naïve. Many *taotie* designs share the same primitive, simple, and innocent beauty.

But it is far from true that anything mysterious and ferocious can become an object of beauty. Those sculptures of gods and men or of animal images with such threatening features made in later periods, however much they may be flaunted for their power and fierceness, reveal themselves only as things void of substance. For they possessed neither the force of destiny, the historic inevitability that is expressed in bronze art, nor the childlike *naïveté* of primitive men.

The further society and civilization progress, the easier it is to appreciate and evaluate the exalted and ferocious beauty of the ancient bronzes. Bronzes were not objects of aesthetic enjoyment but articles used with fear and apprehension in religious rites. In the middle ages, fear of the hideous images sometimes caused such objects to be destroyed. Only in a civilized society where material culture is highly developed and religious thinking on the wane, where cruelty and barbarism are of the past, can art that represented forces of progress and human destiny in ancient history be understood and enjoyed, and its aesthetic value appreciated.

The Art of Line

Chinese characters developed and matured in the Bronze Age. As calligraphy, they gradually became a peculiarly Chinese form of art and an object of aesthetic study and enjoyment.

Oracle-bone inscriptions, ancient though they are, were already a fairly mature form of Chinese handwriting. In fact, the structure and composition of the characters in these inscriptions established the principles and basis for the development of Chinese characters and calligraphy. Chinese characters on the surface seemingly are basically pictographic symbols. In fact, they seem like paintings, simulations or realistic portrayals of objects, but in fact they are highly generalized. Like the practice of tying knots in a string as a memory aid, Chinese characters had, from the very beginning, symbolic meanings above and beyond the objects being depicted. A single character could represent not just one object or one kind of object, but also a category of facts or processes. It could even express subjective feelings, hopes, and desires. In other words, such 'pictography' contained elements of what are now called *zhishi* and *huiyi*.[8]

In this respect the pictography of Chinese characters differs from painting and drawing because it possesses the abstract significance and function of symbols. But since Chinese characters in the very beginning were tightly connected with pictography, and in the course of their development have never fully departed from pictographic principles, the forms of the characters, on which their symbolic function depends, have developed more or less independently of their symbolic meanings, there being so many different ways of simulating the forms of objects. Over time, the pure linear beauty of Chinese characters—freer and more varied in spacing and arrangement of lines than the abstract geometric patterns on pottery—made it possible for them to express or represent shapes, emotions, and ideas of all kinds, eventually becoming the art of line that is uniquely Chinese: calligraphy.

In his preface to *Shuowen Jiezi* (*Book of Chinese Characters and Phrases*), Xu Shen wrote: 'When Cang Xie[9] first invented writing, he relied entirely on pictography.' Many calligraphers of later periods have also pointed out that Chinese characters contain both imagery and simulation:

> They are like the lines on a tortoise shell or the scales of a fish. They have extended bodies and elongated tails, or long wings and short trunks. They resemble the glumes of the millet or clusters of insects. (Cai Yong, [132–192]: *The Seal Script*)

[8] *Zhishi* is to define (an object idea, etc.) by appropriate symbols, e.g., ' 上 ' for 'above' and ' 下 ' for 'below.' *Huiyi* is to define by combining characters, e.g., ' 日 ' (sun) and ' 月 ' (moon) written together (明) means brightness.

[9] According to tradition, Cang Xie was an official who served the Yellow Emperor and invented Chinese characters.

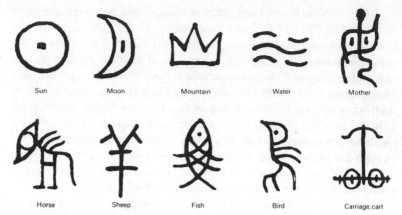

| Sun | Moon | Mountain | Water | Mother |

| Horse | Sheep | Fish | Bird | Carriage,cart |

Pictographic characters.

> [The strokes are] compact like needles placed side by side, straight
> and level like a rope, winding and twisting, or long and angular.
> (Cai Yong: *The Official Script*)

Ever since the creation of the seal script,[10] Chinese calligraphers
have had to pay close attention to the simulation of the forms and
appearances of real objects and the assimilation of their properties in
the formation of characters, even though great freedom of abstraction
and generalization was fully permitted in such simulation and
assimilation. The beauty of Chinese characters is indeed based on
properties that evolved from pictography, that is, on the form, structure,
and composition of lines. For example, in Chinese characters, the
curves and straight lines must be appropriately placed; the height and
breadth proportionate; the combination of parts, free and natural; the
layout, well-arranged. This beauty was already visible in the oracle-
bone inscriptions, of which Deng Yizhe wrote, in *Appreciation of
Calligraphy*:

> Strokes like suspended needles or hanging chives; curves, turnings,
> horizontal and vertical lines, closely knit; uniformity and
> coordination like the angles of an equilateral triangle; balance
> between density and sparseness—such features [in individual
> characters] can enhance the beauty of a whole piece of writing.
> Evidently, such beauty comes from artistic conception and has been

---

[10] A style of Chinese calligraphy much used on seals. It has several varieties,
for example the great seal script and small seal script. Broadly speaking, the
inscriptions on ancient oracle bones and bronzes are all in this style.

reproduced in the exquisite structure of Chinese characters by contemporary calligraphers.

It should be noted, however, that in the beginning such pure beauty of lines—calligraphy—was far from a conscious pursuit. Although the bronze inscriptions had developed, over several hundred years, from pictorial forms into the manipulation of lines, and from individual totemic symbols into lengthy accounts of wars and exploits, it was not until the Spring and Autumn period that the deliberate pursuit of calligraphic beauty became apparent. This pursuit was in accord with the expanded content of the bronze inscriptions and the search for better literary styles. Guo Moruo noted:

In the Eastern Zhou and later dynasties, the nature of calligraphy changed, becoming literary embellishment. For example, the inscriptions on bells were mostly in rhyme and were carved in a regular pattern; the style of the script showed a preponderance of right-falling strokes and a deliberate seeking of excellence. . . . All this comes under literary embellishment in the realm of aesthetic awareness; its effect is the same as design. The tradition of regarding written characters as works of art in this country must have begun at this point.

(*The Bronze Age: An Evolutionary View of the Inscriptions on Ritual Vessels of the Zhou Dynasty*)

Before this, both the *taotie* and calligraphic symbols—often inscribed upon the bottom of a vessel where they were seldom noticed—had had only a solemn, sacred connotation and had never been considered for their aesthetic values. But by the Spring and Autumn and Warring States periods, Chinese characters had come to be viewed as possessing aesthetic value of their own. It was alongside this, and only at this point, that works of art of a somewhat independent character, as well as aesthetic awareness, really appeared.

If we compare the bronze inscriptions of the Shang Dynasty with those of the Zhou which followed, we find that the former more closely resemble oracle-bone inscriptions: they have more straight lines and fewer round corners, and the tips and ends of strokes are often sharp and pointed. Though there was as yet no conscious effort to beautify the structure and arrangement of characters, signs of this were in the offing. By the time of the Zhou Dynasty, whose bronze inscriptions were generally long passages, more attention was paid to the art of composition; the characters became long or round; their strokes were smooth and flowing; various schools and styles emerged; and engraving was light or heavy according to preference. The art of bronze

Divinations inscribed
on an ox bone,
believed to have been
unearthed at a Yinxu
site in Henan
Province.

inscription reached its summit with the famous *maogong ding* (a cooking vessel) and *sanshi pan* (a tray), both of which were bronzes cast in the late Western Zhou (c. eighth century B.C.). Some of the inscriptions on these were round or square, orderly in structure, firm and close-knit in composition, with a solemn aura. Others were round with a seemingly loose though actually compact structure, presenting a free and easy appearance. Their overall smoothness, naturalness, and subdued power distinguished them from the sharp, pointed, straight, and awkward inscriptions of the Shang.

> The compositional beauty of the ancient bronze inscriptions of the Shang and Zhou causes us to believe that Cang Xie has indeed detected the mysteries and wonders of the universe and grasped the secrets of the most extraordinary and wonderful forms in the world of nature.
> (Zong Baihua [1897–1986]: *The Aesthetics of Chinese Calligraphy*)

> Variations in density of composition, light and heavy strokes, slow or fast brushwork. . . . It is like picking out notes from the myriad sounds of nature in musical or artistic creation, developing laws of combining those notes, and using variations in volume, pitch, rhythm, and melody to express images in nature and society and the feelings in one's heart.
> (Zong: *The Aesthetics*)

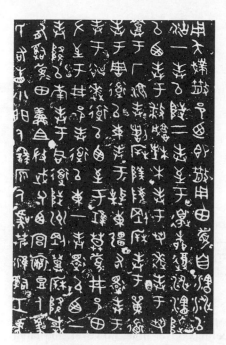

Detail of a rubbing from the *sanshi pan*, Western Zhou, unearthed at Fangxiang, Shaanxi Province. The inscription records an alliance between states and the fixing of state boundaries.

These somewhat exaggerated statements show us some of the characteristics of Chinese calligraphy considered as the art of line. Like music, which is the extraction of musical notes from the world of sound and the working of them into melodies and harmonies according to laws, purified lines were extracted from the simulation of forms by means of freely developed brushstrokes. They were used to produce on paper—character by character—rich, intricate works of soundless music and motionless dancing that express human feelings and ideas.

Thus oracle-bone and bronze inscriptions opened the path for the development of Chinese calligraphy by transforming pictographic imitation into purely abstract lines and structures. Such purified lines—calligraphy—do not represent formal or ornamental beauty, as do designs and patterns in general, but are 'significant forms' in the true sense. While ordinary formal beauty is often static, stylized, standardized, and void of life and vigour, 'significant form' is the exact opposite—it is vigourous, moving, and beautiful in its expression of and allusion to life. Chinese calligraphy, the art of line, is the latter kind of beauty. It is not formal beauty, characterized by orderly, uniform, balanced, and symmetrical lines, but free beauty, with far more varied and changing properties. Its beauty can be compared to floating clouds

This character contains all the basic
strokes in Chinese handwriting.

and flowing water, with strokes as strong and swift as the wind, with
firmness as well as suppleness, with the square in harmony with the
round. In every character, in every piece of writing, and on every page,
there can be creativity, change, and individuality, without mechanical
repetition or rigid standards.

Because Chinese characters incorporate elements of both imagery
(generalized simulation) and expressiveness (of emotions), they can
describe objects and express feelings. Over time, however, the latter
became the dominant factor (see Chapter 7). Though originally closer
to painting and sculpture, calligraphy became an art aligned with music
and dance. It is not calligraphy that should look to painting for
experience, skills, and strength but rather the reverse. Painting should
look to calligraphy for the use of the brush—lightly or heavily, swiftly
or slowly, with or without force or effect; for the making of curves,
turns, pauses, and transitions; for rhythm and cadence. In all these
respects, lines play the leading role, like the melody in music. In fact,
lines have become the soul of many types of visual and performing arts
in China.

Bronze inscription was succeeded by *xiaozhuan*, a style of
calligraphy adopted in the Qin Dynasty. It consists of elongated
characters with curves, executed in strokes of uniform width. The next
development was the *lishu*, the official script of the Han Dynasty, in
which round corners were replaced by square ones and continuous
strokes by separate ones. Further changes resulted in the running,
cursive, regular, and other styles. All possessed a high aesthetic value.

Seal-carving, another kind of uniquely Chinese 'significant form,'
also originated in bronze inscriptions. In a tiny, limited space, different
styles and moods are created using the knife, brush, and structure of the
characters.

Disintegration and Emancipation

The conscious expression of beauty in bronze inscription and calligraphy, as well as in the whole realm of bronze art, began during the Spring and Autumn and Warring States periods, for this was when art and aesthetics were gradually freed from the clouds of magic and religion, just as society was gradually freed from the system of primitive communes that had continued into early aristocratic society. This emancipation, however, resulted in the decline of bronze art, because the epoch of savage terror it mirrored had become a thing of the past and rational, analytic, refined, and worldly ideas and interests were spreading. The early bronze vessels that had been used in sacrifices lost their sacred splendour and their power to inspire awe, and later bronze objects were very different in imagery and design.

Guo Moruo's (1892–1978) four stages in the evolution of bronze in the Shang and Zhou Dynasties, first defined in the 1930s, are still accepted as valid:

1. The stage of excessive production of wine cups. Bronze had just appeared and bronze objects (mostly wine cups) were roughly made; the designs were crude and had no beauty to speak of.

2. The stage of prosperity for bronzes. It lasted from the late Shang to the reigns of kings Cheng, Kang, Zhao, and Mu (c.10th century B.C.) of the Western Zhou and marked the zenith of Chinese bronze art. Bronze objects produced during this period had a higher aesthetic value than those made earlier or later. The most representative product is the *ding*, a uniquely Chinese three-legged vessel of heavy and powerful build, with mystic and fierce-looking images carved in high relief. In the words of Guo Moruo, the bronze objects of this period have been

> treasured by admirers of the antique down the ages. They were mostly *ding* . . . of solid and heavy build. When there were designs, these were carved deep or in high relief. On most vessels, *taotie* images were carved upon the cloud-and-thunder pattern that covered the surface. The *taotie* and cloud-and-thunder decoration were generally regarded as the principal design, with the *kui*-dragon, *kui*-phoenix and elephant in lesser roles. . . . The first three [*taotie*, *kui*-dragon, *kui*-phoenix] were mythical creatures of the imagination. The elephant image decoration, too, was only a figment of the mind; it was not a realistic portrayal.
>
> (*The Bronze Age: A Study of the Images on Sacrificial Vessels*)

Another notable vessel of this stage is the Shang Dynasty *gufu yiyou*, a kind of wine container:

> Its neck and circular base were ornamented with patterns of strange-looking beasts. On the body of the container is a large ox head carved in high relief, its horns projecting and its huge eyes in a fixed gaze. It has an aura of power and mystery. The inscription on the vessel is in a style typical of the late Shang Dynasty.
> (*Selected Bronzes of the Yin and Zhou*, Cultural Relics Press, 1976)

The Zhou Dynasty cooking vessel called *bojuli* also featured a prominent ox head with sharp protruding horns that exudes an awesome and mystical feeling. These objects are among the finest examples of beauty in bronze.

3. The open stage. This was the stage of disintegration of the Bronze Age. Society was progressing and civilization advancing in rapid strides. Productive forces were being improved through the large-scale use of iron tools and of oxen in plowing. In the face of all this, early (tribe-clan) aristocratic society was replaced by new commercial owners and newly emerging forces, systems, and reform movements whose authority lay in their written codes of political and legal justice.

Bojuli cauldron with
sculptured ox head,
Western Zhou.

The disintegration of this early society was linked to ideological emancipation. Skepticism and atheism became the vogue as the magical and religious traditions of remote antiquity which had prevailed throughout the Shang and early Zhou periods died out. With them also died mystical ornamental designs. No longer was it possible to intimidate and rule people by means of primitive, irrational, and inexplicable terror and mystery. Thus, the bronze *taotie*, as an artistic symbol of an earlier epoch, lost its power and was relegated to a secondary role. Ideologically, Chinese society had entered the first era of rationalism by this time.

As Guo Moruo said:

> The vessels of the open stage were simpler in form and shape. If they had pictures or ornamental lines, these were usually crude and in low relief, or only shallowly incised. The cloud-thunder decoration that had been in vogue during the preceding stage virtually disappeared by this time. The *taotie* had lost its power and in many cases was relegated to a subordinate role, for example to ornament the legs or base of a *ding* or *gui* (food container). In general, the vessels of this stage were free of the inhibitions of myth and tradition.
>
> (*The Bronze Age: A Study of the Images on Sacrificial Vessels*)

4. The new-style stage. We are now at the Warring States period, a time of transition reflected in the bronze objects of this stage, which were basically either degenerate or progressive:

> The degenerate type followed the path of the preceding stage, becoming even cruder and simpler, and largely unorna-mented. . . . Articles of the progressive type were light, handy, and generally bizarre; the designs were more refined but less deeply engraved. . . . The designs on a vessel were usually repeated impressions from the same block, but they were varied and intricate because using set patterns was in disfavour. This was a great contrast to the fixed styles of the second and third stages. A common design of the fourth stage was the *panliwen*, a pattern of stylized coiling dragons and snakes, which was actually a refined version of the earlier *kui* pattern. The inlaying of gold pieces was a new phenomenon of this stage, and the depiction of winged men and flying beasts was a leap forward. The animal images depicted on vessels were mostly realistic portrayals.
>
> (*The Bronze Age: A Study*)

These degenerate and progressive types aptly reflect the defeat of the old and the triumph of the new. The degenerate type represented the decay of the old magical and religious concepts, while the light, ingenious progressive type represented newly emerging interests, standards, and ideals.

The progressive type, though ostensibly only variations of earlier designs and objects, had connotations that were completely new. It represented a new kind of bronze art and a new form of beauty that consisted in the removal of religious constraints. Human interests were expressed more freely in the bronze ritual vessels. The method of expression changed from symbolic to realistic; the shape, from thick and heavy to light and handy; the imagery, from stern and solemn to ingenious and bizarre; the carving, from deep and dull to shallow and free; and the designs, from simple, rigid, and mystical to intricate, varied, and rational. Secular wars, horses and chariots, spears and halberds, all were realistically portrayed in new styles that were free and uninhibited on the bronzes of this period.

The bronze objects recently unearthed from tombs of the kings of Zhongshan[11] in southwestern Hebei Province are typical of the progressive type. Though the 卅-shaped ritual vessel resisted changes in form and retained the intimidating features of the ancient totems, other objects were rationalized and secularized. The bronze structure of four deer, four dragons, and four phoenixes forming the support of a

Bronze table with group sculpture of four dragons and four phoenixes, Warring States period, unearthed in Hebei Province.

[11] An ancient kingdom set up by a minority nationality called the Beidi during the Spring and Autumn period. It was annexed by Zhao, one of the Warring States, in 296 B.C.

square table and the series of 15 copper lamps discovered in the tombs are of ingenious and extraordinary craftsmanship. Though unique in structure and very beautiful, they communicate any sense but seriousness. These dragons and phoenixes, like the *taotie*, have lost their traditional power to control human destinies. They retain only a faint aura of the supernatural, and that only for enjoyment and decoration.

Evidence that aesthetic interests of an entirely new kind were spreading widely can be seen in the portrayals of banquets and of land and sea battles that adorn the bronze vessels of this period. These images—vivid worldly scenes of feasting, picking mulberries, archery, hunting, soldiers fighting, cities under attack, and naval battles—affirm the value of secular life, the casting off of the fetters of tradition, and the emancipation of the mind, spirit, and passions.

Like the lamps unearthed from the Zhongshan tombs, the immediate predecessors of the Han Dynasty palace lanterns, and the Han sculpture of a horse treading on a swallow, the low-relief bronze sculptures of the new-style stage were the forerunners of Han Dynasty art, such as the famous brick pictures. Indeed, the bronzes of this stage are more closely related to the art of the Qin and Han than to that of the dynasties that preceded it, just as the society of the Warring States as a whole is similar to that of the Qin and Han but very different from that of the Shang and early Zhou.

By the time bronze art had reached the stage when works of high craftsmanship but no other significance were being produced, it was drawing near its end. The craftsmanship of the bronze objects of the Warring States was superb indeed—the portrayals are so shallowly engraved that the images appear to be floating on the surface of the vessels—but the differences in power and aesthetic value are obvious when they are compared with the ferocious beauty of the Shang and Zhou bronzes. The sublime beauty of the bronze *taotie*, with all its fierceness and mystery, is more appealing because it was after all an expression of the beauty of the flaming social spirit of its time. Thus, it is the earlier works that exemplify the best in bronze art.

Bronze flask with engraved hunting scenes, Spring and Autumn period,
unearthed at Luoyang, Henan Province.

3

Rational Spirit of Pre-Qin

Confucianism and Taoism: Complements and Supplements

THE TERM 'Pre-Qin' generally refers to the Spring and Autumn and Warring States periods (770–221 B.C.). This period, marked by the disintegration of the clan communes, witnessed the most violent changes in ancient Chinese society. In the ideological realm, it saw the most active creative development, as numerous schools of thought emerged and scholars, each claiming to represent the truth, contended ceaselessly. However, the one main trend that ran through all this was rationalism, which freed itself of primitive magic and religion and laid the foundations of the Han people's cultural and psychological structure. This was manifested primarily in the school of thought represented by Confucius (551–479 B.C.) and the opposing but supplementary doctrine of Taoism represented by Laozi and Zhuangzi (c.369–286 B.C.). The mutual and complementary roles played by Confucianism and Taoism are an important thread that has run through all Chinese aesthetic thinking for the past 2,000 years.

The ideological basis of Chinese culture—what makes it different from other cultures, what makes the Chinese people different from other peoples and Chinese art different from other arts—must be traced back to Pre-Qin Confucianism. Whether viewed as good or bad, whether accepted or repudiated, the historical role of Confucius and Confucianism in shaping the Chinese character, culture, and psychology is an undeniable reality. It is not incidental that Confucianism has become synonymous with Chinese culture all over the world.

Confucius acquired his present place in Chinese history in part because he redefined primitive culture, rites, and music by bringing them into the domain of 'practical rationality,' meaning rationality in daily life, human relations, and political concepts, instead of viewing rationalism as an abstract and abstruse theory. His followers, Mencius and Xunzi, extended and completed the Confucian line.

The basic features of the Confucian outlook combine a skeptical or atheistic world outlook with a positive, energetic attitude towards life. It combines psychology and ethics as its core, as Confucius elucidated in his reply to Zai Wo[1] on the question of three years of mourning for a deceased parent:

> Zai Wo asked whether three years of mourning was not too long. He said that if a gentleman neglected rites for three years, the rites would be ruined; if he neglected music for three years, the music would be gone; and that when the last harvest was gone and a new one brought in, it was time to strike the flint and start a new fire. Confucius replied: 'If you ate rice and wore brocade during this time, would you feel easy?' 'Yes. I would,' Zai Wo answered. 'If you do feel easy, then do it,' said Confucius, 'but when a gentleman is in mourning, good food does not taste good, music is not pleasant, and living in the normal way makes him uncomfortable, so he refrains from all these things.' When Zai Wo had left, Confucius said, 'Zai Wo is not a virtuous man. When a baby is born, it cannot leave the bosom of its parents until after three years, so three years of mourning is a universal custom. Did not Zai Wo have three years of such love from his parents?'
>
> (*Lun Yu*, or *Confucian Analects*)

Leaving aside, for the present, the question of whether the three-year period of mourning was a custom instituted by the Confucian school, the important thing here is that Confucius explained a traditional ritual by relating it to a universal psychological principle, the love between parents and children. He gave a rational psychological explanation to the apparently arbitrary custom questioned by Zai Wo. The consequence was that something that might have been viewed as a social compulsion was transformed into something ethically motivated and intrinsically valuable. Confucianism turned the rites, which formerly served and were subordinate to the gods, to the service of human beings. Confucius did not try to orient human emotions, concepts, and rites—the three elements of religion—towards some external object of worship or supernatural realm. Rather, he directed and incorporated them into worldly relationships and human life, modeled on the blood ties between parents and children. Human emotions were diverted from their alien theological objects and from idol-like symbols, and instead found expression and satisfaction in the practical psychology and ethics of social life. This also became an important characteristic of Chinese art and aesthetics.

Take, for example, the difference between the Chinese philosopher Xunzi's (c.313–238 B.C.) *Yuelun* (*On Music*) and

[1] Zai Wo (522–458 B.C.), Confucius's disciple.

Aristotle's *Poetics*: the former stressed the influence of art on common everyday feelings; Aristotle attached more importance to the cognitive and imitative functions of art and its purifying role, thus turning it into a quasi-religious form. The Pre-Qin Chinese philosophers attached importance to the integration of reason and emotion, with reason holding emotion in check. They stressed psychological experience and satisfaction in social and ethical issues, not an ascetic suppression of sensory desires, nor rational cognitive pleasure. Still less did they stress the need to evoke some mystical emotion (Plato) or to purify the soul (Aristotle).

Along with the redefining of rites as 'benevolence' or 'humanity' (Confucius), and as an expression of 'the quality of mercy possessed by all' (Mencius, 372–289 B.C.), music, too, was freed from primitive magic, songs, and dance, redefined and given practical and rational qualities: 'When we speak of rites, do we just think of jade and silks?[2] When we speak of music, do we just think of drums and bells?' (*Confucian Analects*); 'Music has been created, how can it be dispensed with? It cannot be, and the hands and feet will involuntarily begin dancing [to music]' (Mencius); 'All tongues have the same liking for taste; all ears have the same receptivity for sound; all eyes have the same sense of beauty in colours' (Mencius).

Here art is no longer an external form of rites: (1) it must appeal to the senses and be of a general nature; (2) it must be related to social ethics and consequently to current politics. The new rationalistic definition of rites and music initiated by Confucius reached its apogee among Xunzi and his followers, and *Yueji* (*Notes on Music*), a section of the *Book of Rites* devoted to the principles of music, became ancient China's earliest and most specialized collection of documents on aesthetics.

> Music is joy, a human passion that cannot be dispensed with; so man cannot do without music. . . . Its sound should create joy without degeneracy; its words should be discriminating but not reprimanding; its straight or winding movements, elaborate or simple composition. Simple or rich tones and rhythm should be such as to awaken the goodness in man and prevent evil and corruption.
> (Xunzi: *Yuelun*, or *On Music*)

> Music is born in the heart. When a person's emotions are aroused, they turn into sound, and sound that has been refined is called music.

---

[2] 'Jade and silks' is a general term for objects used in rites and ceremonies. Here it is meant that the internal emotions are more important than external objects, even jade and silk.

Thus the music in times of peace and prosperity is tranquil,
expressing pleasure over good government; the music in troubled
times is resentful, showing displeasure over misgovernment; and the
music of a conquered nation is mournful, dwelling on the sufferings
of the people. The way of sound and music is therefore one with
politics.
(Xunzi: *Yueji*, or *Notes on Music*)

Guo Moruo wrote: 'The word *yue* covered a very wide field in
ancient China. It goes without saying that music, singing, and dancing
were included, as these are three in one; but painting and the plastic arts
such as sculpture, engraving, and architecture were also included. Even
hunting, good food, and ceremonial rites were implied by the word. *Yue*
meant joy, so broadly speaking anything that made people happy, that
provided sensory enjoyment, could be called *yue*. But there is no doubt
that it referred primarily to music' (*The Ten Critiques: Gongsun Nizi
and His Theory of Music*).

Thus what is summarized in *Yueji* is not only a theory of music but
aesthetic ideas covering every realm of art, with music as the chief
representative. *Yueji* links music and the arts closely with
the senses: 'The eye wants the best colours, the ear the best sounds, the
mouth the best flavors . . .' and emotions: 'Pleasure comes from it
[*yue*]. . . . When people can sense what is good or bad but there is no
way to voice their joy or anger, things will be difficult.' It asserts that
'*yue* is akin to humaneness as *yi* (righteousness) is to rationality' and
that '*yue* evokes the same [emotional response] in all humans, while *li*
(rites) distinguishes what are different [right and wrong].' These
statements stress the emotional characteristics of art in contrast with the
objective codes and standards of rational systems. But the emotional
influence exerted by the arts and aesthetics is closely related to both
social life and political activities, for 'it lifts the hearts of the people
and easily changes customs and habits' (all quotes are from *Yueji*).

Chinese aesthetics, like Chinese philosophy, stresses not cognition
or imitation, but emotional communication. So it pays less attention to
the object and substance and more to function, relationship, and
rhythm. From *yin-yang* (and the duality of 'to be or not to be,' figure
and spirit, real and empty of later generations) and *he-tong* (harmony
and identity) to atmosphere and artistic appeal, the nature, principles,
and laws of classical Chinese aesthetics were generally functional. In
dealing with opposites, the stress was on blending and harmony more
than on conflict. Regarding the question of realism, the expression of an
intrinsic interest in life was seen as more important than exact imitation

and faithful reproduction. In effect, the stress was on the integration of emotion and reason and on the intuitive wisdom of emotions that could achieve harmony and satisfaction in life, rather than on irrational fantasies or supernatural beliefs. In imagery, the emphasis was on emotional beauty (feminine grace) and grandeur (masculine strength) and not fatalistic terror or tragic, if noble, acts. All these 'self-balancing' principles and artistic components of classical Chinese aesthetics may be traced back to the rational spirit of the Pre-Qin era.

The general trend in the Pre-Qin was towards a rational spirit, whether noted scholars were working on logic or Laozi, legalists, and the militarists were initiating the political strategy. Taoism, as represented by Zhuangzi, was as closely associated with aesthetics and the arts and had as far-reaching an influence as did Confucianism. Laozi and Zhuangzi both opposed and complemented the Confucians, and they played a no less decisive role in forming the Chinese people's world outlook, their attitude towards life, their cultural-psychological structure, and their artistic ideals and aesthetic interests.

We must, however, begin by comparing them with Confucius. Confucian skepticism and its positive world outlook—'Respect ghosts and angels but keep away from them' (Analects)—on the one hand developed into Xunzi's optimistic and progressive atheism—'Be the master of your fate and make use of it'; 'Heaven moves with vigorous strides, the gentleman makes unremitting efforts to improve himself.' On the other hand, they evolved into Zhuangzi's philosophy of aesthetics.

Confucius's respect for the individuality of the members of a clan—'You can capture the commander of an army, but you cannot deprive an ordinary man of his will'—developed into Mencius's idea of a noble character, one that 'wealth cannot corrupt, poverty cannot change, power cannot subdue.' But it also led directly to Zhuangzi's idea of independent individuals who abandon the world and isolate themselves from secular concerns: 'vacillating beyond the dust and dirt of the world; free and unfettered in inactivity.'

At first glance, Confucianism and Taoism appear diametrically opposed: one enters the world while the other rejects it; one is optimistic and active, the other passive and retiring. But actually they balance each other in many ways. Sayings such as 'Save the world at the same time [as you save yourself]' (Confucian) and 'Live a good life by oneself' (Taoist) have often been adhered to simultaneously by scholars and officials of later generations as complementary guidelines in life. Likewise, compassion and magnanimity versus hatred of the dirty world and avoidance of the vulgar, and the idea of being physically among the people while spiritually in an imperial palace, are opposites that have blended and become integrated into the normal psychology and artistic concepts of Chinese intellectuals through the ages.

In the final analysis, however, Confucianism and Taoism do remain fundamentally different philosophies. For example, Xunzi stressed that 'man's nature cannot be beautiful on its own without artificiality,' while Zhuangzi argued that 'there is great beauty on earth [in the natural state] though it does not speak.' The Confucianist formulation stresses the creation of art by man and its practical utility, while the Taoist gives prominence to the independence of art and beauty in nature. Confucianism, bound within its framework of narrow, practical utility, frequently inhibited and disrupted art and aesthetics. Taoism, on the other hand, negated that framework and extricated art— romantic, uninhibited, and imaginative. It promoted an ardent expression of feelings and a search for individuality that gave new momentum to the development of Chinese art, in both form and content. Though Zhuangzi shunned the world, he did not negate life but rather cherished and valued humanity's natural life. (This is basically different from the Nirvana of Buddhism.) This makes his philosophy, as an aesthetic view of life, scintillate with emotion; it is that part of Taoism that supplements and deepens Confucianism and is one with it. This is why we say the Taoism of Laozi and Zhuangzi is both the opposite and the complement of Confucianism.

> What can be described in words are the generalities of a thing; what is understood in meaning is its essence. What cannot be described in words nor understood in meaning is neither general nor essential.
> (Zhuangzi: *Autumn Waters*)

> What the world values are books. Books are only words, so it is words that are valuable. The value of words is in their meaning, but there is a source to the meaning and this source cannot be described in words. The world cherishes books because it values words. Although the world values them, I do not; for what it considers valuable is not the real value.
> (Zhuangzi: *The Way of Heaven*)

These enigmatic, paradoxical statements express the basic characteristics of art, aesthetics, and creativity in a way no scholar of Confucianism or any other school has ever done. They imply that images are greater than thoughts, that imagination is more important than concept, that too much ingenuity may turn into clumsiness, and that words cannot fully express meaning. What is imagined or emotionally felt is often richer than what can be verbally expressed or rationally conceived. And imagination or images that cannot be expressed in words can still be apprehended emotionally.

The Confucians stressed the normal gratification and expression of the senses and feelings, the practical utility of art in the service of the social order and politics. The Taoists, on the other hand, stressed a *laissez-faire* relationship between humanity and the external world that transcended utility. They focused on an aesthetic relationship, on inner, spiritual, and substantive beauty, on the non-cognitive laws of artistic creation. If the influence of the Confucians on later literature and art lay mainly in the theme and content, that of the Taoists lay mainly in the laws of creativity—in aesthetics. And the importance of art as a unique form of ideology lies precisely in its aesthetic laws.

The Principles of *Fu*, *Bi*, and *Xing*

Art forms that appealed to the senses of sight and hearing probably began in the Old and New Stone Ages. But literature in the form of script that conveyed concepts and appealed to the imagination developed much later. While the ancient oracle-bone inscriptions (divinations), bronze inscriptions (on bells and tripods), certain sections of the *Book of Changes*, and the *Daya* and *Song* sections of the *Book of Songs*[3] all contained passages of aesthetic significance, they can hardly be regarded as real works of literature. It is difficult for readers to read, much less comprehend, these ancient writings, which makes it almost impossible for them to arouse any aesthetic response.

The earliest real literary works are the *Guofeng* section of the *Book of Songs* and the various prose writings of the Pre-Qin scholars. It was during the Spring and Autumn and Warring States periods, or perhaps a little earlier than these two eras, that primitive writings changed from pure records of events and hymns addressed to the gods to lyrical and argumentative writings that expressed the rational spirit of their time. The popular love songs and the odes and laments of the clan aristocracy in the *Guofeng* laid the foundation of Chinese poetry and established its aesthetic keynote, which was mainly lyrical, as the

---

[3] *Shi Jing*, or the *Book of Songs*, is China's earliest collection of songs and poems. It was compiled during the Spring and Autumn period and comprised 305 pieces divided into three categories: *Feng* or *Guofeng* ('Styles' or 'National Styles,' a collection of popular songs), *Ya* ('Elegance,' courtly songs) and *Song* (Odes). *Daya* and *Xiaoya* are subcategories of *Ya*.

following examples show:

WIND AND RAIN

Long and loud the rooster crows
  In the cold of wind and rain,
But my troubled soul is calm once more,
  For my good man is here again.

Long and loud the rooster crows
  In the storm of wind and rain,
But my aching heart shall ache no more,
  For my good man is here again.

Unceasingly the rooster crows
  In the gloom of wind and rain
But there's only gladness in my heart.
  For my good man is here again.

THE REEDS (first stanza)

Luxuriant are the slender reeds,
  Like frost the dew so pure;
Somewhere across the waters
  Is the one to me so dear.
I seek him up the river,
  So long and hard the way;
I seek him down the river,
  Midstream he seems to stay.

GATHERING VETCH (last stanza)

The willows were softly swaying,
When I left home years ago;
Now rain and snow are falling,
As I trace my footsteps home.
The way is long, our pace is slow,
Thirst and hunger our load;
My heart is heavy with sorrow,
Who is there to share my woe?

It does not matter who or what is being praised, mourned, or remembered in these pieces—the genuine feeling of joy or sadness they evoke, their vivid and realistic images, the singing, sighing, repeating style, and mild and lingering rhythm remain much appreciated even today. Unlike the ancient epic poems of other nations, they are short verses that, from the very beginning, influence and inspire people by their lyricism and practical rationality. They are works of art that embody the national characteristics of Chinese aesthetics.

From the many pieces collected in the *Book of Songs*, later generations have summed up the aesthetic principles of *fu*, *bi*, and *xing*, whose influence has lasted for more than two thousand years. The best-known exposition of these principles was made by Zhu Xi (1130–1200) of the Southern Song, who said: '*Fu* is the direct statement of facts; *bi* is to compare one object to another; *xing* is to mention something else first in order to bring out the subject by association' (*Commentaries on the Book of Songs*). However, many other explanations have been offered by ancient and modern scholars. Since the meaning of *fu* is relatively simple and clear, the discussions were mainly on *bi* and *xing*, both of which are concerned with how to express one's feelings in order to create artistic effects.

Chinese literature (prose or poetry) is largely lyrical. But not every work that expresses the author's feelings can be considered art. To become a work of art with certain general and necessary artistic qualities and a corresponding artistic appeal, subjective feelings must be made objective, incorporated with some kind of imagination and understanding. *Bi* and *xing* are the means by which feelings can be transformed into art, that is, incorporated with imagination and understanding and consequently objectified.

In *Wenxin Diaolong*, a book on literary theory by Liu Xie (c.465–532, a literary critic of the Northern and Southern Dynasties), are definitions of these two terms: '*Bi* is to compare, *xing* is to arouse. . . . The *bi* way of writing appeared because of the need to compare the natures of different things; the *xing* style was established because of the need to arouse the feelings.' In practice, the two are often used in conjunction with each other, it being difficult to distinguish fully between them. Both are ways to generate, alleviate, express, or transmit one's feelings and ideas through reference to external scenes or objects. Only in this way can subjective emotions be integrated with the imagination and understanding (some measure of which must be present irrespective of whether the integration is made through comparison or contrast) and thus be made objective, becoming an artistic image coloured by reason and emotion. No longer is the object or scene a thing in itself; it has been glazed with emotion, which in turn is no longer just subjective, for it has been transformed into an objective image by human imagination and understanding. Literary images created in this way are neither simple, direct models of external objects nor arbitrary expressions of personal feelings; still less are they instances of rational knowledge accessible through the intellect only. They have an emotional appeal that mere intellect cannot fathom nor cognition fully grasp.

Said Wang Fuzhi (1619–1692): 'The song "The Crane Sings" in *Xiaoya* uses the *bi*-style throughout; not a single line is expressed plainly' (*Jiangzhai's Notes on Poetry*[4]). 'Not a single line is expressed plainly' has always been a major tenet of Chinese aesthetics. Such sayings as 'to get the best with a minimum of words' (*On Poets and Poetry* by Sikong Tu, 637–908) and 'when the antelope hangs itself by the horns, it cannot be tracked' (*Canglang Notes on Poetry* by Yan Yu, Southern Song) are references to this special artistic-aesthetic quality, which is inaccessible to conceptualization and cognition.

Bi and *xing* permit writers to combine subjective feelings with objective scenes and objects. The earliest examples of this appeared in the *Book of Songs*, which has therefore become an authority on the uses of *bi* and *xing* down the ages. Wrote Li Dongyang (1447–1516), a poet of the Ming Dynasty:

> There are three ways of writing poetry and *fu* is only one of them. *Bi* and *xing* are the other two. In both, feelings are embedded in an object. It is easy to cover a subject through direct narration but hard to move and influence people in this way. Only when a veiled meaning is conveyed through descriptions and simulations that are repeated with expression and intonation until the reader grasps them on his own, when words may end but the meaning is unlimited, will the spirit be released and the hands and feet involuntarily dance with joy. That is why in poetry the emphasis is on thought and feeling, not facts.
> (*Notes on Poetry of Huailu Hall*)

Here the importance of *bi* and *xing* to poetry (art) is explained concisely: they are the epitome of emotion, imagination, and understanding. 'Embedding feelings in an object' and 'releasing the spirit' are preferred to 'direct statement,' for the latter too easily turns into pure conceptual knowledge, in which meaning stops when the words do. Even direct statements of feelings too often become items of conceptual knowledge that have no emotional effect on others. The exclamation, 'Ah, how sad I am!' is only a concept, not poetry. Direct expressions of feeling have an aesthetic effect only when their context is in *bi* or *xing*. This is what Wang Fuzhi implied in his advice to 'use a scene to produce a feeling' and 'to enhance the effect, describe sorrow in a joyful scene and joy in a sorrowful one' (*Jiangzhai's Notes on Poetry*). He, like many others, adhered to the belief that emotions can be made objective through scenes and objects, which in turn contribute to both imagination and understanding.

[4] Wang Fuzhi was styled Jiangzhai.

Thus both *bi* and *xing* should be defined as aesthetic principles that concern the characteristics of images of artistic creation. One cannot clearly distinguish betweeh the two or delve too deeply into their literal definitions, as annotators in the old days tried to do. There is, however, a historical significance worth noting in those attempts to distinguish between *bi* and *xing* and to give them exact meanings. This significance lay in the linkage of writings in *bi* and *xing* with social, political, and historical events, which masters of the classics of the Han Dynasty accomplished by expanding the connotations of words. This practice prevailed for more than 2,000 years, from the Western and Eastern Han, the Tang and Song, down to the Ming and Qing Dynasties. For example, some scholars insisted that the first piece in the *Book of Songs*, 'Crying Ospreys', was a tribute to the virtues of empresses and imperial concubines, a view that even Zhu Xi, a man quite liberal in his artistic and literary thinking, readily supported.

Of course, the equating of art to political enigmas as in the example cited above rested purely on guesswork and was only an arbitrary comparison. But there is a reason, a historical reason, for this practice when it is viewed in its entirety.

The stretching of meanings in *bi* and *xing* by Han Dynasty scholars was essentially a reflection of an important historical process, in which primitive songs and poems that served primitive magic and rites evolved into lyrical literary works. In the days of the clans and tribes, the phrase 'poems speak the will' meant that poems 'describe the way' (*On 'Poems Speak the Will'* by Zhu Ziqing) (1898–1948) and 'record events' (Meng Wentong's article in *Scholarly Monthly*, No. 8/1962). In other words, in remote antiquity so-called 'poems' were actually the historical, political, or religious documents of a clan, tribe, or nation, not writings to express the feelings of individuals. There are many historical materials to show that poetry and music were originally inseparable and in the beginning were used as offerings to the gods or to celebrate victories or successes. The *Daya* and *Song* sections of the *Book of Songs* still contained vestiges of this, but by the time of the songs in the *Guofeng* section, the ancient clan society had completely disintegrated, rationalism was on the upsurge, and both art and literature were being freed from ritual and evolving into relatively independent fields of human endeavour. They were no longer religious or political works to chronicle events or eulogize the gods, so it was wrong for the Han Dynasty scholars to continue to relate them to political events.

To understand correctly the origin and cause of the stretching of the meanings of *bi* and *xing* writings, it is necessary to review the whole ideological trend of the Pre-Qin era. A scientific understanding of why such stretching of meanings was made will help us to a true picture of the process of emancipation of literature (poetry) from being an appendage of religion, history, and politics to a free lyrical art.

Relatively little attention or controversy has centered on *fu*, which refers to the recording of events, description of objects, and expression of ideas and feelings in a simple and direct way, especially the recording of events. If the *Guofeng* section of the *Book of Songs* represented a break with primitive ways of recording events and expressing ideas, all of which were associated with religion, to become pure lyrical art with *bi* and *xing* as its principles and methods of creation, the prose of the Pre-Qin era in a sense used the principles of *fu* to break with religion and become a tool of logic and reason. The fact that some of these argumentative prose writings could be regarded as literary works must again be attributed to the law of emotion already described, that is, the objectifying of the emotions and their imaginative empathetic incorporation into the text. It was this law that gave works of ancient Chinese prose, which lacked imagery, the elegance and power that turned them into lasting works that were read, enjoyed, and imitated by later generations.

Some sections of these Pre-Qin works, for example, some of the settings, stories, and fables recorded in the *Confucian Analects*, in Mencius and Zhuangzi, and some of the battle scenes described in *Zuozhuan*,[5] did contain imagery. On the whole, however, the writings of Mencius and Zhuangzi, of Xunzi and Han Fei, and the *Zuozhuan* achieved literary distinction not because of their imagery, but because of the force and style of their arguments and reasoning: the power and grandeur of Mencius, the weirdness and cunning of Zhuangzi, the precision and care of Xunzi, and the sharp, penetrating style of Han Fei. It was these that made them aesthetically appealing. Power, grandeur, weirdness, cunning, precision, care, sharpness, and penetration communicate certain emotions or qualities through the writers' choice of words. It is the emotional quality of the words, more than their imagery, that gives the writings their appeal. This is one of the most prominent features in Chinese prose literature. This fully accords with the difference between China's *Notes on Music* and Europe's *Poetics*— a difference in basic aesthetic theory.

[5] *Zuozhuan* is a commentary on the *Spring and Autumn Annals*. It is attributed by some to Zuo Qiuming, a historian of the Spring and Autumn period.

To sum up, both prose and poetry need the amalgamation and interweaving of emotion with imagination and understanding and with psychological function. But the element of understanding is more important in prose than in poetry.

> Said King Hui of Liang, 'I'm ready to listen to your advice.'
> 'Is there any difference between killing a man with a club and with a knife?' asked Mencius.
> 'No,' said the king.
> 'Between a knife and tyranny. Is there any difference?'
> 'No.'
> 'There is good meat in your kitchen and fat horses in your stable, but the people go hungry and some starve to death in the cold. This is as bad as leading beasts to devour men. We abhor beasts that devour each other; yet as the people's paternal rulers you are leading beasts to devour men. How can you be called a paternal ruler of the people?'
> (Mencius: *King Hui of Liang*)

> In the North Sea there is a fish called *kun*. It is so large that no one knows how many miles its body extends. It has been changed into a roc [a legendary bird] and no one knows how many miles long the back of the roc is. When it is angry and flies, its wings are like clouds hanging from the sky. . . .
> (Zhuangzi: *Travelling at Leisure*)

The excerpt from Mencius uses orderly parallelism to intensify the emotional colour and power of its logic and inferences, giving the process of reasoning an irresistible force. The quote from Zhuangzi is characterized by an extraordinarily exaggerated imagination; it incorporates its statements in specific images. In both cases, the effect comes from the coordination or integration, in different proportions, of emotion, imagination, and understanding. It is because of the presence of emotion and imagination that such writings, though expository or argumentative in nature, came to be recognized as prose literature. Like songs and poems, they too are in full accord with the national aesthetic characteristics of Chinese literature.

Architectural Art

Line—the linear element—is as basic to and expressive of Chinese aesthetics in the visual arts as emotion is in prose and poetry. Indeed, the art of line is closely associated with emotion because visual lines can unfold and express tension, climax, and resolution just as musical compositions do. Lines, too, can express emotion while subject to the restraint and control of rationality. Such characteristics are visible in Chinese architecture, whose abstract lines and forms have been the objects of aesthetic study. Many of China's basic aesthetic features are revealed in her architecture as well as other art forms.

Relics discovered at Banpo and other Neolithic sites tell us that square and rectangular structures of wood and stone, which later evolved into the principal forms of Chinese architecture, were already being built in the New Stone Age. The *Book of Songs* uses such phrases as 'like a pheasant flying' and 'temples built like wings' to describe buildings, showing that even in early times large-scale structures were being built and that they possessed aesthetic qualities. Such terms as 'wings' and 'like . . . flying' probably referred to the building extensions and eaves that tilted like the wings of a bird in flight.

The demand for aesthetic beauty in architecture reached a high point during the Spring and Autumn and Warring States periods. By this time, society had entered a new phase. To the emerging new commercial aristocracy, buildings were no longer mere shelters against the wind and rain—they offered an opportunity to inspire admiration and awe. So the demand for grandeur and magnificence spread rapidly. The *Zuozhuan* and *Guoyu*[6] contain many allusions to this: 'What beautiful rooms; can anything be better?' and 'What beautiful terraces!' In *Mocius: Feile* (*Speaking Against Pleasure*), it is recorded that King Fuchai of Wu ordered the building of a terrace at Gusu (another name for Suzhou) that was still unfinished after a whole decade. In *Zuozhuan: 31st Year of Duke Zhuang*, there is a story of a terrace whose construction began in the spring and lasted through summer and autumn; and in *Guoyu: Qiyu* (*Sayings of the State of Qi*) we read that Duke Xiang had elaborate terraces built.

The enthusiasm for building probably peaked with the construction of the fabulous Epang Palace by Qin Shihuang, the first emperor of Qin, after he conquered the other six states[7] and unified the country. According to historical documents, palace-building took place on a truly astonishing scale in the Qin Dynasty, more than 2,000 years ago. The following excerpts from the *Historical Records: Biography of Qin Shihuang* shed some light on this:

> Whenever Qin conquered another ducal state, it would make models

[6] *Guoyu* (*National Language*), a book attributed to Zuo Qiuming, is a collection of sayings by aristocrats of the various ducal states of the Western Zhou and Spring and Autumn periods.

[7] Qi, Chu, Yan, Han, Zhao, and Wei. Together with Qin, they are called the seven Warring States.

of the latter's palaces, which would be reconstructed upon the northern slopes of Xianyang [near present-day Xi'an], facing the Wei River to the south. From east of Yong Gate to the waters of the Jing and Wei was a continuous chain of halls, pavilions and winding paths. . . .

Shihuang, the First Emperor, felt that the palaces built by his predecessors were too small because Xianyang was such a populous place. . . . So he ordered a new palace built in the woods and gardens south of the Wei River. The first part to be built was the front hall called Epang, which measured 500 steps east-west and 50 *zhang*[8] north-south. The upper floor could seat 10,000 people while a 50-foot flag could be hoisted on the lower floor. On all sides were balconies and pathways that led from the foot of the hall to the Southern Hills, whose peak stood like a watchtower.

These passages show that from its very origins Chinese architectural art focused not on single, independent buildings but on vast complexes with interconnected and well-coordinated parts spread out over a large area. Chinese architecture stressed the organic arrangement of the parts into a coherent, harmonious horizontal complex. While no above-ground buildings of the Qin are extant, Qin Shihuang's underground tomb offers us a good example of such complexes. Though extremely fragmentary, the pits of terracotta soldiers and horses unearthed from around the perimeter of the tomb in the 1970s—one of the world's great archaeological discoveries— suggest that the tomb in its entirety must have been of unbelievable magnificence and splendour. The size of the terracotta figures and the thickness and hardness of the building materials (bricks fired in the Qin Dynasty) also testify to its grandeur. It compares well with the Egyptian pyramids in beauty and power, and both are tombs, but a major difference is that Qin's tomb was a very complicated system of intricate and interconnected parts that extend horizontally rather than an independent structure simple in form and tapering to a point.

'One hundred generations followed the Qin system' (from Mao Zedong's poem). In architecture, this was also true. Chinese architecture probably never departed from the basic standards of style and structure established in the Pre-Qin era. A fairly consistent aesthetic style was maintained throughout the Qin, Han, Tang, Song, Ming, and Qing Dynasties.

How might we characterize this aesthetic or artistic style? In essence, it embodies the spirit of practical rationality that characterizes the Chinese nation. Whereas the principal historical buildings of most

[8] A Chinese measure of length, about 12 feet or 3.3 meters.

countries are temples and churches constructed to enshrine supernatural beings—the temples of the Greek gods, the Islamic mosques, the Gothic churches—China's major architectural works were palaces built for emperors and kings, in other words, for humans. In all probability, since the construction of the so-called 'large mansion'[9] of the New Stone Age, worship of gods and spirits in China has taken place not in independent, free-standing sanctuaries, but in worldly dwellings that were also the setting for everyday life.

This practice of housing humans and gods under the same roof developed further once primitive religion was superseded by Confucianism. Thus, Chinese architecture throughout history is typified not by religious buildings isolated from the world at large and symbolizing things beyond human experience, but by palatial ancestral temples linked to secular life and the human environment. As a result, the artistic features of Chinese architecture are associated with the human, earthly plane and grounded in reality; the spaces are not void and solemn so as to instill terror in the hearts of those who enter, but rather arranged so as to be plain, natural, and closely related to everyday life. Space is not conceived of as something creating mystery or tension, or evoking excitement or repentance; it is used to produce a sense of clear, harmonious and practical values.

Just as the basic theory of Chinese landscape paintings, as we will see later in Chapter 9, is that they can have many functions—they can be 'viewed,' 'travelled through,' and most importantly, 'toured,' or 'lived in'—so the emphasis in Chinese architecture is not on intense stimulation or perception, but on the evocation of ordinary human sentiments. Buildings are not places to be visited once a week for the cleansing of the soul, but are to be revisited constantly or used as a home. Unlike many Western churches, where visitors on entering find themselves in a vast cavernous space that evokes feelings of smallness and helplessness and the wish to call to God for protection, the horizontal expansion of Chinese buildings into an organic complex virtually transforms spatial consciousness into a concept of time. Chinese complexes, with their broad horizontal dimensions, permit visitors to stroll at their leisure through an uninterrupted procession of varied and intricate halls, balconies, pavilions, and terraces that epitomize the ease and comfort of life and evoke a feeling of mastery. Although the amount of space taken up by the complex may be

[9] A public place for meetings, festivities, and worship in the very primitive group society.

enormous, space is turned into time as one moves along leisurely at one's own pace. In such complexes, practical, worldly, rational, and historical elements dominate, not the supernatural awareness that is the basic aesthetic focus of many purely religious buildings.

Chinese rationality is also expressed in the rigid symmetry of its architecture, which is solemn, regular, and orderly. When compared to a Christian, Muslim, or Buddhist building, any individual building in a Chinese architectural complex does appear to be small, low, plain and, perhaps, inferior. But when the complex is viewed as a whole, its orderly composition and meandering and interlocking parts give it an obvious power and grandeur. Simple basic units are put together to form an intricate whole, with variation in the symmetry and a uniform style in the variation.

Parenthetically, it is worth noting that though the Great Wall, a classic example of Chinese architecture, is lacking in strict symmetry, its different sections are identical in structure. It, too, is horizontal, meandering over thousands of miles, and though its height may not be impressive, its remarkable power lies in the way it stretches uninterruptedly over peaks and ridges, like an infinitely long dragon flying and dancing. Its continuity in space is an expression of continuity in time, and a symbol of the vitality of the Chinese nation.

This quality—a mobile beauty that unfolds through time—is also revealed in the spatial characteristics of individual buildings within the complexes. Here the artistic characteristics of lines are again revealed, for it is through lines that beauty is expressed. The shape and ornamentation

Hall of Supreme Harmony, Palace Museum (former imperial palace), Beijing. Built in the Qing Dynasty, it is the largest wooden building in China today. Here the Qing emperors performed their most important state ceremonies, including coronations, birthday celebrations, festivities, and the launching of military expeditions.

of the roof play an important role in Chinese wooden buildings. The curves of the roof and the slightly upward tilting eaves of the post-Han period give a light and uplifting appearance to an otherwise exceedingly heavy and oppressive canopy. Moreover, with a wide and thick body and a broad base to match, the whole structure does not appear top-heavy,

Great Wild Goose Pagoda, Xi'an, Tang architecture. This is a seven-storied structure that stands 64 meters high. Each side of the base is 25 meters wide. The Buddhist scriptures that Xuanzang brought back from India were stored here at one time.

simply solid and stable. What is evoked is a feeling of harmony, comfort, and practicality and a clear rhythmic effect.

Even the religious pagodas introduced into China from India became Sinicized over time. They were no longer randomly piled structures that were both intricate and repetitious in composition, nor straight vertical columns of uniform width. Instead, they acquired distinct levels, which gave them a rhythmic beauty as clear and simple as whole numbers in mathematics. They thus differ greatly from complex, piled-up structures like the Wuge Temple in Cambodia.

Comparing the Great and Small Wild Goose Pagodas built not far from each other in Xi'an, we find that the Great Wild Goose Pagoda is a more typical example of a Chinese-style pagoda. Its simply graded and clearly defined stories and the obvious differences in proportions between adjacent stories are quite unlike the Small Wild Goose Pagoda, whose stories are narrower and less distinctly marked off. The style of the latter, though also Sinicized, may be closer to an original exotic style.

Similarly, if we compare the Yuan Dynasty city gate discovered in Beijing in 1968 with the city's more familiar Ming Dynasty gate, the artistic features of the architectures of different nationalities are apparent. The Yuan gate is thinner and more slanted, which is a somewhat exotic style, and resembles in some respects a Muslim city gate. The Ming gate and wall, which resembles the city wall of Nanjing, are on the contrary thick, straight, and powerful. Even though these Ming features are the result of modifications and developments in later generations, the main threads can still be traced back to the rational spirit of the Pre-Qin era.

Because Chinese architecture ever since the Pre-Qin era consisted of palatial buildings in which people were to live and enjoy themselves not just worship, the buildings have always been richly decorated with fine paintings and carvings for the free enjoyment of all who had access to them. The *Confucian Analects* mention 'shaped brackets and embellished upright pieces' which evidently are references to architectural decoration. The abundance of paintings and carvings in Chinese architecture is also referred to in Han Dynasty prose. The meticulous care in decorating eaves and brackets, the free and varied shapes of doors and windows, and the use of brilliant colours are represented in such phrases as 'golden beds and jade doors,' 'double-eaved buildings with carved banisters,' 'carved beams and painted rafters.' Such methods of decorating buildings have continued up to the modern era.

Landscape gardening developed steadily in the later period. The

law of symmetry that gave palace architecture its dignity and solemnity
was finally broken with the introduction of a new style of architectural
beauty, which aimed to simulate the natural world and was
characterized by capricious twists and turns and unpredictable changes
in layout. This allowed more room for the architect or designer's
imagination and feelings to exert themselves. The following lines from
a poem by Lu You (1125–1210) are a good example:

> Where hills are thick and rivers wind, the path there seems to end;
> Yet beyond the shade of willow and flowers bright another
>   village stands.

This style of landscape architecture, though still characterized by
an overall organic arrangement, was an expression of the greater
freedom in artistic conception and aesthetic ideals enjoyed by scholars
and officials in the later stage of Chinese society. Heavily influenced by
the aesthetics of landscape painting (see Chapter 9), it sought to bring
the human and natural worlds closer together by 'naturalizing'
artificially designed grounds so that they would become as much one
with nature as possible. Through such ingenious methods as 'borrowing
scenes' and 'combining the real with the imaginary,' architectural
complexes were integrated with natural landscape beauty to form an
organic whole whose beauty was far more free and open than that of
purely artificial works. Distant hills and bodies of water were

Qing Dynasty garden architecture built around the Lesser West Lake, Yangzhou.

'borrowed' and integrated into the overall concept; mountains, clouds, trees, sails, ripples, bridges, streams, and villages were all encompassed. But the principle of horizontal expansion, the transformation of spatial awareness into a process of time still predominated, as did the endeavour to cultivate and express ideas about life in the present world as opposed to transcendent religious mysteries.

4

Romanticism of the Chu and Han

The Traditions of Qu Yuan

THOUGH the rational spirit rapidly gained ground in the north, with everything from Confucius to Xunzi, the Logicians to the Legalists,[1] bronze to architecture, poetry to prose gradually being freed of the fetters of magic and religion, the picture in the south was a different one. Here, what remained of primitive clan society was still relatively strong and it maintained and developed the colourful traditions of remote antiquity. In all ideological realms, it was still a world of extraordinary imagination and violent emotions, whose chief exponent in literature, art, and aesthetics was the culture of Chu,[2] represented by Qu Yuan.

Qu Yuan (c.340–278 B.C.) was China's earliest and greatest poet. His works were the expression of a deep-rooted cultural system that had originated in prehistoric times. The Confucians in the north rationalized, one by one, all the ancient traditions, myths, and magic. They humanized the gods and transformed legends into a worldly order of kings and subjects, fathers and sons. For example, the legendary saying that the 'Yellow Emperor had four faces' (or a four-sided face) was interpreted by Confucian scholars to mean that he had dispatched four ministers to 'govern the four parts of the country.' And the equally incredible saying that the Yellow Emperor lived for 300 years was, according to Confucian scholars, a reference to the man's influence, which lasted through three centuries. In the version of the *Book of Songs* edited by Confucius, who had made deletions, there were no allusions to strange powers or gods and demons. As opposed to all this, in southern culture represented by Qu Yuan vestiges of such unworldly things were clearly retained.

[1] The Logicians represented a school of thought of the Warring States period, whose teachings centred on the relations of names to things. The Legalists formed one of the principal schools of the same historical period. They advocated a policy of farming and war—wealth through farming, strength through war—and called for a rigidly enforced legal system.

[2] Chu was the largest of the seven Warring States. Its territory at one time covered nearly all of central and south China, from the Yangtse River valley to the southern provinces of Guangdong and Guangxi.

The long poem *Li Sao* (*The Lament*), now generally recognized as Qu Yuan's major work, shows us a riotous world of imagination and sentiment, rich, poignant, and profound—a world of beautiful women, fragrant grass, fields of irises and orchids, lakes full of lotus, lustrous perfumed gowns, gods, supernatural beings, soothsayers, quicksands, poisonous water, and dragons:

> Oft I looked back, gazed to the distance still,
> Longed in the wilderness to roam at will.
> Splendid my ornaments together vied
> With all the fragrance of the flowers beside.
> All men had pleasures in their various ways,
> My pleasure was to cultivate my grace.
> I would not change though they my body rend;
> How could my heart be wrested from its end?
>
> . . . .
>
> At daybreak from the land of plane-trees grey,
> I came to paradise ere close of day.
> I wished within the sacred grove to rest,
> But now the sun was sinking in the west;
> The driver of the sun I bade to stay,
> Ere with the setting rays we haste away.
> The way was long, and wrapped in gloom did seem,
> As I urged on to seek my vanished dream.[3]

In the midst of this world of myths and fantasies, the poet stood alone: staunch, defiant, resentful, and grief-stricken—an earnest seeker of truth who hated the existing social order and refused to compromise with his time. *Li Sao* fused the unbridled romantic fancies of primitive myth and the fiery individual character and passions that appeared with the awakening of man's rational nature into a perfect, organic whole that marked the real beginning of Chinese lyric poetry. Perhaps the only other work of equal artistic calibre is the novel *A Dream of Red Mansions*, by Cao Xueqin (?–1763).

Tian Wen (*Asking Heaven*), another work generally attributed to Qu Yuan, probably retained more of the mythical traditions of antiquity and in a more systematic way than any other work of literature. It mirrored the transition from mythology to history as a result of the emergence of rationality and raised questions about the continuum of mythology and history. In *Tian Wen* these questions were wrapped in a

---

[3] From *Li Sao and Other Poems of Qu Yuan*, English edition, translated by Yang Xianyi and Gladys Yang.

multi-layered blending of rich sentiment and imagination:

> Where are the forests made of stone?
>   What animals can speak?
> Where do dragons carrying bears
>   Roam over hills and creek?
> The savage nine-head cobras—
>   Where do they dart and play?
> Where live people who never die?
>   And where do giants stay?

Li Sao, *Tian Wen*, and the other works which came to be known collectively as *Chu Ci* (*Songs of Chu*) made up the prominent romantic system that dominated southern culture. In essence, these writings continued the traditions of the songs and dances performed at sacrifices to the gods in what had been Chu territory in ancient times. This continuity is seen clearly in the following passage about the 'Jiu Ge' (Songs of Nine Virtues), from the book *Chuci Zhangju* (*Analyses of the Songs of Chu*) by Wang Yi of the Han Dynasty: 'Belief in ghosts and a love of temples were common in the city of Nanying, between the rivers Yuan and Xiang, in the former state of Chu. To please the gods, there had to be singing, dancing, drums, and music in the temples . . . and so the songs were composed.'

Wang Fuzhi (1619–1692), in explaining the 'Jiu Bian' (Nine Pieces), also part of *Chu Ci*, wrote:

> *Bian* here is the same as *bian*, a unit. A piece [of a poem] is a *bian*. The title 'Jiu Bian' was borrowed from King Qi of the Xia Dynasty. The pieces carried on an old style in a new form. They can be set to the music of strings and winds, and their language is stimulating and fast-flowing, unlike the *Feng* and *Ya*, for they were the voice of Chu. The *fu*-style of later generations originated from them.

This passage is important because it clarifies several key issues. First, it points out that the songs of Chu 'carried on an old style' that was as old as the beginning of the Xia Dynasty, thus establishing their origin and antiquity and proving that they were the descendants of a style that originated in primitive society. Second, the songs could be set to music, which meant that they could be sung and could accompany dancing. Modern scholars believe that compositions like the 'Jiu Ge' were sacrificial songs, dances, and music related to primitive rites. They were collective activities and not the creations of individuals. Third, the comments on the language suggest outpourings of feelings, richness of imagination, and strange imagery uninhibited by Confucianism's practical rationality and, consequently, untrammelled by so many moral codes and so much reasoning as in the so-called teachings of the *Book of Songs* and other Confucian classics. Primitive vitality, fantastic ideas, unbridled imagination—all were freely and fully expressed. Fourth, and most important, Wang Fuzhi points out that the songs of Chu were the origin of the *fu*-style literature of the Han Dynasty.

As a matter of fact, Han culture was identical with Chu culture, the Han and Chu being inseparably linked. Although in their political, economic, and legal systems, the Han rulers basically retained Qin Dynasty patterns, in certain ideological spheres, especially in literature and art, they preserved the features of southern Chu, which was their ancestral home. The Han Dynasty originated in Chu and most of the inner circle and basic corps of the two rival camps of Liu Bang and Xiang Yu, who contended for power after the fall of the Qin Dynasty, came from what was once Chu territory. Thus, when Xiang Yu was finally defeated and encircled at Gaixia, he heard Liu Bang's soldiers singing 'songs of Chu on all sides.' And when Liu Bang returned in triumph to his native place, he composed a song called 'The Great Wind' in traditional Chu style. From beginning to end, voices representing the interests of Chu dominated the Western Han court. The two cultures had the same origins, at least in the realm of literature and art, and shared much in both form and content. They differed from the culture of the northern states of the Pre-Qin era.

Chu-Han romanticism was ancient China's second great artistic tradition. It emerged in the wake of the rational spirit of the Pre-Qin and both paralleled and complemented that spirit. This romanticism was the aesthetic trend that dominated the art of both the Western and Eastern Han Dynasties; unless this vital point is grasped, it will be difficult to understand the basic features of Han Dynasty art.

The distinctiveness of the art of the two Hans, the Western Han in particular, is obvious if it is compared with the *Book of Songs* or the prose writings of the Pre-Qin period, except of course Zhuangzi, which belongs to the same—southern—cultural system. The similarity between Zhuangzi the philosopher and Qu Yuan the poet as revealed in the former's *Travelling at Leisure* and the latter's *Wandering Afar* has long been recognized.

Han art and the ideas of the Han people were pervaded by ancient myths and legends, which became almost indispensable themes or subject matter during this period. Fuxi and Nuwa with their human heads and snake bodies; Dongwanggong and Xiwangmu, the fairy king and queen; Wangziqiao the deathless, whose arms were transformed into wings; and the host of fabulous birds and beasts—red hares, golden crows, lions, tigers, fierce dragons, mammoth elephants, giant tortoises, mythical beings with hog heads and fish tails—all retained in Han art and given deep allegorical meanings and mystical symbolism. The artistic content and aesthetic value of such depictions lay not in their images of the animal world, but in the world of myth and magic, of which those marvellous beings were the signs and symbols.

From worldly temples to underground palaces, from the silk painting of Mawangdui in the south to the Tomb of Buqianqiu[4] in the north, what is revealed to us in the art of the Western Han is precisely what is recorded in the *Songs of Chu* and *Book of Mountains and Seas*, where heaven, earth, and the underworld meet. In both aura and imagery, the Mawangdui silk painting with its dragons, snakes, nine suns, owls flying and hooting, giants holding up the sky, pious master and servant, and the Buqianqiu sepulchre murals that show Nuwa with her snake body and beautiful face, hog heads chasing away ghosts, heaven-sent demons devouring gods of drought, monstrous beings and animals, have an obvious kinship with the pieces 'Wandering Afar' and 'Recalling the Soul' from the *Songs of Chu*. All describe a world in which gods mixed with men, a world that was vast, bleak, and abounding in wild animals and uncanny beings. The following are excerpts from 'Recalling the Soul':

> Return, O soul! O soul return!
>   In east you cannot stay.
> There giants loom ten thousand feet,
>   On wandering souls they prey.
> There ten suns rising one by one,
>   Melt rock and gold away.
>
>   .   .   .   .   .   .
>
> Return, O soul! O soul return!
>   In south you must not be.
>
>   .   .   .   .   .   .
>
> There vipers swarm and foxes huge
>   Hold sway a thousand *li*.
> Nine-headed serpents come and go,
>   On human flesh they feed.
>
>   .   .   .   .   .   .
>
> Return, O soul! O soul return!
>   There're quicksands in the west.

---

[4] An ancient tomb of the Western Han, discovered at Luoyang, Henan province, in 1976.

Torn to bits in thunder pits,
  You'd never find your rest.
Return, O soul! O soul return!
  To north you must not go.
There icebergs rise like mountains high,
  In a thousand *li* of snow.

. . . .

Return, O soul! O soul return!
  Do not to heaven ascend.
There tigers, leopards guard the gates.
  Where mortals meet their end.
A nine-head giant plucks up trees
  Nine thousand with his hands;
And wolves and jackals roam at large,
  As countless as the sands.

. . . .

Return, O soul! The world below
  Is not where you belong.
The Guardian there nine tails wears,
  And horns so sharp and strong.
With shoulders broad and bloody hands,
  He stalks you where you go;
Three eyes upon his tiger head,
  A bull-like frame below.

Here we have a description of a terror-filled world stalked by man-eating beasts, to be avoided by humans. The Mawangdui painting and Buqianqiu murals depicted a somewhat more benign world in which men sought immortality, received blessings, and prayed for divine protection. Still, both were romantic worlds, full of myth, magic, and illusion, of eerie beings and mystic signs and symbols. In both, the primitive vitality and savage traditions of remote antiquity were preserved and carried on.

The Western and Eastern Hans witnessed a momentous, ideological reform in the reign of Emperor Wudi (156–87 B.C.), who 'banned all schools and worshipped only Confucianism.' In this way, the rational spirit of the Pre-Qin, whose hallmark was Confucianism and whose content was historical experience, gradually pervaded the south's art and literature and the thoughts of its people, resulting in the fusion of northern and southern cultures into a unique heterogeneous congeries. The myths and fantasies of southern Chu and the historical tales of the north, the absurdities disseminated by the Taoists and the moral principles of the Confucians were interwoven, and in a parallel way they fluctuated, mixed, and were expressed in human thought and the world of art. The dead, the living, fairies, ghosts, historical figures, worldly scenes, myths, fantasies—all existed together; and primitive totems, Confucian teachings, divinations, and superstitions lived side by side in a process that was more amalgamation than supplantation. It was still a romantic world of the imagination, rich but chaotic, and of passions ardent and undisguised.

Described in *Selected Paintings of the Han Dynasty* (pages 2 and 4) are some Eastern Han Dynasty stone pictures that reflect this romantic imagination:

> First row: Fuxi, Nuwa, Zhurong, Shennong, Zhuanxu, Gaoxin, Emperor Yao, Emperor Shun, Emperors Yu and Jie of the Xia (all are myths).
> Second row: stories of the dutiful sons Zeng Sen, Min Ziqian, Lao Laizi, and Ding Lan (all are legends).
> Third row: stories of the political assassins Cao Mo and Zhuan Zhu (all are historical tales).
> Fourth row: men, horses and chariots.

> The pictures are arranged in four rows. In the first row are pictures of the gods riding winged dragons in the clouds. In the second, from left to right, the Wind Chief sends forth a blast, the Thunder God is seated in a carriage beating a drum; the Master of Rain holds a water jar; the rainbow is a ringlike figure with four drooping dragon heads; the Lightning Girl stands above the rainbow holding a whip; the Thunder Spirit is under the rainbow with a hammer and chisel striking a human. . . . . In the third row are seven men with weapons and farm tools fighting off monsters. In the fourth are people hunting tigers, bears, and wild oxen.

Though history, reality, and the world of man became increasingly important in works of art as a natural consequence of the progress of society and civilization, Chu-Han art never entirely lost its romantic, fantastic elements. They were, on the contrary, its very soul—a fact that is manifested not only in the dazzling, fantastic world described above but also in the mobility, power, and crudeness of its artistic style.

A Dazzling World

Although the Confucian influence was quite prevalent during the Han Dynasty, and Confucian precepts such as 'foster human relations, teach and reform' and 'punish the evil, praise the good' were expressed and extolled in every realm of art from literature to painting, Han Dynasty art was not limited by this narrow utilitarian creed. On the contrary, through graphic representations of myth and history, fact and fiction, humans and beasts, it created with breadth and power a dazzling world in a riot of colours, one that consciously or unconsciously objectified the human innate character and symbolized the organic or inorganic body. The human conquest of the material world was the real, dominant theme of Han art.

The supernatural world depicted in the art of this period differs greatly from the Buddhist fanaticism of the later period known as the Six Dynasties (see Chapter 6). Here, there are no moans or groans of the distressed—only a pleasant yearning, a seeking of happiness in both life and death. Eternal life, immortality, was the wish and goal. The people of the Qin and Han did not negate or abandon their present life, as Buddhists did in later generations, at least not after Emperor Shihuang of Qin and Emperor Wudi of Han dispatched messengers to seek out the gods and obtain the 'elixir of life.' They loved life, viewed it optimistically, and sought by all means to perpetuate it. To them, the world of immortals was not on some far-off shore, remote and unattainable; rather, it seemed to be just across the bank, not far from the world of reality. It is not surprising, therefore, that at this stage of history, the old, primitive myths of humans and gods dwelling together, of creatures with human heads and snake bodies (Fuxi and Nuwa), of beings with leopards' tails and tigers' fangs—the image of the fabulous Queen Xiwangmu as described in the *Book of Mountains and Seas*—should have been interwoven with true historical tales and real people.

But the supernatural beings in Han Dynasty art were conceptually different from both primitive totems and the bronze *taotie*. They had lost the latter's coercive power over people, and instead reflected human hopes and desires. That is, this world of the gods was no longer a force that acted upon and dictated reality, as it had been in primitive art; rather, its force was of hope and imagination. The world of humans and the world of gods were in direct contact and were members of an intricate relationship that existed not in real life but in the imagination, not in theory and ideas but in art and fantasy. The union of human and god in primitive art, in which dream and reality were fused, had changed into a unity of hope and sentiment in the world of imagination. Instead of mortals beseeching the gods and spirits to dominate, control, and rule their world, people wanted to ascend to heaven to partake of the deities' joys.

Though some of the themes and scenes in Han Dynasty art are absurd and full of superstition, their artistic style and aesthetic keynote are neither terrifying, threatening, nor decadent; rather, they are pleasant, cheerful, optimistic, and positive. Moreover, interest in human life did not lessen because of the longing for the land of immortals. On the contrary, life on earth became more vigourous and buoyant, so much so that heaven, too, was filled with earthly joys and became just as innocent and naive. The gods did not conquer humanity—humanity instead conquered the gods. Providence, at this stage of history, was but an extension of humanity.

Interwoven with and parallel to this longing for the land of immortals was a keen relish for a confirmation of the real world. This is shown, on the one hand, by the prominence given to Confucian values and to historical tales that extolled dutiful sons, chivalrous men, wise rulers, and capable ministers, and, on the other, in the many descriptions of secular life and the natural environment. It might be said that these two aspects were the two wings of Han Dynasty art, if fantasies and supernaturals were the main body.

The themes of many Han Dynasty stone engravings were taken from historical tales: 'Zhou Gong, Regent to King Cheng,' 'Jing Ke's Attempted Assassination of the King of Qin,' 'Nie Zheng's Assassination of the Prime Minister of Han,' 'Guan Zhong Shoots Duke Huan,' 'Zhao Dun Bitten by a Dog,' 'Lin Xiangru Returns the Jade to Zhao,' 'Hou Ying and Zhu Kai Steal the Wei Command,' 'Emperor Gaozu Kills a Snake,' 'The Hongmen Banquet.' Historical personages from Confucius the sage to Lao Laizi the pious son, from chivalrous warriors to women martyrs, from ancients to contemporaries—all who deserved a place were duly pictured. The focus in all such depictions was on people, scenes, and actions that had an intense emotional and dramatic appeal. So, despite the sobering influence of Confucian precepts and moral teachings, Han art's vigourous and deep-rooted romanticism was not overwhelmed.

In addition to but in contrast with the historical tales, which looked back over time, there were depictions of secular life, or expansion in space. Of these, the many, varied, and realistic scenes carved on the stones and bricks unearthed in Shandong (Wuliang Temple), Henan (Nanyang), and Sichuan furnish some of the best examples.

> In the category of genre pictures, there were [in Shandong] scenes of feasting, hunting, travelling, the performing arts, warfare, cooking, and daily chores. Arrayed before us are snake-charmers, wrestlers, horse-and-carriage processions, grand ceremonies, simple household tasks, cultural systems of all kinds.
> (Li Yu: *An Outline History of Chinese Fine Arts*)

There were pictures of fighting on foot, on horseback, on chariots, and on water. Bows, arrows, slings, crossbows, swords, spears, and halberds were used.

. . . Depicted in the two lower layers of the second half were chariots, riders, and kitchen scenes. In the upper layer were scenes of music and dancing. There were both men and women, some of whom were playing on stringed instruments, some blowing bamboo or clay pipes, and some doing acrobatics.

A work process in metallurgy was portrayed. From left to right were first the smelting and then the hammering and chiselling. It was tense, strenuous work performed collectively (this was actually slave labour).

The forests were full of wild beasts. Peasants were diligently opening up virgin land. . . . One man is leading an ox; another is holding the plow; and a third, whip in hand, is hallooing.
(Chang Renxia: *Selected Paintings of the Han Dynasty*, pp. 4–5)

In Sichuan, the paintings are described thus:

. . . another square brick, on which are two pictures. The upper picture shows two men with backs bent and bows stretched sitting beside a pond. In the background are a number of startled water birds, some with their wings spread as if about to fly off. . . . Swimming fish and lotus blossoms in the pond, and some withered trees on the shore, round off the scene. The lower picture is a scene of farm work.
(Li Yu: *An Outline History of Chinese Fine Arts*)

Is this not a dazzling world? From the imaginary land of immortals to the world of aristocratic pleasures to the slave labour of the lowest social echelons; heaven and earth, past and present, the whole world and otherworld—all are the subjects of Han Dynasty art. The customs, indulgences, and superstitions of the upper classes: banquets, carousing, ceremonies, horses and carriages, hunting, travelling, food, housing, daily life, sacrifices, seeking immortality, exorcising ghosts, averting misfortunes. The life, work, and play of the lower classes: harvesting, smelting, husking rice, slaughtering animals, woodcutting, carrying loads, sword dances, rope walking, theatrical performances. Animals of all sorts, from the domesticated hog, ox, dog, and horse to the hunted tiger, deer, wild goose, and fish. Men grappling with animals and animals fighting each other. . . . When we add to all this the myths, legends, and historical tales, we have a true universe that vibrates with life and vigour.

Seventeenth-century Dutch genre painting depicted with painstaking care scenes and episodes of everyday life—ordinary rooms

'Shooting Wild Geese,' brick engraving of the Han Dynasty.

in which ordinary people carried out ordinary tasks using ordinary
utensils. This school was a reflection of the Dutch people's zest and
love for life and their pride in their conquest of nature (the sea). It was
a style that found greatness in the commonplace.

Similarly, in Han Dynasty art, ordinary scenes, situations, people,
and objects like granaries, kitchen stoves, pigpens, and chicken coops
were often painted or sculpted with painstaking care. Even funerary
objects to serve the dead were important—another reflection of the
era's positive and total concern for life, for only those who love life,
and believe in its values, can truly appreciate the world of reality and
will use art to describe, preserve, and perpetuate it. The richness and
variety of Han art were almost unique in Chinese history. Just as the
depiction of highly ordered daily life in Dutch genre painting was a
confirmation of man's triumph over the sea, so the copious scenes
depicted in Han art reflected the artists' pride in man's conquest of the
material world. But in force, power, value, and theme, Han art far
surpassed Dutch genre painting. For it was the art of a vast, populous,

great empire that had become united and highly centralized for the first time in history and was enjoying an era of prosperity. Vast scenes of reality, centuries-old traditions, and primitive myths and fantasies combined in glittering, colourful images that reflected man's conquest of the material and natural world—these are the basic features and the essence of Han Dynasty art.

The stone (or brick) pictures of this historic period that we see today are monochrome, but we know from the murals and clay figurines unearthed from Han tombs that the architecture, sculptures, and wall paintings of that period were gorgeously coloured. Wang Yanshou of the Eastern Han, in 'Song of the Lulingguang Hall,' described the paintings and sculptures on the architecture of his time in terms such as: 'tiger leaping upon its prey,' 'coiling dragon, galloping horse,' 'red bird spreading its wings,' 'white deer and solitary rainbow,' 'immortals standing high,' 'beautiful girls peeping through windows,' 'a world of pictures; things of all sorts, sundries and oddities; mountain spirits and watersprites', 'five dragons wing to wing, the Emperor of Men[5] with nine heads, Fuxi with scales, Nuwa with a snake's body,' 'loyal ministers and dutiful sons, martyrs and virgins, wise men and fools, victors and vanquished—all are depicted.' This again shows that it was a world of magnificent colours and romantic art, a three-part heterogeneity of myth, history, and reality.

The branch of literature that best parallels such art is the Han Dynasty *fu* which, though evolved from the songs of Chu, was a pure form of literature that had broken away from primitive song and dance in that it was composed not for singing but for recitation. And though later generations sometimes considered them dry and 'as tasteless as wax,' like dictionaries or reference books, *fu* writings remain an imposing expression of the spirit of their time. '*Fu* describes objects in clear details,' commented Lu Ji (261–303), a man of letters of the Western Jin, in his *Wenfu* (*On Literature*).

Virtually all *fu* writings of the Western and Eastern Han were descriptive or narrative, and so extensive in scope that they 'encompassed the universe and overviewed the world' (*Wenfu*). There were satires, allegories, and admonitions, too, but the main content and purpose of *fu* was to describe and celebrate real and imaginary things, especially material objects, life, and its environs: mountains, water,

[5] One of the three legendary emperors called the Emperor of Heaven, Emperor of Earth, and Emperor of Men. The last-named had nine heads and nine brothers, who ruled over the nine divisions of the country in China's legendary epoch.

trees, birds, beasts, cities, palaces, beautiful women, clothes, ornaments, trades, professions.

Unlike painting, literature is not bound by the size of the paper it is written on. It can, therefore, describe more and larger things. Magnificent hills and rivers, towering palaces, spacious fields, armies of people—all can be recreated under the writer's brush. Han *fu* is a good example. Though clumsy, stereotyped, and overladen with trivialities and ornate phrases, *fu* writings describe in scrupulous detail almost everything under the sun: the splendour of nature, the prosperity of cities, thriving trade, abundance of produce, majestic halls, lavish costumes and ornaments, human behaviour, strange birds and beasts, the excitement and dangers of hunting, the joys of singing and dancing. In artistic spirit, this literature is in full accord with the murals, stone sculptures, and other artworks of the Han Dynasty, for *fu* writing also aimed to describe a rich, powerful, and prosperous world full of vitality and self-assurance, a world with a deep interest in and love for the living present. Despite its now stereotyped and florid style, no later Chinese dynasty produced anything to match it in range and diversity of subject matter.

Han art and literature reflected the Chinese people's triumph over the natural world, a triumph that artists and writers continually confirmed and eulogized in contemplating the world around them: the hills, mountains, and rivers; houses and palaces; material objects and living creatures. All these were reproduced in art as direct or indirect objectifications of human life. People no longer existed in their own spiritual world but were fused with external life and their environs, with a dazzling world of reality. This is the basic reason Han art and literature, though crude and clumsy in structure, is so clear in content and so impressive in style. It is from this viewpoint that Han Dynasty visual arts should be appreciated and Han Dynasty *fu* writings interpreted if their significance as the standard form of literature of their day is to be understood correctly.

The Han Dynasty's exquisite handicrafts, especially its lacquers, bronze mirrors, and brocades, are comparable to the *fu* writings, stone pictures, and mural paintings in reflecting the spirit of their time. In form, pattern, technique, and conception they are unrivalled in Chinese art history, and excel even the handicrafts of the later Tang, Song, Ming, and Qing dynasties, except for ceramics and wooden furniture. They were the consummate works of a collective craftsmanship engaged in by slaves, which began during the Warring States period and reached full maturity and its highest point in the Western Han. This was a craftsmanship that was handed down from generation to generation, without regard for time and labour, and it resulted in skill and ingenuity of the highest order. Neither the state-owned nor the private handicrafts of later periods attained the superb workmanship of such articles as the brocade unearthed at Mawangdui, the jade garments sewn with gold thread supposedly used to keep a corpse from decaying, discovered in Hebei Province, and the world-famous Han mirrors and lacquer ware, which are still as bright as new. These objects might be said to parallel in miniature the pyramids of ancient Egypt, because both are the products of the immense collective labour of generations of slaves. Han handicraft articles are a tangible but minute representation of a great and dazzling world in which, amid a vast assortment of objects, is revealed the power of human beings and humans' triumph over nature.

Powerful Crudeness

In Han Dynasty art, conquest of the material world and manipulation of the grand variety of worldly objects were expressed in scenes and images of strength, motion, and speed. These give Han art the power and primitive crudeness that constitute its basic aesthetic style.

In typical works of this period, such as the brick carving of men shooting at birds; the sculptures of galloping horses, enraptured storytellers, and dancers with long sleeves; the pictures of horse-and-chariot battle scenes and the assassination attempt on the Prince of Qin; and the processions of people, gods, and animals in tomb murals, there are no details, no ornaments, no individuality, no personal emotion. Rather, what is most striking in all these art works are the highly exaggerated forms and postures, the large, sweeping movements, the full-length images, and scenes depicted clearly but in rough lines and contours. This is the very essence of Han art, for it is through these exaggerated forms and un-embellished movements and in these rough-contoured figures that strength, speed, motion, and aesthetic power are generated.

Motion, strength, and power are often expressed through a sense of speed, which may be defined as a concentrated expression of motion and strength in a fleeting state. The well-known sculpture of 'a horse treading upon a flying swallow' suggests speed; so does the instantaneity with which the assassin's dagger hits the post in 'Jing Ke's Attempted Assassination of the Prince of Qin.' In tense, violent struggles and in dramatic stories and scenes, power is always revealed through fast action and strength. In this style, therefore, animals are made to appear wilder than usual—far from being quiet and docile, they charge frenziedly, leaping and bounding. This is the opposite of Tang art, which depicts grandeur with stillness and tranquillity. In Han art, whether the theme is a myth, fantasy, historical tale, or human figure, there is a sense of speed through inner strength and motion even when the subject is in an inactive state. Human characters in Han art show their worth not by their spirit, soul, individuality, or inner quality, but by their deeds and actions, that is, by their direct, external relationship with the world, whether historically or in the living present—in a form of motion. This is why actions, deeds, events, and dramatic plots became the dominant themes in this period; their inherent motion, strength, and power is in sharp contrast to the tranquillity, frozen forms, and inner spirit of the art of later periods, such as the Six Dynasties (see Chapters 5 and 6).

Just as conquest of the material world is expressed through action, movements, and plot rather than through spiritual aspects or facial expressions, so realistic portrayals characterized by rough outlines but paying little attention to details give Han art its 'primitively crude' outward appearance. Indeed, the images in Han art appear clumsy and antiquated, badly proportioned, and unnatural in posture. They are noteworthy for their predominance of straight lines, sharp angles and squares, and lack of smoothness. All this, however, instead of detracting from their beauty, only enhances it. 'Primitive crudeness' becomes an intrinsic factor and feature whose absence would have made it difficult to bring out the sense of motion, strength, and power. Contorted bodies, over-long sleeves, exaggerated actions: though awkward and unrealistic, these were very appropriate for portraying motion and strength. Straight lines and right angles had the same effect: neither soft nor smooth, they enhance the feeling of strength; 'power' and 'primitive crudeness' were one here.

If we compare the stone pictures of the Han Dynasty with those of the Tang and Song, and the clay figurines and engravings of the Han with those of the Tang, we can see that in all cases the Han works, though still in a budding stage and consequently simple and crude, are nonetheless superior to the later products by virtue of their sense of motion, rhythm, vigour, and power. Though some Tang figurines also suggest motion, they lack the sense of freedom that characterizes Han works. On the other hand, though some Han figurines depict inactive postures such as sitting and standing, they still possess vigour, power, and the possibility of motion. Thus, the tricoloured horse figures of the Tang, though brightly coloured, are much inferior to the crude horse figures of the Han if power, sturdiness of form, and sense of motion are the criteria. The Tang sculptures of Mount Tianlong, despite their bulging muscles and terrifying appearance, cannot match the clumsy stone sculptures of the Han. And the brick pictures of the Tang and Song, notwithstanding their exquisite workmanship, beautiful facial features, and elegant colours, are inferior to those of the Han in vitality and artistic value. The throbbing vitality of Han art, the fullness of its rendering of strength and power, were difficult for later generations to emulate.

As it was in imagery, so was it in composition. Artists of the Han Dynasty had not yet learned the laws of contrast, how to use void to express solids or white to accentuate black. So they filled whole sheets and surfaces with their drawings, paintings, and engravings, leaving very little blank space. While this may be a sign of clumsiness and *naïveté*, it gives the viewer a sense of fullness and natural simplicity that latter-day art, with its cleverly planned empty spaces, does not. Han art is obviously clumsy and rough when compared to the ingenuity and delicacy of later periods, but it is plain rather than garish, pure and unburdened with details. Because the image in a Han Dynasty work was not regarded as an end in itself, it gives the impression of being in a free and open style. And because the image is in simple contours, the rough and bold atmosphere is uninhibited, possessing a romantic rather than a realistic quality. But it is by no means related to the *xieyi*[6] school of romantic art of later periods. Han art owes its romanticism to its fusion of powerful atmosphere with primitive crudeness, and to its overall sense of motion and strength. This is different from the expression of personal emotion that came to the fore in the art of later periods. During the Han, clear demarcations between folk art and belles-lettres had not yet been drawn. In stone engravings, in the songs of *Yuefu* (*Repository of Songs*, the best example of Han literature), in wall paintings, in handicrafts, in clay figurines, in *lishu*, the official script—Han art represented, above all, a national spirit. If Tang art expresses the interaction between Chinese and foreign arts, and consequently has an alien tinge, Han art is the repository of the native tones and traditions of China: the innocent, bold, and uninhibited romanticism that evolved from Chu culture, and the beauty of the crude and primitive power of humanity in its conquest of the material world.

---

[6] *Xieyi* is a style of Chinese painting characterized by bold outlines and spontaneous expression.

5

The Style of Wei and Jin

The Human Theme

THE WEI and Jin Dynasties were a period of important changes in Chinese history. In economics, politics, military affairs, culture, and the entire ideological realm, including philosophy, religion, art, and literature, there were great turning points brought about by a second change in social formation since that of the Pre-Qin era. The urban prosperity and commodity economy of the Warring States and Qin-Han periods had declined, but the manorial economy that began in the Eastern Han consolidated and expanded steadily as thousands of small farmers and industrial and commercial slaves became serfs or quasi-serfs tied to land owned by landlords and held very much in bondage. Conforming to this standard form of natural economy, a hereditary and rigidly stratified class of great families and aristocratic clans, each with its sphere of power, now occupied the centre of the stage of history. Thus the curtains were raised on the first stage of China's feudal society.

The impact of the social changes on ideology, culture, and psychology brought about the collapse of the study of Confucian classics that had prevailed during the Western and Eastern Han Dynasties. The tedious and absurd *chenwei* (a kind of divination associated with Confucian beliefs) and *jingshu* (dogmatic Confucian thinking and teaching) that had neither scholarly nor theoretical value collapsed at last amid the turmoil of the times and the storms of peasant revolutions. In their place emerged the world outlook of the feudal landlord class, a new ideological system.

The Wei-Jin era (A.D. 220–420) witnessed a re-emancipation and great activity in the ideological domain where many questions were put forward and much progress was made. Though in duration, breadth, scope, and diversity of schools it could not match the Pre-Qin, nonetheless the profundity and purity attained by its speculative philosophy were unprecedented. The *xuanxue* (abstruse learning, metaphysics) of the Wei and Jin represented by the talented young man Wang Bi[1] not only

---

[1] *Xuanxue* was a philosophical school of the Wei-Jin. It was basically Taoist but incorporated some Confucian teachings. Wang Bi (226–249), one of its chief exponents, was the author of *Annotations to the Book of Changes* and *Annotations to Laozi*.

outclassed the tedious and superstitious Confucianism of the Han, but also surpassed the thought of the clearheaded mechanical materialist Wang Chong.[2] This period saw a process of liberation from an ideology that had dominated the stage for several centuries, a process that sought to establish new theories and ideas.

This process began in the last years of the Eastern Han. Wang Chong's philosophical work, *Lun Heng* (*On Equilibrium*), buried for more than a century, was resurrected on the recommendation of Cai Yan, marking a rediscovery of rationalism. At about the same time and shortly after, the theory of practical politics of men like Zhongchang Tong, Wang Fu, and Xu Gan, the legal concepts of Cao Cao and Zhuge Liang, Liu Shao's *Biographies* and the numerous translations of Buddhist scriptures, all at variance with what was considered proper during the two Han periods, emerged to form a new and progressive ideological trend. The Pre-Qin schools of Logicians, Legalists, and Taoists, suppressed for centuries by a decree issued by Emperor Wudi of the Western Han banning all schools except Confucianism, again became the focus of attention and study. With no excessive control or criteria ordained by an emperor, the realms of culture and ideology were relatively open and debates and discussions were very much the vogue. It was under these conditions that, in contrast to the Confucian classics and the art and literature of the two Han periods, which extolled feudal merits and virtues and stressed practicality, a genuine speculative and rational 'pure' philosophy and a genuine lyrical and perceptual 'pure' literature and art were born. This was a leap forward in Chinese ideological history. The most celebrated figures in history who symbolized this leap and opened up the new era of the true, the good, and the beautiful in the various branches of ideology were He Yan and Wang Bi in philosophy; Cao Cao, Cao Pi, Cao Zhi, Ji Kang, and Ruan Ji in literature and art; Zhong Yao, Wei Li (Madame Wei), Wang Xizhi, and Wang Xianzhi[3] in calligraphy.

[2] Wang Chong (27–c.97) was a philosopher of the Eastern Han.

[3] Biographical notes: Cai Yan, also called Cai Wenji, daughter of the famous scholar and poet Cai Yong (132–192), was a talented woman poet of the Eastern Han. Zhongchang Tong (180–220), Wang Fu (c.85–162), and Xu Gan (171–218) were philosophers of the Eastern Han. Cao Cao (155–220) was a poet, politician, and military strategist of the Eastern Han; he was prime minister to the last Han emperor, Xiandi. Zhuge Liang (181–234), politician and military strategist of the Three Kingdoms, was prime minister of the kingdom of Shu. Liu Shao, whose dates of birth and death are unknown, was a scholar of Wei of the Three Kingdoms. He Yan (?–240) was a philosopher of the Three Kingdoms. Cao Pi (187–226) and Cao Zhi (192–232), sons of Cao Cao, were

What was the basic feature of this new ideological trend, that is, the new outlook on life and the world that lasted from the last years of the Eastern Han through the Wei and Jin, the same trend reflected in literature and art and aesthetics?

Briefly, it was the awakening of humankind. It was the voice of history on the march as people gradually extricated themselves from the bonds of ancient society. Such an awakening had been impossible during the two Han dynasties, when human activities and concepts were entirely subject to theological activities and dominated by *chenwei* teleology. This awakening began, progressed, and was realized through various tortuous paths. In literature, art, and aesthetics, the awakening was more sensitive, direct, and clear than in other spheres. *Nineteen Poems*[4] and the poems misattributed to Su Wu and Li Ling[5] that were similar to the former in style heralded a new era in both (poetic) form and content. Whether singing of daily life, passing events, human affairs, the climate, fame, wealth, or pleasure, they voiced the writer's thoughts directly and expressed his feelings profoundly. Most prominent in such expressions of feeling was sorrow over the brevity and uncertainty of life. This is the keynote of the *Nineteen Poems*, as the following lines show:

> We live not more than a hundred years,
> Yet our grief may last a thousand.

> Man lives but a single life,
> That passes like floating dust.

> Life is not rock or gold,
> How can it be lasting?

poets; Cao Pi, the elder son, later became the first emperor of the kingdom of Wei. Ji Kang (224–263) was a thinker, scholar, and musician of the Three Kingdoms; he was executed for opposing the powerful Sima family, the virtual rulers of the kingdom of Wei. Ruan Ji (210–263) was a thinker and man of letters of the Three Kingdoms. Zhong Yao (151–230) was a calligrapher of the Three Kingdoms and Wei Li (272–349), often referred to as Madame Wei, a calligrapher of the Eastern Jin. Wang Xizhi (321–379) and Wang Xianzhi (344–386), father and son, were calligraphers of the Eastern Jin; they were popularly called the 'two Wangs of calligraphy.'

[4] This is a collection of poems in five-character lines composed in the last years of the Eastern Han; authors unknown. In a plain and natural style, they exerted a considerable influence on poetic works of later periods.

[5] Su Wu (?–60 B.C.) was a celebrated envoy and Li Ling (?–74 B.C.) a famous general of the Western Han. Both were literary men as well, but the poems were not written by them.

Life is short like a sojourn,
Not stable like rock and gold.

No more do I meet old acquaintances,
Am I not aging fast?

We may wish each other ten thousand years,
But neither saint nor sage can reach it.

Looking beyond the city gates,
I see nothing but graves and mounds.

In these poems that Zhong Rong[6] extolled as 'gentle and beautiful in language, profound and sorrowful in meaning, breathtaking and soul-stirring, virtually every word worth a thousand catties of gold,' how many words were used to lament the uncertainty of life! If each word is worth a thousand catties of gold, as the old saying goes, the burden must have been in hundreds of tons. Mingled with thoughts of friendship, parting, home, loved ones, an unsettled life, and the inevitable end, and with words of advice, comfort, hope, and encouragement, these verses that lament the brevity of life and its frustrations, the paucity of pleasure and the proliferation of grief, seem sadder and more tragic than ever.

Travelling, always travelling,
I part with you in life,
To go ten thousand miles hence,
Far beyond the horizon.
The way is long and arduous,
Who knows if we will meet again.

. . . . . .

I age quickly, thinking of you;
So suddenly the twilight comes;
Speak no more of what is lost,
Do your best and eat your fill.

. . . . . .

The traveller's thoughts are on the road,
He rises to watch the night;
He sees the stars have vanished,
And here the parting begins.
To the wars I am going,
Not knowing when we will meet.
Clasping your hands I heave a sigh,

[6] Zhong Rong (?–c.518) was a literary critic of the kingdom of Liang of the Southern Dynasties.

As the tears begin to well.
Learn to love the springtime,
Forget not the hours of joy.
If I live, I shall return to you;
If I die, I shall think of you always.
(From *Nineteen Ancient Poems*)

From Jian'an[7] through the Jin and the Song of the Southern Dynasties, from royalty and nobility down to the middle and lower social echelons, this anxiety over life and death, survival and extinction, and sorrow over the shortness of life, spread far and wide, becoming the keynote of a whole epoch. Some of the most famous poets and scholars of the time expressed these emotions thus:

Cao Cao:

Drink and be merry,
For life is short,
Like the morning dew,
There is much to regret.

Cao Pi:

As I hear people say,
Worry makes one old.
Alas, my hair is white,
Why comes it so soon?

Cao Zhi:

Man enters into life,
Then passes away like dew.

. . . .

Neither rock nor gold are we—
Alas and alack the day!

Ruan Ji:

Life is like the dust and dew,
Heaven's way is remote and far.

. . . .

The sage laments at the river's edge
That death comes all too soon.

Lu Ji (261–303):

As heaven's will is to change,
How can life be long!

[7] Title of the reign of Xiandi (196–220), last emperor of the Eastern Han.

Sorrowing and sighing always,
Shedding tears alone.

Liu Kun (271–318):

The task is still unfinished,
The sun speeds towards the west;
Time, alas! waits not for man,
It passes like floating clouds.

Wang Xizhi:

Life and death are momentous indeed: it's distressing to think of it.
To equate life with death is ridiculous, and to regard great age and
infant death as the same is absurd. Posterity will view us as we view
those who have gone before. How sad!

Tao Qian (365–427):

I grieve that the morning sun sets quickly,
I sigh for the eternal sorrows of life;
All must end after a hundred years,
Why so much grief and so little joy?

What all these poets expressed in their writings was the same
theme of regret and sorrow, presented in the same vein. Obviously, this
was a question that occupied an important place in the social psychology
and ideology of their time. It was the nucleus of their outlook.

This outlook consisted in a steadfast adherence to life while under
the influence of a philosophical trend based on skepticism. Outwardly,
it appeared to be one of sorrowing and sighing in passive and
pessimistic tones, but inwardly it was actually the opposite: an ardent
love of life, living, and the future, born of the questioning and denying
of an ideology that had prevailed up to that time—the ideology of the
old system that embraced fatalism, Confucian ethics, and belief in
ghosts. This doubting and refuting of external powers gave rise to an
internal moral awakening and an inward search for truth. That is, the
whole body of moral principles, the superstitions, divinations, fatalism,
and Confucian teachings that had been accepted and preached up to that
time were now regarded as false or questionable; they were valueless or
not worthy of belief. Only man's mortality was real. Only the sadness
of parting and the grief and misfortunes that shadowed his brief
existence were real. That being so, why shouldn't he enjoy himself
while he could? Why shouldn't he cherish his life and his own person?
Thus the scholars write: 'The day is short but the night is long; so why
not light a candle and enjoy ourselves.' 'Better drink fragrant wine and

dress in fine silk.' 'Why not mount a fast steed and take to the highroads and waterways.'

The language is frank, direct, and unvarnished. Ostensibly, it was a call for indulgence, dissipation, and degeneracy, but in essence it was not so. It was a revelation, in the light of existing social conditions, to men who loved life and were eager to live. That life is uncertain and old age comes quickly are universal issues, common to all generations. But in the poetic works of the Wei and Jin that sing of these perpetual issues there is an aesthetic charm so persuasive as to render the works immortal. This is because the thoughts and feelings expressed in them embodied the spirit of their time. Since the peasant uprising known as the Yellow Turbans (c.184) in the last years of the Eastern Han, all society had been in a state of growing turbulence. It was a period of incessant wars and plagues that killed thousands upon thousands; not even the greatest aristocratic families were spared. 'All perished, whether they were Xu's, Chen's, Ting's, or Liu's' (Cao Pi: *Letter to Wu Zhi*). Wealth, honour, and power could vanish in a flash. Even Cao Pi and Cao Zhi, heirs of the most powerful family in the land, lived no more than forty years.

In the face of all this, and the fact that established traditions, honour, learning, and beliefs were no longer reliable, most having been forced upon people, the significance and value of the individual's existence now came to the fore; the pervasive question was how to live this short life with its numerous hardships in a conscious and meaningful way, to make life richer and fuller. In essence, this pointed to a kind of human awakening. That is, in the course of questioning and denying old traditions and norms, outworn beliefs and values, people had rediscovered, reassessed, and were again pursuing their own lives and destinies. This was a new attitude and outlook, and so the poems of this period which openly flaunted the seeking of pleasure in life were different in content from the decadent works of later periods. Most of the finest poetic works that have been preserved through the ages, while they lamented the darker aspects of life, revealed nobler, more stimulating thoughts and feelings that varied in substance according to circumstances. Thus, what followed the pessimism of 'drink and be merry for life is short' was the pledge of an old warrior (Cao Cao): 'The stout heart of a hero does not weaken with age.' Similarly, the sorrow over life that characterized the Jian'an style existed in conjunction with an ardour and spirit generated by personal accomplishments. And behind the lamentation that 'life and death are momentous; how sad!' was a more optimistic tone, 'Though the myriad voices of nature may all be different, whatever suits me is always new,' an endeavour to find peace and comfort in the bosom of nature.

The philosophy of the famous scholars of the Zhengshi period, who refused to be constrained by laws and rites, and the political grievances of scholars of the time of Taikang and Yongjia,[8] revealed in such sayings as 'I fondle the pillow but cannot sleep, so arranging my clothes I sit there alone meditating' (Lu Ji), and 'Who had expected that what had been tempered into steel should change into a softness that can be twisted around the finger' (Liu Kun), all had a certain positive content in them. It was this affirmation that prevented 'man's awakening' from going the way of decadence or depression; and it was man's awakening that gave aesthetic profundity to this affirmation. That was why the *Nineteen Poems*, the Jian'an style, and the voices from Zhengshi down to Tao Yuanming's elegy to himself did not dishearten people in spite of their mournful view of life but, on the contrary, produced a certain positive feeling.

Again, the inward search was linked to outward denial and the awakening was achieved through opposition to, skepticism and destruction of old traditions, beliefs, customs, and values. 'Better drink fragrant wine and dress in fine silk' is clearly incompatible with Confucian teachings. The Cao family, father and sons, violated the moral principles and standards of human relations that had been so stressed during the Eastern Han. The Zhengshi scholars went a step further and rejected traditional concepts, customs, and rites. 'Discredit Tang and Wudi, disparage Zhou Gong and Confucius': for this Ji Kang lost his head and Ruan Ji only narrowly escaped death. He Zeng,[9] upholding Confucian ethics, had suggested to the Simas, the most powerful family in the kingdom of Wei, that they should execute Ruan Ji, the pretext being that he was 'indulgent, violated the rites, and corrupted social values.' It was as Liu Ling[10] wrote in 'Ode to the Virtue of Wine':

> [This was a time when] the honourable sons of the nobility, officials,
> and scholars . . . rolling up their sleeves and baring their breasts,

[8] Zhengshi: title of the reign (240–249) of Cao Fang, emperor of Wei of the Three Kingdoms. Taikang: title of the reign (280–289) of Emperor Wudi of the Jin. Yongjia: title of the reign (307–313) of Emperor Huaidi of the Jin.

[9] He Zeng (199–278) was a prime minister of the Western Jin and a man notorious for his corruption and profligacy.

[10] Liu Ling was a scholar of the Western Jin who is said to have had an extraordinary capacity for wine. The exact dates of his birth and death are unknown.

gnashed their teeth in anger as they harangued on the rites and laws, whose pros and cons rose in swarms. . . .

This shows the vehemence of the struggle and antagonism on the ideological front. In the long run, the outdated rites and laws could not withstand the onslaught of new ideas, and political persecution could not stop the change in the general mood. From philosophy to literature and art, from concepts to customs, new things that appeared to be wild and absurd triumphed over and replaced the old and orthodox, which were essentially hypocritical. Talent won against moral codes, simple burial superseded extravagant funerals, Wang Bi surpassed the Han Dynasty Confucians, and the Seven Worthies of the Bamboo Grove[11] became the ideals of the Six Dynasties.[12] Even in the brick pictures in burial vaults, the worthies displaced or forced their way into the ranks of the gods, ministers, and warriors of the two Hans.

People who were not saints and knew no laws, who had been severely censured and put to death, were now enshrined in the wall paintings of underground temples. These people who had done nothing that merited status, who had no legal power, and put forth no moral principles to speak of, became the model for others by dint of their own personality. This can only be explained as the triumph of a new world outlook. People did not necessarily want to follow a life of dissipation or to indulge in wine and pleasure, but they were attracted by talent, character, appearance, and manners. Men were no longer respected for their accomplishments, or show of moral integrity and learning, as they had been during the two Han periods, but chiefly for their inner speculative attitude and spirit. It was the person and the character displayed, not external things, that increasingly became the centre of the philosophy, art, and literature of this period.

Of course, the individual who served as a model still had about him the aura of his class—he could only have been a member of the great families and aristocratic clans whose political system and criteria of talent were the means by which philosophical views of life changed into the stressing and judging of human character. It was through the aristocracy that human awakening passed into the pursuit of life, appearance, and style.

[11] These worthies were seven distinguished scholars of the Wei and Jin, among whom the most prominent were Ji Kang and Ruan Ji. They were said to be friends who loved to wander in bamboo groves.

[12] Six Dynasties is a general term for the Wu (of the Three Kingdoms), Eastern Jin, and Song, Qi, Liang, Chen of the Southern Dynasties. All had their capital at Jiankang (present-day Nanjing).

The criteria for assessing talent, in particular, had a direct bearing on the social atmosphere and psychological climate that turned the spotlight on the inner spirit. From the time Cao Pi decreed the Nine-Grade Zhongzheng system of selecting officials,[13] the judging of men and their character had become the centre of political, social, and cultural discussions. The judgement was no longer limited to ethics, personal integrity, Confucian learning, and moral courage as it had been during the Eastern Han; talent, temperament, ability, style, and features became the most important factors. In brief, the highest criterion and principle was not a man's actions and conduct but his inner spirit (regarded as an unlimited potential possibility). This fully accorded with the aristocratic style of the great families and nobles, to whom refined manners and features represented ideal beauty. What people appreciated, appraised, discussed, and acclaimed was not the general, the temporal, the superficial and external; what they valued had to be expressive of some inner, intrinsic, and unconventional style or quality.

This change, this new attitude of the people, was revealed clearly in the writings of this period, especially in the *Biographies* and *Social Talk* (*Shishuo Xinyu*), works compiled in the Three Kingdoms and the Northern and Southern Dynasties. *Social Talk* recounts many stories and anecdotes that were humorous or otherwise, but not all of them were of the deeds of famous generals or ministers, or of the personal integrity of loyal and righteous people. Far from being so, most were stories of people discussing abstruse subjects nonchalantly but eloquently. What was prominent in them was the revelation of an inner wisdom, a superior spirit, refined words and actions, and a beautiful style—and beauty here means the expression of a person's inner wisdom and character through an outward appearance as beautiful as some natural phenomenon. For example:

> In the eyes of his contemporaries, Wang Xizhi was as fragile as a floating cloud, as graceful as a startled dragon.
> (*Social Talk*)

> Ji Kang, the man, was as lofty as a solitary pine. When drunk, he was as confused and disorderly as a jade hill about to collapse.
> (*Social Talk*)

[13] This was a system of selecting civil servants in the Wei, Jin, and Northern and Southern Dynasties. Under this system, scholars were divided into nine grades according to their ability, on the basis of which the selections were made. Over time, the system was corrupted and family connections instead of ability became the chief consideration. Thus, the system became a protector of the special rights of the great families.

'Bright as if the sun and moon were clasped in one's bosom,' 'eyes gleaming like lightning seen from under a cliff,' 'smooth and bright like willow under the spring moon,' 'straight as a sturdy pine in the wind,' 'dark and deep like looking down from a mountaintop,' 'clear and towering like a ten-thousand-foot cliff.' The aim of such exaggerated descriptions was to express a lofty inner character through an impressive outward appearance, this being the aesthetic ideal and interest of the then ruling class.

With a self-sufficient manorial economy and their social position and political privileges secured by a hereditary system, it was not surprising that the attention of the great families and nobility should be turned from their environs inward to the heart, from society to nature, from Confucian classics to the arts, from external to subjective existence. 'Watching the returning wild geese, playing the five-stringed fiddle, glancing around with self-satisfaction, mentally roving the mysteries of the universe' (Ji Kang)—this was their world outlook. They were afraid of an early death, so looked for ways to prolong life; they took medicine and made 'pills of immortality'; they drank freely, then talked loudly about the philosophies of Laozi and Zhuangzi and studied the rites and abstruse learning; they indulged in pleasures on the one hand while thinking philosophically on the other. This seemingly aloof, careless, and self-satisfied attitude, caring for nothing and for everything, constituted the so-called Wei-Jin style; medicine, wine, appearance and scenery, along with discussions of Taoism and the abstruse, were the necessary contents of such a style.

All this of course had repercussions in the realms of philosophy and aesthetics. The main subject of discussion in philosophy was no longer the numerous and complex external phenomena but internal nihility, not man's view of nature (theory of primeval forces, or *yin-yang*) but ontology. The doctrine was that a rich and diversified reality could be attained only when all the potential possibilities were there. And so, writes Wang Bi in his annotations to the thirty-eighth chapter of *Laozi*: 'Nothingness is the root'; 'respect the root and nurture the ends'; 'doing nothing is the root, being nameless is the parent; when the root and parent are discarded to suit the offspring, there will be failings, however great the achievement.' He expounds further in *A Few Examples of Laozi's Philosophy*: 'Things are born out of the formless and meritorious deeds of the nameless; formlessness and namelessness are the origin of all things.' There is a limit, an end, to all external things and achievements; only the internal spiritual being is primary, fundamental, limitless, and endless; the former is impossible without the latter (the parent). And this is their definition of 'sages': 'Sages are superior to men in their godly spirit; they are similar to men in their human feelings. Because of their superior spirit, they understand the Great Harmony and nihility. Because they have human feelings, they are not without joy and sorrow in respect to worldly objects' (He Shao quoting Wang Bi in *Biography of Wang Bi*).

This, then, was the speculative philosophy of the Wei-Jin style. To do nothing and do everything, to be superior in spirit and still possess human joys and sorrows, not to seek external, limited, superficial deeds and merits but to possess a spirit and style with unlimited possibilities— this was the nihilistic theme in philosophy and the model of beauty in art in this historical period. Thus the dazzling world (of action) of the two Hans gave way to a richness of character, marked by quiet, abstruse thinking. Lyric poetry and figure painting began to mature, replacing the long-winded, narrative, and clumsy Han Dynasty *fu* and the Han brick pictures, in the same way as *xuanxue* (abstruse learning) replaced the Confucian classics and ontology (seeking the inner being) replaced the concentration on nature (exploring the outer world).

Clearly, it was not incidental that 'expressing the spirit through figures' and 'rhythmic vitality' should be put forward as aesthetic theories and artistic principles at this stage. 'Rhythmic vitality' requires that a painting vividly express a person's spirit, temperament, style, and bearing. How to depict environs, events, forms, and postures (the aim of Han art, as explained in Chapter 4) was not the point. 'Express the spirit through figures' had the same meaning. As Gu Kaizhi[14] put it, 'Whether the four limbs are beautiful or ugly has no bearing on the excellence of a work. It is in the eyes that the spirit is expressed.' That is to say, the spirit, which is the most important thing, is transmitted through a person's eyes, not by the shape of his/her body or his/her actions. The eyes are the windows of the soul, and external actions are only subordinate and secondary. This aesthetic interest and criterion that stressed the seeking of a person's aura and spirit fully accorded with the ways of judging people in *Social Talk*, and with the demand for speculative wisdom in the abstruse learning of the Wei-Jin. All are expressions of the spirit of their time—the Wei-Jin style.

Corresponding to the precepts of 'rhythmic vitality' and 'express the spirit through figures' in the visual arts, and having a similar meaning, is the idea that 'words cannot fully convey the meaning' in the art of language. This is philosophy, but it also has a profound implication in grasping the aesthetic laws of literature. What it implies is that one must express meanings which conceptual words and phrases

[14] Gu Kaizhi (c.345–406) was a painter of the Eastern Jin.

cannot fully convey. The saying was originally used in reference to abstruse philosophical principles, such as 'Nothing can more fully express meaning than imagery; nothing can more fully express imagery than words' and 'Words are to clarify the image; when the image is there, the words are forgotten; the image is to embody the meaning; when the meaning is understood, the image is forgotten' (Wang Bi: *Zhouyi Lueli*, or *Some Examples from the Book of Changes*). Both words and images are tools of transmission with limitations. The important thing is to try to grasp by means of these tools the unlimited thing-in-itself, abstruse principles and profound meanings that can never be fully fathomed. Like expressing the spirit through form and creating a rhythmic vitality, the aesthetic implication here is to transmit and express by means of the limited and exhaustible words and images some kind of inner quality belonging to the 'sages' that is unlimited, inexhaustible, and beyond the reach of ordinary people; to express by means of passions (joy, sorrow, etc.) that are common to all, a godly spirit that transcends the ordinary. Or, we might say that it calls for the creation of an ideal character with unlimited possibilities that manifests itself as stillness, but embodies various actualities of motion (passion, function, phenomena). The statues of the Buddha sculptured in later generations are the best expressions of this ideal character in art.

'Words cannot fully convey meaning,' 'create a rhythmic vitality,' and 'express the spirit through figures' are Chinese artistic-aesthetic principles formulated during the Wei-Jin that have had a far-reaching influence. Their emergence was inseparable from humankind's awakening, for they were a concrete aesthetic expression of this human theme.

Literary Awareness

The modern writer Lu Xun (1891–1936) once made a pithy remark concerning the literature of the Wei and Jin: 'Cao Pi's epoch may be called the epoch of literary awareness or, as modern critics put it, the epoch of art for art's sake' (*And That's That: The Wei-Jin Style and the Relationship Between Medicine and Wine*). 'Art for art's sake' was in contrast with the utilitarian principle 'to foster human relations, to teach and reform' of the literature and art of the Han dynasty. If the human theme was the new content of the literature of the early stage of feudalism in China, literary awareness gave literature a new form. The two, closely linked and integrated with each other, became the criteria for all the arts of this period. They were the new Wei-Jin style, with Cao Pi as its earliest exponent.

Lu Xun: 'The Han language developed gradually in the course of time. Not all the credit for this should be given to the Cao family, father and sons, but the language does owe its elegance and beauty to the initiative of Cao Pi' (*And That's That*). Cao Pi had a very good social position and later became emperor. He enjoyed the highest honours the country could give and one might suppose that for him the highest ideals in life had been attained. But he did not think so himself: 'Life has its end and honour and pleasure end with the body; the normal span of such things cannot compare with the infinitude of literature.' Emperors, kings, ministers, generals; wealth, nobility, glory, and honour, all quickly turn into dust. What is truly imperishable, passed on from generation to generation, are the products of the spirit. These live on through the ages without the help of a good historian or the push of some external force. An illustrious emperor can be buried in oblivion, but a beautiful piece of literature will long be read and recited in its own right. Thus, Cao Pi stressed and called for beauty in literature because it was related to his world outlook, to his quest for immortality. Immortal writings mean immortality for the writer.

In form, role, or value, the literature of the Wei-Jin was vastly different from that of the Han period. In the Han Dynasty, literature was only a plaything of the imperial court. The great masters of language Sima Xiangru (179–117 B.C.) and Dongfang Shuo (154–93 B.C.) were little more than court jesters, whose position was 'betwixt and between entertainers and pets.' And *fu* writings, however impressive, were but songs of praise or odes to peace, seasoned with a little satire to humour the emperor. Still less could be said of Han painting and calligraphy, for in that society such arts could play no independent role.

Literature was virtually synonymous with the Confucian classics during the Han. In the book *Salt and Iron*,[15] for example, the term 'literature' referred only to Confucian scholars and their writings. Jia Yi (200–168 B.C.), Sima Qian (c.145–?B.C.), Ban Gu (A.D. 52–92), and Zhang Heng (A.D. 78–139), now rated among the greatest writers in Chinese history, were never regarded as men of letters in their day. They were politicians, ministers, or historians in both name

[15] A collection of documents of argument on governmental policies in politics, economics, culture, and military affairs during the reign of Emperor Zhaodi (reigned 86–73 B.C.) of the Western Han. It was compiled by Huan Kuan, a high-ranking Han Dynasty official.

and position. Awareness of literature as a form of art to be appreciated for its own sake began only in the Wei and Jin.

Stress on beauty in language, on the distinguishing of literary forms and styles, on processes of literary thought, on literary criticism, on the study of literary theories, and on the compilation of literary collections—all these were unprecedented phenomena of the Wei and Jin down to the Southern Dynasties. They were a prominent feature of the ideology of this historic epoch. The differentiation of literary styles and the description of literary thought in Lu Ji's *Wen Fu* (*On Literature*) are familiar to many:

> Poetry originates from emotions and is beautiful: *fu* describes objects in detail; a tablet inscription presents the essential merits of a person; *lei* (funeral prayer) is both lingering and sad. . . .
>
> Follow the four seasons and sigh for what is gone: scan the universe and meditate on its profusion; lament over fallen leaves in the height of autumn; praise the soft willow in the fragrance of spring. The heart is serious when one thinks of the frost; the intentions remote and uncertain as they soar into the clouds. . . . In the beginning, all is looking and listening, thinking and questioning, the spirit seeking the farthest corners of the earth, the heart roving ten thousand feet high. In the end, feelings that are vague become clearer; objects clear and distinct spur each other forward. . . . Past and present are seen in one instant; the four seas are taken in at a glance.

This was probably the first time in Chinese aesthetic history that such a special study and description of the categories of creative writing, and of creative psychology in particular, had ever been made. It was a clear indication of literary awareness. Scholars of the Southern Dynasties continued this study after Cao Pi and Lu Ji. Zhong Rong in *Shipin* (*On Poets and Poetry*) evaluated the artistic merits of his contemporaries and raised the question: 'In the case of writings that concern the governing of a nation, one should make reference to the ancients . . . but when voicing our moods and feelings, what need is there to quote the classics?' Here he stressed again the difference in creative features between poetry that expressed one's feelings and practical Confucian classics for directing world affairs. Liu Xie in *Wenxin Diaolong*, a book on literary theory, not only made a special study of such creative laws and aesthetic qualities as style, spirit, thought, elegance, feeling, and time sequence, but stated at the very beginning of his book: 'The sun and moon are like jade, illuminating heaven; the mountains and rivers in their splendour give shape to the earth. This is literature representing the way' and 'Literature gives expression to the quintessence of the universe.' Relating the origin of prose and poetry to Zhou Gong, Confucius, and the Six Classics,[16] elevating literature to the philosophical height of the 'way' of nature— this may be regarded as an aesthetic summary of the literary awareness that characterized the Wei-Jin period.

A reflection of this awareness in the theme of creative work was the change from poetry in mystic language to poetry on natural scenery (idyllic poetry). But such creative works that described nature, from the writings of Guo Pu (276–324) of the Western Jin to those of Xie Lingyun (385–435) of the Southern Dynasties, though celebrated in their time, were not truly a success in themselves. What such works pursued in content was identical to the aim of ontology: the human theme appeared as the seeking of identity with the way—nature. In form, they were parallel to painting; literary awareness was manifested as a desire to use imagery to discuss the abstruse and to depict scenes and objects. However, nature here was only something for the physical enjoyment of the aristocracy, or only a means for them to seek the remote and abstruse, a way of achieving a so-called 'transcending spirit and easy conscience.' Nature was not intimately and tightly associated with their life, mood, and feelings. Consequently, in their art, nature was mainly a lifeless, ossified environment to be depicted in painting, plated in colour, engraved in gold. In Han Dynasty *fu*, nature was used to externalize or express men's achievements and activities; in the idyllic poetry of the Six Dynasties, nature was used to externalize or express men's ideas or their visual enjoyment. The subjective and the objective were not mixed but separated from each other. Thus, however meticulous Xie Lingyun's descriptions may have been, the natural scenes he described did not come to life. His idyllic poems, like some of Gu Kaizhi's paintings (for example, 'Admonitions of the Palace Instructress'), were merely conceptual descriptions; they lacked both feeling and individuality. But, by means of such descriptions, literature enriched itself in form through the accumulation and creation of styles patterns vocabulary, rhythm, and rhetoric, providing valuable reference material for later generations.

One example of this was the emergence of poetry with five-character lines, which established itself and matured from the abstruse poetry and idyllic poetry of the reigns of Jian'an and Zhengshi. The

---

[16] The Six Classics are the *Book of Songs*, *Book of History*, *Book of Rites*, *Book of Changes*, and *Spring and Autumn Annals*, commonly called the Five Classics, plus the *Book of Music*. Some scholars object to this classification, saying that the contents of the *Book of Music* are already included in the *Book of Songs* and *Book of Rites*.

change from the four-character lines in the *Book of Songs* to the five-character lines of the Wei-Jin, though only a matter of one more character in each line, made a great difference in capacity and power of expression. What took two four-character lines to express could be adequately expressed in one five-character line. This was a big stride forward. Moreover, the five-character poem made regular, standard, and patterned the irregular poetry of the Han Dynasty (in which a poem was a medley of three-, four-, five-, six-, and seven-character lines) and became the standard style. It dominated the poetic realm and was regarded as the principal orthodox form until the last years of the Tang Dynasty, when it was finally superseded by the seven-character *jue* poem and seven-character *lu* poem.[17]

Pianti (a rhythmic prose style) of the Six Dynasties and the 'four tones, eight flaws' theory[18] of Shen Yue (441–513) also consciously developed to a high degree the aesthetic quality of Chinese rhetoric. They explored and utilized in an unprecedented way the various laws of formal beauty such as symmetry, balance, coordination, harmony, complexity, and unity in the meaning, tones, and rhythm of Chinese characters. They were an expression of literary awareness through outward form. To this day, the flexible but orderly matching of sound and sense is still an important aesthetic factor in Chinese literature.

In actual creative activity and in literary criticism, the principles and criteria were much the same. One important reason why Cao Zhi was regarded with such high esteem at the time, Zhong Rong comparing him to 'Zhou Gong and Confucius in the sphere of human relations,' was that attention to the choice of words and structure of lines in poetry began with him. It was he who formulated such principles as 'extra effort should be spent on the opening note,' 'words must be selected with the utmost care,' 'orderly matching of lines,'[19]

---

[17] A *jue* poem has four lines and a *lu* poem eight lines, each with the same number of characters, five or seven.

[18] The four tones in classical (not modern) Chinese pronunciation are the *ping* (even tone), *shang* (rising tone), *qu* (falling tone), and *ru* (abrupt tone). The eight flaws all refer to incorrect uses of tone and rhyme in poetry.

[19] The orderly matching of lines is a feature peculiar to classical Chinese poetry. A Chinese poem in classical style is made up of couplets, two in a four-line poem, four in an eight-line one. In some of these couplets (the second and third in an eight-line poem), each character in the first line must be suitably matched in meaning and part of speech by the character in the corresponding position of the second line. The following couplet (translated character by character) from a poem by Cao Zhi may illustrate this kind of matching:

'harmony in tone,' 'a profound and far-reaching conclusion,' all of which show that he was both deliberate and meticulous in writing poetry, a characteristic quite different from earlier poets. This made him a pioneer of latter-day poetry, which was clearly different from the poetry of the Han and Wei that had no strict tonal patterns or rhyme schemes. Actually, in terms of artistic merit, Cao Zhi's numerous poetic works may be less than a match for Cao Pi's one piece, 'Song of the Swallow,' which Wang Fuzhi of the early Qing acclaimed as the 'optimum in feeling, intensity, colour, and sound; peerless through the ages.' But 'Song of the Swallow' was in the style of a folk song composed on the spur of the moment and, in the words of Wang Fuzhi, was 'virtually a gift from heaven, not a product of human effort' (*Jiangzhai's Notes on Poetry*). By the aesthetic standards of the Wei-Jin, this was only 'mediocre, more like a casual talk' (Zhong Rong: *On Poets and Poetry*), very much below the 'rich, colourful, and copious writings' (ibid.) of Cao Zhi with their carefully chosen words and well-composed sentences. It is not surprising, therefore, that Zhong Rong, in his *On Poets and Poetry*, should list Cao Pi as a poet of only average calibre and place many poets whose works were relatively insubstantial but who emphasized rhetoric in a higher class. This was a period that stressed the beauty of well-matched words and sounds, and set a high value on a single well-composed sentence. It manifested to the extreme the seeking of formal beauty. Thus, in addition to wine, medicine, appearance, and spirit, beauty of language was a major component of the Wei-Jin style.

So-called 'literary awareness' is an aesthetic concept that refers not to literature alone. In other arts, especially painting and calligraphy, such an awareness also began in the Wei and Jin and manifested itself in much the same way, that is, in the tendency to stress, study, and discuss creative laws and aesthetic forms.

Second only to 'rhythmic vitality' in the six principles of painting formulated by Xie He is 'disciplined brushwork,' which was a conscious summary of the traditions and functions of lines in the Chinese visual arts and, for the first time, clearly established the theory and importance of the art of line that is unique to China. 'Disciplined

Hidden-fish-leap-clear-ripples;
Good-bird-sings-high-branch.

The two first characters are modifiers; the second characters are nouns that mean living creatures; the third characters are verbs of action; the fourth, modifiers again; and the fifth, nouns denoting inanimate objects in nature.

brushwork' (linear representation) was placed before 'proper representation of objects,' 'specific colouration,' 'good composition,' and 'copying the old masters.' Immanuel Kant, too, once said that the aesthetic quality of lines surpasses that of colours. This point was well understood in ancient China, for the art of line (in painting), like lyric poetry, is the most developed part of Chinese art and literature and the richest of its characteristic features. The art of line and lyric poetry are expressions of the cultural-psychological structure of the Chinese nation.

Calligraphy, also unique to China, is the art of line in a highly concentrated and purified form. Awareness in calligraphy also began during the Wei-Jin. It was in this period that the rigid, orderly, and imposing style of handwriting gave way to the running, cursive, and regular scripts. What used to be a little known and unimportant occupation of the middle and lower classes now became a skilled and absorbing pastime of the great families and distinguished scholars. Brush skill, form of characters, structure, composition—all were enriched, diversified, and rendered more sophisticated. Such calligraphies as those of Lu Ji, Wang Xizhi, and Wang Xianzhi are among the most valuable relics of fine handwriting that are extant. Through beautiful lines, they reflect the writers' moods, spirit, and feelings:

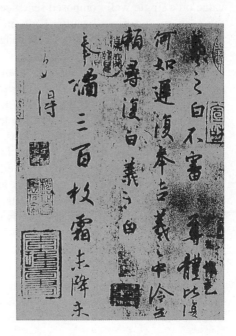

Fengjutie, running script, specimen of Wang Xizhi's handwriting, Eastern Jin.

Lines that express happiness are continuous and flowing, with no
pauses or breaks, and no sharp turnings. Lines that express unpleasant
feelings usually have stops in them, suggesting difficulty or
impediment. When there are too many stops, it is a sign of grief and
anxiety. . . .
(Lu Fengzi: *A Study of Chinese Caligraphy*, a good reference work
that explains concretely how lines give expression to one's feelings)

In the main, what calligraphy expressed was the free, flowing, romantic,
and lofty style of the Wei and Jin, a clear and open atmosphere that
differed from that of the Han Dynasty and was even reflected in stone
tablets and engravings that appeared at a slightly later date.

Ruan Ji and Tao Qian

Art is often incongruous with politics and the economy, so it is not
strange that a style as free, complacent, romantic, and out of the
ordinary as that of the Wei-Jin should appear in a society and era
marked by turbulence, disorder, disaster, and bloodshed. But because of
this, what appeared to be free and easy on the surface often veiled an
inordinate sorrow, fear, and inward anguish.

From the Wei and Jin through the Northern and Southern
Dynasties, the imperial household changed hands again and again and
upper society was a scene of constant fighting and killing. The political
struggle was extremely acute and ruthless. Many famous scholars of the
time, as prominent members of the great aristocratic families, were
sucked into the political eddies, from which they were sent, one after
another, to the execution ground. He Yan, Ji Kang, Lu Ji, Lu Yun,
Zhang Hua, Pan Yue, Guo Xiang, Liu Kun, Xie Lingyun, Fan Ye, Pei
Wei: all these first-rate poets, writers, and philosophers were either
executed or murdered. It was a shocking list of victims, of whom the
ones mentioned were but a representative few.

'The Guanglingsan is gone forever.' 'The song of the crane at
Huating will not be heard again.'[20] What remained were only tales of
grief and suffering. Wealth and comfort on the one hand, an impending
doom on the other—this was the lot of the sons of the great families,
embroiled in political struggles. 'In constant fear of being ensnared;
worried that disaster will come any day' (He Yan). 'The worried heart

[20] These are lines lamenting Ji Kang and Lu Ji. Guanglingsan was a piece of
lute music played by Ji Kang just before his execution. Huating was Lu Ji's
native place.

is forever moaning and howling' (Ji Kang). These are the feelings constantly revealed in the writings of these scholars. Ruthless political purges coupled with personal and family misfortunes caused their world outlook to be heavily weighted with sorrow and dread; and because of the political content, their 'laments on life' took on a greater gloom and solemnity. Irrespective of whether they followed the trend of the times to save their necks or sought refuge in nature to calm their souls, their feelings were in an extremely controversial and complex state because of the fear and anguish ever present in their lives. Outwardly they could affect a contempt for worldly affairs, a free and easy manner above the common run; but inwardly there was great mental suffering as they clutched frantically at life. This was the inner and deeper aspect of the Wei-Jin style.

Ruan Ji (210–263 A.D.) was a typical scholar of this period. 'However impassioned he may have been, he tended to veil many of his ideas' (Lu Xun). His 82 lyrical pieces are indeed in veiled language; yet they are also very clear, for what is mirrored in their artistic conception and poetic sentiments are the sorrow and sighs of people closely involved in the political struggles and persecution of their time:

(1)
That which flourishes must wither,
Brambles will grow in the hall.
Spurring the horse I take my leave,
To the western hills I go.
My own body I cannot save,
What can I do for my wife?
Frost covers the wild grass,
As the year draws near its end.

(2)
There's a raging fire in my heart,
And changes beckon to me;
There's never an end to worldly things,
The wise know suffering always.
I dread that in some instant,
The soul will leave with the wind;
Forever walking upon thin ice,
Who knows my worries within.

Regret, sorrow, fear, love, anxiety, worry: Ruan Ji was unable to extricate himself from these mental problems and unwilling to go with the tide. On the one hand, he wanted very much to live long: 'Only the art of prolonging life can bring comfort to my heart.' On the other, he sighed: 'People may wish to live long, but what use is there in a long life?'

> I would fly up into the skies above,
> Where the earth would be heard no more,
> Why stay and play with the quail here,
> Flapping their wings in the yard?

> I would hide myself within the clouds,
> No nets can ensnare me there;
> Why spend my time with the philistines,
> Hold hands and make pledges with them?

Thus he revealed his hatred of the times and his desire to free himself. But then he writes:

> I would glide with the swallow and sparrow,
> Than soar with the yellow crane;
> The crane may fly the seven seas,
> How will it return again?

Ruan Ji had to submit to reality in order to live. He was forced to write appeals for the advancement of others, appeals that to him were stupid and boring. But he was extremely cautious, never openly criticized anyone, and on one occasion went drunk for sixty days in order to avoid an undesirable marital connection with the emperor. His poems were veiled in meaning, because they embodied the man's great mental agony and keen dilemma: to write or not to write. As a member of the famous group of scholars of the Bamboo Grove, he is said to have been very romantic and uninhibited in his ways, but in fact the conflict and suffering in his heart was unusually great.

> I grieve for the siskin,[21]
> Can't help shedding tears.

> Who says jade and stone are the same?
> I cannot keep the tears from falling.

Lines like these often appeared in his poems. Probably nobody else has ever expressed the pain and sorrow of a ruthless political persecution in a strong but indirect way with such depth and beauty. It was this that gave true substance to the Wei-Jin style and the human theme, and it is only from this point that we can more fully apprehend the positive significance and aesthetic power of the Wei-Jin style.

The Wei-Jin style originally endured over a relatively short period.

---

[21] The 'siskin' was a veiled term for victims of political persecution.

In this book, however, we have extended it to the Eastern Jin and the Song,[22] so Tao Qian[23] may also be regarded as a personified ideal representative of this style.

Tao Qian's aloofness, like Ruan Ji's indulgence in wine, was only an outward phenomenon. The real Tao Qian, like Ruan Ji, was a man who evaded the political struggles of his day. He did not come from as distinguished a family as Ruan Ji, nor was he forced by circumstances into the struggles at the highest social level. But his family background and the ambitions of his youth interested and involved him in politics, and it was characteristic of the man that he later retired very willingly from the political arena. As to why he did so, his poetic works, whose tone is quite similar to that of Ruan Ji and other poets of his time, may provide the best answer.

(1)
Fish frighten when the net is laid,
Birds startle when the cage is built,
And man when conscience is awakened,
Leaves office to take up the plow.

(2)
Famous scholars in days of old
Eagerly fought for power;
But when they've lived a hundred years,
All must return to the grave.

. . . .

Wealth and fame may be valued;
Regrets they bring as well.

(3)
The stems are about to blossom,
But the hills and rivers change;
Stalks and leaves fall on their own,
As trunks are swept away.

. . . .

They shouldn't have grown on the highland,
So why regret it today?

These and many of Tao Qian's other poems all had a political meaning. As his personal status, position in life, circumstances, and experience were different, his sorrows and regrets were not as poignant

---

[22] The first of the four Southern Dynasties, not the Song that preceded the Yuan.
[23] Tao Qian (c.370–427), also called Tao Yuanming, was a poet of the Eastern Jin.

as those of Ruan Ji. Still, such feelings were the main reason he waived 'wealth and fame' and returned to the plow. He withdrew resolutely from the politics of the upper classes to seek spiritual comfort in a country life of wine, reading, and poetry-writing. But he did not have the feeling of nullity towards life and society that characterized most scholars and officials of late feudal society. On the contrary, he had a great interest in life and society. He did not share their belief in Buddhist meditation to seek some sort of total enlightenment, but was very much interested in the vicissitudes of life and the problem of death. He had much the same outlook as expressed in the *Nineteen Poems*: 'Life seems to change and disappear; eventually it returns to nothing.' 'If I do not enjoy myself today, do I know if there is a tomorrow?' Though he followed Taoism, he adopted essentially the stand of an atheist and skeptic, questioning many issues: 'Contentedly I have followed Laozi and long endured hunger; yet I return to poverty and an early death. . . . Though I loved to study and did what was right, why is life so hard? I question that virtue should be rewarded in this way, and dread the falseness of the word.' And in summary: 'So remote is heaven, so endless human affairs; some are clear, some very obscure, how can one really seek out the truth?'

Ruan Ji had this same skeptical outlook. He writes: 'Fame and honour are not one's treasures; sound and colour do not mean enjoyment; he who goes to find the elixir does not return; the will of the gods has not been met. Realizing this, I am perplexed; I have hesitated a long, long time.'

However loudly these scholars might talk of Laozi and Zhuangzi, they knew in their hearts that 'to equate life with death was absurd, to regard great age and infant death as the same was illusive.' The Lao-Zhuang philosophy (atheism) was not for them. The mysteries of life still haunted them and could not be solved. And so regrets over the uncertainty and brevity of life continued, from the *Nineteen Poems* to Tao Qian, from the last years of the Eastern Han to the Jin and Song (of the Southern Dynasties) and later. It was not until after the Qi and Liang Dynasties, when Buddhism reached its prime and most people were converted to it, that an apparent solution to the mysteries of life was seemingly found.

Like Ruan Ji, Tao Qian took the path of withdrawing from politics. But he was the only one who succeeded in doing so. With a world outlook based on skepticism and atheism, he chose to return to the plow, despising fame, honour, and riches: 'I would rather be poor and relieved in mind than stoop to compromise and amass a fortune.

Since crowns and carriages do not mean honour, ragged garments are
no disgrace. It may seem foolish to choose the humble, yet happily I
return to stay.' The correct path in life was not to seek riches and
honour, carriages and crowns, or fame, merit, and academic rank, but to
cultivate one's character instead of stooping to personal gain. Thus it
was he alone who found physical pleasure and spiritual comfort in
pastoral life. And thus, under his brush, pastoral scenes were no longer
objects for philosophical thought or mere enjoyment; they had become
a part of the life and interests of the poet. This was very different from
the lot of men like Xie Lingyun. In Tao's poetry, hills, water, grass, and
trees were no longer lifeless things; they possessed a deep emotion and
a real meaning; they were plain and unadorned, but full of life.

> We spend our days in the hamlet,
> Clad in grass we wander about,
> When we meet we waste no idle words,
> But ask how the mulberry grows.
> The hemp and mulberry are growing tall,
> My land extends with each new day.
> I dread the coming of frost and sleet,
> When all will wither away.

> So dim is the distant village,
> So thin is the hamlet smoke;
> Dogs bark deep in the village lane,
> Cocks crow on the mulberry tree.
> No speck of dust in the courtyard,
> Much leisure in the empty room;
> Long was I in a cage confined,
> To nature I now return.

This is beauty that is real, commonplace, but hard to attain. Ostensibly,
it is only an objective description of country life, but it was the feelings
of a man with a high degree of personality that made such a description
possible.

Tao Qian and Ruan Ji represented two distinctly different
approaches to artistic creation in the Wei-Jin era. The one was plain,
moderate, and above worldly things; the other bitter, vehement, and
impetuous. But both were the finest representatives of the Wei-Jin style.

6

The Buddha's Worldly Countenance

A Miserable World

RELIGION is a very complex phenomenon. So is religious art which, generally speaking, is an object of faith and worship, not of enjoyment. Beauty and aesthetic form in religion are to serve its spiritual content.

In China, the main form of religious art handed down from ancient times is that seen in the Buddhist rock grottoes. Buddhism gained a wide following in this country during the Northern and Southern Dynasties, an era plagued by incessant wars, during which it became the ideology of the great families and the landlord class and played a dominant role in society. The kingdoms of Northern Wei and Southern Liang of this period formally adopted or restored Buddhism as their state religion, giving legal endorsement to its dominance. It continued to develop through the Sui and Tang, reached the zenith of its power and influence with the emergence of Chan (Zen) Buddhism, a Sinicized sect, and then gradually declined. Its rise and fall virtually coincided with those of the great families and landlord class.

Buddhist rock grotto art also changed and developed along with the changes in the times, the rise and fall of social classes, and the progress of social life, reflecting in its imagery how the Chinese nation accepted Buddhism, assimilated and reformed it. This was an important ideological process, through which the Chinese tradition of practical rationalism and historicism eventually triumphed over mysticism and fanaticism. Consequently, though the same giant Buddhist image and the same colourful murals are represented again and again, the secular content was not the same in different historical periods. An important example of this can be seen in the Dunhuang murals, in which the differences are clear in the world of the gods as depicted in the different dynasties of Northern Wei, Sui, Tang (early, prime, middle, late), the Five Dynasties, and Song. There were changes not only in theme and subject matter but also in appearance and style. Religion, after all, was only an anaesthetic and 'heaven' merely a reflection of the human world. There were three general epochal divisions in Buddhist religious concepts and their representation in art: Northern Wei; early Tang; and late Tang, Five Dynasties, and Song.

Buddha, stone carving of the Eastern Han at Lianyungang, Jiangsu Province. The earliest Buddha image discovered in China.

China's earliest rock grotto art, whether at Yungang, Longmen, Dunhuang, or Maijishan,[1] dates back to the Northern Wei. Rock grottoes were easier to preserve than wooden temples and palaces, especially in times of war, and the Northern Wei was a dynasty plagued by wars. The principal themes of the murals in the grottoes of this period are either the Buddha himself or Buddhist legends spread from India. Among these, the most popular are the stories of the man who cut off his own flesh to save a dove, the man who sacrificed himself to save a hungry tiger, Sudatta, a man who loved charity and charitable acts, and the five hundred bandits whose eyes were gouged out.

[1] The Yungang grottoes are in the Wuzhou (also called Yungang) Mountains of Shanxi Province. The principal grottoes here were built in the years 460–494. Fifty-three large ones are still extant and these house a total of 51,000 statues, of which the tallest is 17 meters high. The Longmen grottoes are in the mountains of Longmen and Xiangshan, Henan Province. The first grottoes were built in the period 477–499 and new ones were added over the next 400 years; 1353 grottoes with 785 niches and over 97,000 statues are still standing. The Dunhuang grottoes are in Dunhuang county, Gansu Province. Excavations here began in the Eastern Jin, and repairs and additions were

The story of the man who cut off his own flesh to save a dove is actually a story of the 'prince of the Sakyas,' one of the many mortal forms Sakyamuni is said to have passed through before he became a buddha. According to the story, one day a dove pursued by a hungry eagle flew into the prince's bosom and begged him to save its life. The prince turned to the eagle and said. 'Do not eat this little dove.' 'If I don't get any fresh meat to eat, I shall die myself,' answered the eagle. 'Why don't you pity me a little?' Thereupon, the prince picked up a balance scale. He placed the dove on one of the pans and ordered pieces of flesh to be cut from his legs and placed on the other pan, hoping to save the dove by giving the eagle an equivalent in his own flesh and blood. But strange to say, after all the flesh on both legs and both arms had been cut off and placed on the balance, the dove was still heavier. And so the prince with his last ounce of energy threw himself upon the pan, ready to give up his life and everything for the dove. At that instant, the earth shook and both dove and eagle disappeared. The whole affair had been an act devised by the gods to test his faith.

In most of the mural paintings of this story, the scene is of the prince having the flesh of his leg cut off. The prince is shown seated cross-legged, a large figure with head turned slightly to one side and eyes downward, calm, fearless, determined. One of his hands is placed before his chest; on the palm of the other is the dove that has come to him for help. Below, a small fierce-looking butcher is cutting the flesh from his leg, from which the blood is dripping. Around him are people with different expressions on their faces, some terrified, some compassionate, some sorrowful. On each side are bodhisattvas dancing and flying in a carefree manner, as if emitting some smooth but powerful sound like music, in contrast to the solemnity of the dominant theme. The portrayal was intended to be an expression of the calmness and sublimity of the soul under extreme physical suffering. 'Sacrificing Oneself to Feed a Tiger' is another story of the pre-enlightenment Buddha. It tells of three princes of the state of Maha Bodhi who went out travelling. Arriving at the foot of a crag, they saw seven newly born tiger cubs and in their midst a mother tiger, hungry, emaciated, and on

made in succeeding dynasties down to the Yuan; 486 grottoes are still extant. Besides 2415 statues, they contain mural paintings that cover 120,000 square meters of wall space. Maijishan is a mountain in Tianshui county, Gansu Province. Construction of rock grottoes here began in the 4th century and additions were made in later periods down to the Ming and Qing; 194 grottoes are still extant. They house over 7000 statues, of which about a thousand are over one meter in height.

the point of death. The youngest prince secretly made up his mind to sacrifice himself in order to save the tiger. He sent his two brothers home and then threw himself into the tiger's jaws. The beast, however, did not even have the strength to bite him, whereupon the prince pricked himself until the blood flowed and then jumped down from the top of the crag. He fell at the side of the tiger which, after licking up the blood, regained its strength and devoured the prince, leaving behind only a pile of bones and hair. When his brothers returned and saw the remains, they wept bitterly and told their father, the king, who ordered a pagoda built upon the spot to the memory of his son.

The mural painting of this story consists of a series of pictures showing various details of the horrible event: the seven cubs around their famished and dying mother; the young prince leaping down from the crag; the hungry tiger eating the prince; the king and queen weeping for their son; and the building of the pagoda. The chief scene is the one that shows the prince being devoured by the tiger. Both the story and the scenes in this mural are sadder and more gruesome than the first story.

Ostensibly, the story was intended to show the goodness and beauty of the soul in a situation of great misery. But what was there to be pitied about a tiger? The real purpose was to trumpet the spirit of self-sacrifice: A man willing to sacrifice himself in such a situation would of course be ready to lay down his life for any cause of humanity. And when princes and kings were so 'self-sacrificing,' what about the ordinary people? Clearly, this was self-assurance and self-deception on the part of the ruling class and an opiate dealt out to the masses. It was a perfect example of counter-rational religious fanaticism, whose artistic tone was marked by vehemence, passion, tension, and crudeness.

The murals we see today have long faded in colour and lost their original appearance. Yet in those rough contours that can still be made out, we may sense the fanatic aura and tone with their disquieting effects: the desolation of the countryside, the vivid images of men and beasts, the bold and uninhibited rhythm of lines, and forms and postures that suggest motion. The artistic style successfully brings out the fanaticism of theme and subject matter that is the basic aesthetic feature of murals of the Northern Wei.

Another story tells of a prince called Sudatta, who loved charity and never refused anyone who begged him for help. But one day when he gave away a white elephant, a national treasure, to an enemy country, his enraged father, the king, sent him into exile. Together with his wife and two children, he left home in a two-horse carriage. They had not gone far when two men appeared and begged him for horses and he gave his pair to them. Soon after, another man came up and asked for the carriage and he gave that away too. He and his wife now went their way on foot, each carrying one of the children. Other beggars came along and begged for clothes and he gave what he had to them. By the time he had given away just about everything—horses, carriage, clothes, money—the family reached a mountain, where they made their home. It was not long before another beggar arrived. The two children hid themselves for fear that their father would give them away this time, but the prince found them, tied them up and handed them over to the beggar. When the quaking children refused to leave their parents, the beggar lashed them until the blood flowed. The prince looked on with tears in his eyes but refused to take back his word and his children were led away.

The bandit story is about five hundred bandits who rebelled and fought the king's soldiers. They were defeated and captured, and their eyes were gouged out as punishment. As they wept and wailed in the cold, the Buddha appeared and with some magic ointment restored their sight, whereupon all were converted to Buddhism.

The last two stories, though also gross exaggerations, are a more direct reflection of reality. Property confiscated, children seized and taken away, rebellion, torture—such things were often seen or experienced by the common people in those days. Here, however, they were used to praise suffering, endurance, and self-sacrifice, to admonish people not to oppose pain and injustice, in return for which they could expect Buddhist enlightenment after several cycles of life based on severe self-discipline. But the grim reality was that for nearly four hundred years, from the disintegration of the Han empire to the reunification of the country in the Tang Dynasty by the House of Li, society as a whole was in a constant state of war, famine, plague, and disorder with only intermittent spells of peace and regional stability. Such respites came during the Western Jin, the Early Qin,[2] and the Northern Wei, when the cities of Chang'an and Luoyang enjoyed short periods of prosperity. But for the most part, class and national oppression and exploitation were carried out in the most savage, ruthless, and primitive ways. Massacres were a common occurrence. A whole historical epoch was permeated with repeated slaughters and

[2] The Early Qin (350–395) was one of the small, short-lived kingdoms in the northern and western parts of China during the epoch in Chinese history known as the Sixteen Kingdoms (304–439). Most of these kingdoms were set up by minority nationalities.

exterminations between classes and nations and within the ranks of the ruling clique and the imperial family. In the last years of the Han and throughout the Wei, it was 'white bones strewn over the wild, no hens cackling within a thousand *li*' (lines from a poem by Cao Cao).

The wars of the eight princes of the Western Jin[3] raised the curtains on a period of still greater social upheaval, during which the most common scenes were 'white bones in the wild, not a thing standing' (*Book of Jin: Biography of Jia Shu*); 'all roads blocked, no smoke over a thousand *li*' (*Book of Jin: Records of Fu Jian*); 'personal disaster, downfall of family, doors closed on all rooms' (*Book of Song: Biography of Xie Lingyun*); 'men starved to death on a thoroughfare, none to identify or remove the bodies' (*Book of Wei: Records of Gaozu*[4]). Records like this were numerous in the history of that period. The Sixteen Kingdoms (see footnote on the Early Qin) that occupied the northern and western parts of China rose and fell by turns as a result of incessant wars and ruthless killing. The Eastern Jin and the Southern Dynasties, located in relative security on the northern bank of the Yangtze, were nonetheless plagued by warlords displacing each other, by intrigues and murders within the imperial family, and by frequent dynastic changes. Very often, a prestigious imperial or aristocratic family would collapse after only a short period of prosperity and all its members would be sentenced to death or slavery. The lot of the common people was, of course, even worse. To escape conscription and oppression, many left home to take religious vows, 'feigning a love of monastic life, but actually to escape forced labour or military service' (*Book of Wei: Sakyamuni and Laozi*). In short, life was miserable, as insignificant as the dew, with no security for oneself and one's family, with the future full of uncertainties, with nothing to live for. Life was only sorrow, suffering, fear, and sacrifice, for there was no right or reason in the world and events did not follow the normal laws of cause and effect. The good suffered while the wicked triumphed. Home, self, and family were in constant danger. It was pain and hardship all the way. Why was it so? Why must it be so?

These were questions which, it seems, could not be answered by rationalism, nor expounded upon by traditional Confucianism and Taoism. So Buddhism, which offered an answer, entered into men's hearts. Since there was no right or reason in this world, men looked to

---

[3] This refers to the civil wars between rival factions of the imperial family in the early years of the Western Jin.

[4] Gaozu was a title of reverence for the first emperor of a dynasty. Here it refers to Cao Pi.

samsara, or transmigration, for the fulfillment of cause and effect, putting their hopes for justice in heaven and a future life.

> Says the (Buddhist) scripture: There are three ways of requital. The first is present requital; the second, requital by birth; the third, requital later on. In the first case, good or evil done in this life is repaid with happiness or suffering in this life, too. In the second case, requital comes with the next birth, that is, in the next life. In the third case, the requital may come with the third, fourth, or even hundredth or thousandth life.
> (*Guang Hongmingji*,[5] Vol. 8)

Subjected as they were to savage wars, unrest, and exploitation, it is not hard to imagine with what fanaticism and mixed feelings the poor, helpless people sought to 'cleanse their souls' as they knelt or sat before the religious images. The so-called 'sitting in meditation, totally transfixed' practiced by many monks and Buddhist disciples was actually a great ordeal of suffering and duress. The monks and laymen who practiced Buddhism could only regard religion and the rock grottoes as ornaments of their present life, as a sacred haven amid human suffering where they could lay down their beautiful hopes, lighthearted dreams, and sighs and sorrows, and possibly forget the injustices and irrational things of the world. It rendered them more humble and subservient, more willing to resign themselves to adversity and make greater sacrifices in order to receive the blessings of the gods. Today, hundreds of years later, we can still sense the human life and historical reality that have been aesthetically condensed in those artistic scenes and images; it is like reading a tragic poem or a tale of suffering. In those melancholy stories expressed in such an intensely violent way, we can well appreciate the aesthetic, emotional power that attracted and deceived people into believing in Buddhism and heaven.

The real achievement of the rock grottoes was not the murals but the sculptures, for which the former were only a backdrop. The purpose of the scenes and stories on the four walls was only to bring into sharper focus the body of the Buddha in the centre, for there had to be an object of faith and a physical form for worship. As the person dwindled proportionately in significance, the Buddha increased in physique. In artistic terms, there was a very powerful contrast: mural scenes of ardour and agitation surrounding a master figure of extraordinary tranquillity.

---

[5] *Guang Hongmingji*: a collection of essays on Buddhism in 30 volumes, by Dao Xuan.

The beauty of Chinese sculptural art reached a climax in the creations of the Northern Wei, from the early sculptures at Yungang, which were solemn and dignified, to the more matured works at Longmen, Dunhuang, and especially Maijishan, which were graceful and elegant with their thin faces, small necks, flowing robes in many folds, and a mood that suggests ease, vitality, and complacency, as if all the smoke in the world had been cleared away. People concentrated their hopes, ideals, and concepts of beauty in these images, which were gods that embodied a broad and infinite range of spiritual possibilities. But these gods did not manifest any love, kindness, or concern for the world, only a transcendent attitude that was above secular things. Though the figure of an image may be bent and its eyes cast downward in a condescending manner, it appeared to be uninterested in or unmoved by worldly affairs. It had an air of contempt for the world of reality, expressed in a sagacious smile as if it had seen through everything. Thus the figures displayed composure, aloofness, grace, and wisdom amid the miserable world of terror, bloodshed, and chilling brutality portrayed in the surrounding murals.

Whatever they may symbolize, the sculptures were actually a representation of what was considered the ideal human form, spirit, appearance, and style in those days. The features of the buddhas in the Yungang caves, down to the black moles on their faces and feet, were a faithful reproduction of the earthly king. 'There was a mandate that year for the making of a stone image, which must have a body like the emperor's; when completed, there were black stones on the face and feet, like the black marks on the emperor's body' (*Book of Wei: Sakyamuni and Laozi*).

The numerous Buddhist images of the Northern Wei were carved entirely according to the aesthetic ideals of the great families of the nobility: an emaciated body that suggested some illness, a faint smile with a hidden meaning that could not be divulged, the wise look of a philosopher who had found the truth, the carefree manner of one above secular interests. All these represented the highest standards of beauty pursued by the ruling class since the Wei-Jin era. *Social Talk* recorded many legends, anecdotes, and humorous tales the purpose of which was to extol the ideal character of this upper class. When Buddhism spread and became the dominant ideology, people began to use Buddhist images to express this ideal character, whose two most important features were an inner wisdom and a refined style.

The combination of faith and speculation was a special feature of the Buddhism of the Southern Dynasties. It was the means by which the

Buddhist statue of the Northern Wei in a grotto at Gongxian, Henan Province.

scholar-officials from the great families and the aristocracy pacified
their souls and relieved themselves of mental suffering. It gave spiritual
satisfaction to these scholar-officials absorbed in thinking and studying.
This found expression not only in Buddhist sculpture (for example,
Maitreya meditating to absolve doubts) but in the whole realm of art.
Lu Tanwei (?–c.485), painter of the Southern Dynasties who was listed
first in Xie He's *A Critique of Ancient Paintings*, was noted for his
portraits of 'graceful figures and delicate looks that seem so real,
causing the viewer to tremble as if he were actually facing the gods.'
Gu Kaizhi, too, was famous for his depictions of 'thin and sickly
characters, with expressions that cannot be described in words.'

Though the Northern Dynasties were superior to the Southern
Dynasties in power and military strength, they recognized southern
culture as orthodox Chinese culture. For many centuries, southern
scholars who went to the north, notably Xi Zaochi of the Eastern Jin,
Wang Su of the Song and Qi, and Wang Bao and Yu Xin of the Chen,
were received there with great honour. As Gao Huan (?–547) of the
Northern Qi once said: 'East of the River[6] people gave all their attention
to clothing, headdress, rites, and music; scholars of the central plains
(north China), seeing this, believed that it was there that these things
originated' (*Book of the Northern Qi: Biography of Du Bi*). Because the
culture of the Southern Dynasties was regarded as orthodox culture to be
studied and emulated, it is not surprising that southern painters and
northern sculptors were so similar in their artistic style and in the general
appearance of their works. The Buddhist art that has been handed down
to the present, though preserved in northern grottoes, should be regarded
as representative of the spiritual aspect of the whole country in those
days. Completely rejected were the kissing, twisted bodies, large breasts,
erotic scenes, overly large forms, and exaggerated actions found in
Indian Buddhist art. Even the external features (structure, colour, lines,
ornament, design) of sculpture and murals were Sinicized. Sculpture,
more than any other branch of art, was a concentrated expression of the
aesthetic ideals of the Northern and Southern Dynasties.

Illusory Praise

The reunification of the country followed by a relatively long
period of peace and stability under the Tang was a marked contrast to

---

[6] East of the River is a popular term that refers to regions along the lower
reaches of the Yangtze.

the long-term disunity and incessant wars of the Northern and Southern Dynasties. Along with the country's unity and stability, there appeared in the realm of art an obvious change in the facial features and body shapes of sculptures, and in the style and subject matter of mural paintings. This change began in the Northern Zhou and Sui, continued through the early Tang, and attained its maturity in the prime Tang, developing into a new type of beauty that was also in marked contrast with the miserable world of the Northern Wei.

As to sculpture, the slender bodies and graceful looks, the gentle, elegant, pretty, and leisurely features disappeared. They were replaced by Sui Dynasty images with square jaws, large ears, short necks, thick bodies, and a plain and clumsy physique. These, however, were only transitional characteristics. With the advent of the Tang, figures had evolved into healthy, robust, and well-developed forms. Tang sculpture differed from the earlier works that portrayed figures so out of the ordinary, so full of unspeakable wisdom and spiritual qualities. Tang figures appeared to possess more human qualities and kindlier feelings. The image of the Buddha became more merciful, seemingly more concerned about the present world and anxious to be close to humankind and to help people. It was no longer a superior, self-satisfied, unreachable divine being, but was looked upon as an authoritative master who administered worldly affairs and to whom petitions could be made.

The Tang grottoes were not like thatched huts or dark caves; they were more like comfortable dwellings. The statues of bodhisattvas did not bend forward but sat or stood composedly. Of still greater importance was that there were no more three-buddha or one-buddha-two-bodhisattva groups with obscure implications and no clear distinctions between them. The Tang sculptures showed either a platform of buddhas or a group of bodhisattvas in an orderly rank, each for a distinct purpose and with a different function. Moods, features, and bodily postures that corresponded to the primary functions and duties of the characters were displayed in a far more definite form than before, for example, the solemn, kind, and propitious look of Bhagavat, the simplicity and docility of Ananda, the serious and earnest attitude of Mahakasyapa, the gentleness and reserve of the bodhisattvas, the strength and power of the 'heavenly generals,' the fierceness of the 'heavenly warriors.'[7] It was a display of strength, of kindliness, of innocence as a model of piety, or of wisdom that could provide leadership and guidance. The images are therefore more concrete and secular and less spiritual, and the ideals they

[7] All the names mentioned here are of Buddhist deities.

represent are more diversified. There is much more than just a mysterious smile of many implications but hard to fathom.

All this, of course, was a further Sinicization of Buddhism, with Confucian teachings infiltrating Buddhist temples. Unlike Europe, religion in China was subordinate and subject to politics. Buddhism was increasingly controlled and administered by feudal emperors, kings, and officials, in whose hands it became a docile tool for the protection of the feudal system. '[It] aided the prohibitory laws of the king's administration, benefited the qualities of benevolence and wisdom' (*Book of Wei: Sakyamuni and Laozi*). 'He would often travel in a carriage to deliver addresses; those who saw him called him the bald official' (*Biography of the Eminent Monk: Hui Neng*). From religious teachings to clerical ranks, Buddhism more and more approximated Confucianism. The Buddhist monk also 'worshipped the king and repaid his parents.' 'Buddhist monks say *Taizu*[8] is the living Buddha, to whom monks must show full respect' (*Book of Wei: Sakyamuni and Laozi*). As a matter of fact, the heads of the Buddhist clergy received salaries from the government and had government rank. 'Yao Qin appointed the monk Lue as the Chief Monk, a rank equivalent to a *shizhong*;[9] this was the beginning of government-paid emolument for priests' (*A Short Monastic History of the Great Song*).

The heated debates and attacks between the Confucianists, Buddhists, and Taoists that began in the Northern and Southern Dynasties subsided during the Tang and was gradually replaced by harmony and coexistence. Religion was made to serve politics and the Buddhist realm was eventually permeated with the human ethics taught in Confucian ideology. Buddhist leaders of all sects entered the imperial court while the upper clergy in the provinces were extolled because they

> Served the Buddha, were sensitively aware of Buddhist laws, thoroughly studied Confucianism in their spare time, and instructed others in the virtues of king and subject, father and son. . . . And so the fierce criminal was moved to embrace Buddhism and to detest killing, and the righteous willingly laid down his life for his country; the benefits were indeed numerous.
> (*The Works of Du Mu*, Vol. 20)

All this conformed closely to Confucianism.

---

[8] *Taizu* was a posthumous title for the first king or emperor of a Chinese dynasty.

[9] *Shizhong* was a high official title in many Chinese dynasties. During the Northern and Southern Dynasties, a *shizhong* was sometimes the prime minister.

The full amalgamation of religion and Confucianism in the Tang Dynasty is mirrored in its Buddhist sculpture, in the moods and smiles of the images that suggest gentleness, honesty, and an interest in worldly things and in the orderly ranks and duties of rulers and subjects. On the one hand, there were the fierce, muscular 'general of heaven' and his 'warriors' with the power to suppress, on the other, the kind and gentle bodhisattvas and Guan Yin (Avalokitesvara), the goddess of mercy, who could pacify. And in the centre was the dignified, magnanimous, all-passive and all-active Buddha himself. The great infinity of the buddhas of past, present, and future was no longer depicted in numerous small images exactly alike, as during the Northern Wei. It was cleverly represented as an organic whole made up of just a few images. This of course was an indication of a further change and development in ideology (of all Buddhist sects) and in art as well. The Buddhist kingdom in heaven conceived during this time was only a replica of the imperial court of the Tang empire, a feudal Chinese Buddhist kingdom, whose art was wholly subordinate to and a representation of this concept. A typical feature of Tang sculpture is that it was not divorced from man's world and yet was above it, above and yet closely related to it. This differs from Northern Wei sculpture, which was wholly above the secular, and from Song sculpture, which was wholly at one with the secular. Many fine examples of Tang sculpture can be found at Longmen, Dunhuang, and Tianlongshan.[10] The Buddhist images in the Fengxian Temple of Longmen, especially the statue of the Buddha that stands over ten meters high, with a kindly and beautiful countenance, are among the finest examples of ancient Chinese sculpture.

Mural painting followed the same path of development as sculpture. There were changes not only in the imagery of a subject— for example, Vimalakirti, portrayed as thin, pale, and sickly during the Six Dynasties, was now depicted as a hale and hearty old man—but in theme and subject matter as well, there was an about-face. The stories of feeding the tiger, saving a dove, giving away one's children, and the scenes of sorrow and cruelty, which spread from India and did not accord with traditional Chinese principles of returning 'good for good, justice for evil,' disappeared at long last. In their place were so-called

[10] Tianlongshan is a mountain south of Taiyuan, Shanxi Province. The grottoes here were constructed over a period of about 400 years, from the Northern Qi to the Sui and Tang. The sculptures in them are of high artistic value, but most of the sculptures have been destroyed by foreign invaders in modern times.

Fengxian Temple, relic of the Tang Dynasty at Longmen, Luoyang. Measuring 34 meters wide and 39 meters deep, it houses eleven statues, of which the one in the centre is of Losana, a dignified and good-looking figure clad in a monk's vestment and standing 17.14 meters high.

pure lands, that is, imaginary scenes of a Buddhist paradise: 'In Buddhist land . . . the earth was of coloured glaze: boundaries were marked with golden ropes; city towers, palaces, balconies, and windows were made of precious stones.' And so in mural paintings we see towers of gold, houses of gems, fairy hills, magnificent pavilions, wood and stringed instruments being played in the halls, music all day long, the Buddha sitting in the centre of the lotus surrounded by divine beings, an orchestra of drums and bells sounding in unison in front, rosy clouds and flying devas behind, exotic grass and flowers below. Here there are no bloodshed and sacrifices, no barren hills and woods, no tigers and wild deer; only magnificent colours, smooth, flowing lines, a well-developed and graceful composition, a boisterous but joyful atmosphere. The beauty of dancing with flying robes replaced the beauty of violent motion. Buxom female figures replaced thin and coldly aloof males. Gorgeous beauty replaced a rough and unconstrained style. Horses, too, were now portrayed as stout and beautiful, not thin and gaunt; and flying deities changed from male to female—the whole scene, atmosphere, rhythm, mood, even costumes and ornaments were completely different from the preceding era. While in the murals of the Northern Wei miserable reality and bitter suffering were depicted in order to seek a respite for the soul and blessings from the gods, it was the exact opposite in the Tang, which sought spiritual comfort and satisfaction through illusions of joy and happiness.

A comparison of the tales circulated in the two different periods makes the difference more clear. Various kinds of Buddhist stories appeared along with the *jingbian*[11] of the Tang Dynasty. The most popular of these is the story of Bad Friend. Good Friend and Bad Friend were two princes who, with 500 followers, set out one day to look for treasure. Unable to stand the hardships, Bad Friend returned home. Good Friend persevered and after many dangers and difficulties found the treasure. On his way back, however, he was robbed of the treasure by Bad Friend, who also put out his eyes. The blind prince learnt to play the zither, wandered into an unknown land, and became a gardener there. One day the king's daughter heard him playing. They fell in love with each other and, in spite of her father's objections, she decided to marry him. After their marriage, the prince regained his sight and together they returned to his own country. His parents, who had also been blinded through grief for their son, recovered their sight

---

[11] *Jingbian* was a style of painting popular during the Tang and later dynasties. It was used to depict Buddhist stories and spread Buddhist doctrines.

too upon his return. Bad Friend was forgiven, the royal family was reunited, and there was rejoicing throughout the land.

When we compare this story with the stories of misery and suffering of the Northern Wei, the contrast in flavour and spirit is enormous. The Chinese optimistic attitude towards life and belief in family harmony and worldly happiness symbolized the spirit of the new era and were expressed through its sculptures and murals.

The change in artistic flavour and aesthetic ideals was not and could not be determined by art itself. In the final analysis, it was real life that caused the change. Gone at last was an era in which human life was as worthless as weeds and disaster could befall anyone any time. In its place was an era of relative peace and stability in a country prosperous and united. People living in the border regions in those days, in their prayers to the Buddha, often beseeched that in their next life they be 'born in China.' Society was progressing and the great families of nobles were on the decline, but non-hereditary, secular, bureaucratic landlords were becoming more and more powerful. Along with this, new factors and new phenomena appeared in economic, political, and military spheres, in social atmosphere, and in psychological moods, and these filtered into Buddhism and its art.

Since the lower social classes were not as miserable during the Tang Dynasty as they had been during the Northern and Southern Dynasties, the upper classes could indulge in such worldly pleasures as singing and dancing with less apprehension. Also, class struggle had taken on a new form, along with which the longing for a Buddhist kingdom and the demand on religion had changed too. It was no longer necessary to frighten people through depictions of cruelty and suffering in order to enforce spiritual control: the allurement of a happy life in heaven was a better tranquillizer. And so sculptures and murals in rock grottoes were no longer characterized by sharp contradictions but by a mutually complementing harmony.

What the Tang Dynasty *jingbian* murals depicted was not the world of reality but idealistic scenes based on conditions in the imperial court and the life of the upper aristocracy. Likewise, statues of the Buddha were not modelled upon the average man; they were specimens of well-fed, well-clothed, and well-built members of the nobility. It was admiration and the seeking of happiness that caused people to prostrate themselves before Buddhist images and the *jingbian*. This was very different in psychological effect and aesthetic feeling from the situation in the Northern Wei when Buddhist stories and images instilled only fear and a feeling of hopelessness. The relationship between heaven and earth now was not marked by confrontation but by proximity. What was being orchestrated was an illusory song of happiness in dreams to enchant the people.

Toward the Secular

There were three epochal social changes in ancient China, apart from the one during the Pre-Qin. These changes commenced in the Wei-Jin, mid-Tang, and mid-Ming respectively, and in each case there were clear repercussions in the whole ideological realm, including literature, art, and aesthetic ideals.

The most important changes that began in the mid-Tang were the suspension of the *juntian* system and the abrogation of the *zu-yong-diao* tax system,[12] which was replaced by payment in money; the development of economic interchange and trade between the north and south; the establishment of the imperial examination system; and a great increase in the power of the non-hereditary, secular landlords,[13] who gradually assumed control of or infiltrated the government at all levels. Among the middle and upper classes, there was a general seeking of luxury, joy, and pleasure. China's feudal society was entering its later stage.

These historic changes, completed during the Northern Song, are clearly reflected in the Dunhuang murals. The rows of bodhisattvas of great stature in the murals of the prime of Tang had disappeared by the mid-Tang. More popular were the *jingbian*, in which figures were secondary, the emphasis being on boisterous scenes which virtually filled all murals. By the late Tang and the Five Dynasties, this change was even more conspicuous; there were many more kinds of *jingbian*, but the images of the gods became smaller and smaller. The colours were garish, changing from luxuriant to gorgeous, with an ever richer ornamental flavour. The smoothness with powerful lines and rhythm that characterized paintings of the early and prime Tang had by this time become fine and soft and sometimes seemed almost cursory.

[12] The *juntian* system was a per-capita system of apportioning land that lasted from the Northern Wei to the mid-Tang. *Zu* was land tax paid in millet, *yong* was tax paid by physical labour, and *diao* was tax paid in local produce (silk, cotton cloth, etc.).

[13] These landlords did not inherit their land as did the monastic landowners and great families. Either because they had performed some meritorious service or because they had passed the imperial examinations and received official appointments, they became richer and obtained land.

The figures of bodhisattvas (gods) became smaller while those of the attendants (humans) became larger, some being of the same size as the bodhisattvas of the prime Tang and, occasionally, even larger. These attendants were sumptuously dressed in the manner of the higher aristocracy of the day and were arrayed according to rank and seniority as in real life. If formerly the intent had been to deify the human world, now it was the human world itself that was made prominent, except that it was only the upper stratum of society that was portrayed. It was obvious that by this time what was of greater interest and attraction to people was real life, not the lavish but repetitious and monotonous portrayals of 'pure lands,' nor 'pictures of the way,' nor some imaginary paradise. Mural painting truly began to take the way of realism: Heaven is in this human world, all joys are in the present.

Examples of this may be seen in two Dunhuang murals of the late Tang and the Five Dynasties: 'Zhang Yichao Leading His Troops on the March' and 'Lady of the State of Song on the Road.' These were pictures of real life having nothing to do with Buddhism, yet they were painted in a temple grotto constructed for worshipping the Buddha and, moreover, occupied a conspicuous position.

Zhang Yichao was a national hero of the late Tang who recovered lost territory west of the Yellow River. In the mural, the impressive spectacle of flags, drums, and bugles, of rows of soldiers and civilians, of war horses in battle formation, was obviously to glorify a real historical figure and event. Likewise, the horse-drawn carriage, acrobatics, music, and dancing in 'Lady of the State of Song on the Road' were all depictions of real life.

Among noted painters of the day, Wu Daozi had to give place to Zhou Fang and Zhang Xuan,[14] as painters specializing in human figures, landscapes, flowers and birds emerged one after another. At Dunhuang, secular scenes had infiltrated on a large scale into the sanctuaries of a Buddhist domain. Everything pointed to the fact that religious art was being ousted by a realistic secular art.

The increasing aesthetic interest in real life resulted in an increasing number of so-called 'everyday scenes' in the murals of this period: the banquets, inspection of troops, and healing of diseases of the upper classes; the plowing, milking cows, towing boats, and travelling of the lower and middle classes. Although some murals were

[14] Wu Daozi, Zhou Fang, and Zhang Xuan were three famous figure painters of the Tang Dynasty. The first excelled in Buddhist and Taoist figures. The other two were painters of real people: scholars and ladies.

still made in conjunction with Buddhist scriptures, many were pure scenery unrelated to religion. They revealed a common interest in the existing secular life.

Alongside this, paintings of landscapes, buildings, and terraces also increased. It was no longer a case of 'men being larger than mountains and water so shallow that a boat will not float' (Zhang Yanyuan: *Famous Paintings Through the Ages*) as in the Northern Wei murals, in which woods and hills were only a symbolic background for a religious theme. Landscape painting became more realistic and could be appreciated aesthetically in itself. A good example is the painting of the Wutai Mountains in a Song Dynasty grotto.

The change is also reflected in the stories that the murals depicted. The most popular story in the *jingbian* murals is 'Laoducha's Duel with a Saint,' which tells of a duel of magical powers. Laoducha, a monster, changed himself into a large tree in bloom, whereupon Sariputra, a buddha, conjured up a storm that uprooted the tree. Laoducha changed into a pond and Sariputra changed into a white elephant that sucked up the water. Laoducha then transformed himself successively into a hill, a dragon, and an ox, and Sariputra responded by changing into a man of enormous strength, a bird with golden wings, and a lion king which, in each case, was able to destroy or devour Laoducha's transformation. A tale like this was more of a theatrical performance to entertain people than a religious teaching, more a storyteller's invention to amuse his listeners than an attempt to preach the power of Buddhism. Thus religion and its piety were gradually forced out of the realm of art.

Things were much the same in other areas. For example, the so-called 'popular teachings' of the temples and monasteries in those days were very common, but their content was no longer the Buddhist scriptures, nor the speculation on 'being' and 'non-being' of scholars of the Six Dynasties, but secular life, folk legends, and historical tales plain and pure. In fact, they had hardly any connection with religion, being designed only to draw in more people so as to fill the temple's coffers. Many were tales of adventure and fighting such as 'The Defection of the Han General Wang Ling,' 'Ji Bu Castigates the Enemy in Battle,' and the adventures of Wu Zixu.[15]

> On the pretext of discussing the scriptures, crowds gathered only to
> talk about obscene and trashy things. . . . Foolish men and seductive

---

[15] Wu Zixu was a high official of the state of Wu of the Spring and Autumn period. He fled to Wu from Chu to escape persecution and had many harrowing experiences on the way.

women enjoyed listening to them, swallowing it all. Rites and
worship were still observed in the temples . . . but the prostitutes
imitated their tones when composing songs and music.
(Zhao Lin: *Anecdotes of the Tang Dynasty*)

The temples' 'popular teachings' were the predecessor of the
storytelling and townsfolk art and literature of the Song Dynasty.

Chan (Zen) Buddhism, which had flourished since the mid-Tang
and prevailed over all other Buddhist sects, was a theoretical expression
of the above state of affairs. The development of art parallels that of
philosophy. From the debate on 'being' and 'non-being' of the Wei-Jin
abstruse learning to the argument over form and spirit of the Buddhist
philosophy of the Southern Dynasties, Buddhism by its meticulous
speculation had captured the imagination of the then representative
class in Chinese culture, the great families and aristocracy, who delved
ever deeper into its mysteries, unable and unwilling to return.
Philosophical speculation actually found abundant material for study in
religious faith; thus the pessimistic view of life that had existed since
the Wei-Jin gradually diminished and men were now intoxicated by a
new and unique narcotic, an integration of speculation and faith.
'Gautama Buddha's merits and salvations are countless; they spread
over the whole secular world. Those who equate life with death are
impressed with his broad vision; those who are deeply read value his
brilliance' (*Book of Wei: Sakyamuni and Laozi*). It was because of this
that a certain measure of rational speculation was preserved in religious
faith, and such extremely mystic and terrifying concepts as those of
Brahma and Siva[16] in Hinduism never appeared in China, while the
non-rational fantastic tales that spread from India quickly vanished
from the Chinese stage of art and history when society had but changed
a little.

Chan Buddhism went a step further and taught the complete
identification of religious faith with daily life. It dispensed with all the
tedious rites and doctrines, asserting that it was possible to become a
buddha without entering a monastery and without strict self-denial and
meditation. Additionally, it asserted that the way to become a buddha
was actually not to become one, for to be a real buddha was to maintain
or possess a high spiritual worth *in one's daily life*. In the transition from
'attaining sudden enlightenment and becoming a buddha' to 'berating
and chastising the Buddha,' from 'all men have a Buddhist nature' to

[16] Brahma and Siva are two of the chief gods of Brahmanism and Hinduism.
Brahma is the god of creation and Siva the god of destruction.

'mountains are still mountains, water is still water,' the important thing was not only to rise 'from mortal to saint' but to a greater degree to descend 'from saint to mortal,' which means to be physically exactly the same as ordinary people in ordinary life, different only in spirit. 'Carrying water and cutting firewood, are these not good acts?' 'Silence, speech, stillness, motion, colour, sound, all are Buddhist things' (*Guzunsu Yulu*, or *The Sayings of Chan Buddhists*, Vol. 3). The conclusion, of course, was that there was no need for any special object of religious faith, nor a physical form for worship. Just as religious art was to be superseded by secular art, so religious philosophy, including Chan Buddhism itself, inevitably would be ousted by the secular philosophy of Song Dynasty Confucianism. Religious fanaticism in China was on its way out. 'Of the 480 temples of the Southern Dynasties, how many towers and terraces are in the smoke and rain!' (from a poem of Du Mu, a famous late Tang poet). Of course, the real, underlying cause of all this was the important changes in the country's economic basis and social relations as Chinese society passed from the Middle Ages to a more recent era—late or post-feudalism.

With the completion of the process of social change, the Song Dynasty rock grottoes at Dunhuang became repositories of religious art divested of everything religious. The grottoes were large but lacking in spirit. There were numerous bodhisattvas in the murals, but they had no vitality and were more like shadows or paper cut-outs pasted on the wall; patternization and generalization were extremely obvious, even in the case of designs that showed pure formal beauty. Completely gone were the liveliness of the designs of the Northern Wei and the free, uninhibited style of the Tang: all that remained was the standardized and stereotyped Muslim script. The grotto as a whole appeared to be cold, barren, dull, and lifeless. The only things worth seeing were the paintings of landscapes, towers, and terraces, which approximated reality, such as the painting of Tiantai Mountain, but they were no longer religious art. Entering such a grotto, one is reminded of the rational poetry and Neo-Confucianism of the Song. These had no religious fervour, nor did they engage in pure rational speculation. They stressed only scholarly discussions and feudal ethics. It is surprising how close art and philosophy are to each other.

The religious paintings of Han Gan of the Tang Dynasty, which are recorded in the *Youyang Zazu* (*Miscellanies of Youyang*), were already 'realistic portrayals of little singing girls' in aristocratic families; the images of gods had been completely humanized and secularized. This characteristic became more prominent in Song

Court Lady, statue of the
Song Dynasty in the Jin
Temple at Taiyuan.

sculpture. The stone carvings of Dazu (in Sichuan Province), the Song sculptures in the Jin Temple,[17] and the rock grottoes of Maijishan, all represented a new type of sculptural beauty very different from the products of the Wei and Tang. They were neither speculative deities (as in the Northern Wei) nor lords of the universe (Tang), but worldly gods, images of humans. They were more real, more concrete, more personable, in fact more lovable. The statues of Guanyin, the goddess of mercy, and of Manjusri and Samantabhadra, on the northern hill of Dazu, all have a soft, delicate complexion, slightly slanting eyes, thin eyebrows, and a frailty that touches the heart. The Song sculptures of Maijishan and Dunhuang are also like this, and more so are the famous statues of ladies-in-waiting in the Jin Temple. In fact, the most successful works of Dazu and Maijishan—very charming images— were depictions of real girls of the people. They do not belong to the category of religious art and have little religious significance.

Chinese Buddhist art, which lasted hundreds of years, cannot be viewed as one homogeneous body. It is important to make a historical analysis and concrete examination of the subject. The transition of heaven and earth from violent confrontation to proximity and harmony, to final amalgamation into one body, the acceptance and development of religious art to its gradual disappearance, was a long, complicated process. However, the ideological trend and aesthetic ideals of this art fully conformed to objective laws in their course of development. In religious sculpture, for example, different aesthetic standards and ideals appeared along with the dynastic and social changes. These may be summed up into three very general categories: Northern Wei, Tang, and Song. In Wei sculpture, idealism was prominent; in Song sculpture, realism dominated; in Tang sculpture, there was an integration of the two. The ideals of beauty in each period were different. All three had their successes and failures, good and poor works, and sometimes it is difficult to distinguish between the three. And as the likes and dislikes of people today are also different, each of us will have his own preference. Without regard for individual pieces, the author would recommend Wei sculpture, in which the special property of sculptural art—expressing a highly generalized subject or ideal that commands respect and admiration by means of a human body at rest—appears to be fully utilized.

[17] This is a famous temple near Taiyuan, Shanxi Province. It was constructed to the memory of the first emperor of the Jin Dynasty, but some of the buildings and statues in it were added during the Song.

7

Voice of the Prime Tang

Springtime and Li Bai

THE STORY of the Tang Dynasty is the most brilliant chapter in ancient Chinese history. The ending of several centuries of national disunity and civil wars and the implementing of the *juntian* land system from the central plains to the northern border brought power and prosperity to the Li-Tang empire[1] politically, economically, and militarily. Along with the development of the economy, the serf-like human bondage of the Northern and Southern Dynasties slackened and eventually disappeared after the mid-Tang, while a series of new factors and phenomena appeared.

'The people east of the mountains[2] are simple and sincere; they value relations by marriage.' 'The people east of the (Yangtze) river are refined; they respect men for their character.' 'The people of Guanzhong[3] are strong and brave and they value crowns and glory.' 'The people north of Daizhou (in Shanxi Province) are militant and they esteem relatives of the imperial family.' (Quotations from *New History of Tang: Biography of Liu Chong*.) Consequently, when the great families of Guanzhong headed by the House of Yang (Sui) and House of Li (Tang) seized power over the whole country, 'crowns and glory' (official rank, title, emolument) prevailed over more typical traditional customs and concepts such as marital relations (stressed by the former great families of the Han, Wei, and Northern Dynasties), personal character (stressed by the great families of the Eastern Jin and Southern Dynasties who valued a person for his style and conduct), and kinship with the imperial family (stressed by minority nationalities who entered the central plains and who valued blood relationships). Officialdom became an important concern of scholars of the Tang, and a 'certificate of appointment,' signifying official rank, title, and emolument,

[1] Li was the surname of the Tang imperial family.

[2] East of the Mountains is a historical geographic term. It referred to regions east of the Taihang Mountains between Shanxi and Hebei Province.

[3] Guanzhong is an ancient geographic term with varying definitions. It generally refers to a region that approximates present-day Shaanxi Province.

increasingly replaced a distinguished family background as the highest honour in Tang society. Social customs were changing.

These changes were linked to the rise and fall of social and political power. The most distinguished families of the Southern Dynasties, such as the Wang and Xie, had already degenerated during the Qi and Liang Dynasties. The die-hard conservative families of the Northern Dynasties such as the Cui and Lu had been suppressed by the new imperial family, the Li, at the very beginning of the Tang. And the Guanzhong families that clustered around the new imperial household, in their turn, were persecuted by Empress Wu Zetian[4] when she usurped power. In contrast, the power of a new landlord class was rising and expanding. This was the class of secular landowners who rose from the common people, as opposed to the monastic landlords and hereditary great families.

Among the large number of auxiliary tombs at the Zhaoling Mausoleum of Li Shimin (599–649, second Tang emperor, posthumous title 'Taizong'), those of officials who had performed meritorious service and were given the surname 'Li' by imperial mandate occupied more prominent places than those of kindred members of the imperial family. This disposition of the dead augured important changes in the world of the living. It was followed by the large-scale 'southern selections'[5] undertaken by Emperor Gaozong (reigned 650–684) and Empress Wu Zetian and the institution of an examination system by means of which large numbers of successful *jinshi*[6] candidates received

---

[4] Wu Zetian (624–705) was the only empress in Chinese history to rule the country in her own right. She was the wife of Emperor Gaozong of the Tang Dynasty. When her husband died in 683, she became regent to his son and heir, Zhongzong, but she deposed him in the following year and placed Ruizong, another of Gaozong's sons, on the throne. In 690 she deposed Ruizong and proclaimed herself the Holy Empress of a new dynasty, called the Zhou. She ruled well for a time but used her power ruthlessly. In 705 Emperor Zhongzong regained the throne for the Tang and retired her under the honourary title of the Great Sage Empress Zetian. She died in the following winter.

[5] In the year 676 Emperor Gaozong of the Tang Dynasty, hearing that many local officials in south China were incompetent, sent a special envoy to Guangxi, Guangdong, and other southern provinces to make personal selections of talented people to serve in government posts. This came to be called the 'southern selections'. Some emperors in later dynasties also adopted the practice.

[6] *Jinshi* was the highest academic degree awarded under the examination system of the Tang. In many dynasties from the Tang onward, a *jinshi* received priority in official appointments.

official appointments, entered into and assumed control over various levels of government without even the need of being granted imperial or aristocratic names. Thus the hereditary monopoly of a few great families was broken up in the new social order, and it was no longer necessary for talented people to sigh hopelessly as the Western Jin scholar Zuo Si once did:

> Luxuriant is the pine in the valley,
> Profuse are the seedlings on the hill;
> With their slender inch-wide bodies,
> They shadow the hundred-foot tree.

For the large number of intellectuals of the secular landlord class, a new path full of hope was now open and waiting to be explored.

It seems that this path led first to military glory on the country's frontiers. 'Would far rather lead a hundred men than be a scholar' (Yang Jiong, Tang poet). During the reign of the 'Heavenly Khan,' a nickname for Emperor Taizong, who waged wars east and west, subdued the Tujues (Turks), reduced the Tufans (Tibetans), and granted amnesty to the Huiqis (an ancient name for the Huns), all society from distinguished families to poor scholars, from the nobility to the lowly tradesmen, was permeated with a sense of honour and heroism born of a desire to win glory on the battlefield. Men of letters practised the martial arts, studied military science, and went off to the borderland. There were very few distinguished poets of the early and prime Tang who had not personally experienced the life of a soldier in the harshness of the great northern deserts. They were soldiers as well as scholars and led highly romantic lives. It was so even with the great poet Li Bai, who lived during the time of Emperor Xuanzong (685–762). He reveals this in his own words: 'I was a man in cotton clothes [a commoner] of Longxi who drifted to Chu and Han. At 15, I loved fencing and offended almost all the feudal lords. At 30, I could write essays but provoked the cabinet ministers' ('Letter to Prefect Han of Jingzhou'). These lines reveal a spirit that was bold to the point of rashness and had even a trace of impudence. It was far different from the conduct of the pale-faced scholars and modest gentlemen of the Song and later dynasties.

Externally, this was an era of extension of the country's frontiers and flaunting of its military prowess. Internally, it was an era of relative unity and stability. On the one hand, the interflowing and fusing of northern and southern cultures enabled the old schools of the Han and Wei (Northern Dynasties) and the new voices of the Qi and Liang (Southern Dynasties) to supplement and benefit each other, in the course of which the old was weeded out to make way for the new. On the other hand, trade and transportation between China and the outside world developed and the Silk Road brought in not only foreign trade fairs but exotic rites, customs, clothing, music, art, and religion. Foreign wines, foreign songstresses, foreign headdresses, and foreign music were the height of fashion in Chang'an (present-day Xi'an). It was an unprecedented blending of past and present, foreign and Chinese. Import and assimilation without fear or prejudice; creation and innovation without restriction or sentimentality for the old; inhibitions shattered; traditions broken—this was the social and ideological atmosphere that gave birth to the so-called 'voice of the prime Tang' in art and literature.

Bodhisattva, stone sculpture of the Tang Dynasty unearthed from the ruins of Daming Palace in Shaanxi Province.

If the art of the Western Han may be regarded as imperial art characterized by an exaggerated presentation of people's external activities and their triumph over nature (see Chapter 4); and Wei-Jin art may be seen as that of the great families and aristocracy, turned inward towards the heart, towards human character and speculation (Chapter 5); then Tang art may well be considered an enhanced amalgamation of the two, that is, it was neither merely an exaggerated depiction of external events and human activities nor just an inward seeking of the soul through speculation and philosophy, but a confirmation and apprehension of, a longing for and emphasis on, the flesh-and-blood world of humanity. Permeating the art and literature of the prime Tang period was a rich ardour and imagination filled with the blooming vitality of youth. Not only pleasure but frustration, anxiety, and sorrow scintillated with the spark of youth, freedom, and joy. This was the art of the prime Tang, a typical example of which is its poetry.

Many people in the past have discussed the differences between Tang and Song poetry. Never since Yan Yu of the Song Dynasty declared in his book *Reflections on Poetry* that 'the people of our dynasty stress reason while the people of the Tang stressed zeal and interest' and poetry was divided into two large categories, Tang and Song, with the Tang further divided into early, prime, middle, and late,[7] have arguments for and against such a division ceased. Professor Qian Zhongshu (1910–?) of modern times, in his book *Tanyi Lu* (*Notes on Art*) summarized the different points of view and put forward the thesis that 'classifying poetry into Tang and Song is a matter of style, not dynasty,' pointing out that 'Tang poems generally excel in spirit, emotion, and rhythm, while Song poems are superior in structure, thought, and reasoning. . . . It is not that Tang poems were written by Tang poets and Song poems by Song poets.' He explained further:

[7] The Tang Dynasty lasted 289 years (618–907). Historians have divided it into four periods: early, prime, middle, and late. Originally, the division was made on the basis of the development of Tang poetry, but later other factors were also considered. The following are the approximate dates of the four periods, on which historians are not fully agreed:

Early Tang—From 618 to the beginning of the 8th century.

Prime Tang—From the beginning of the 8th century, when Xuanzong, surnamed the Brilliant Emperor (Minghuang), ascended the throne, to the An-Shi rebellion that broke out in 755. It was an era of prosperity and progress.

Mid-Tang—From the An-Shi rebellion to the first quarter of the 9th century.

Late Tang—From the first quarter of the 9th century to the founding of the Late Liang, the first of the Five Dynasties, in 907.

'People are different in their natural disposition and this is reflected in poetry: a sanguine nature approaches Tang poetry, a serious one is like that of the Song. . . . Youth is enterprising and uses the Tang style: age is deliberate and prefers the Song.' This is a sound thesis, for Tang and Song poems are indeed different in both style and nature. Poets of all dynasties had their preferences, including those of the Tang and Song, which is to say that Tang poets could and did write in the Song style and vice versa. Moreover, sometimes it was difficult to distinguish between the two styles. In the final analysis, however, each style was the product of its time, for the basis of their differences rested in society. Youth loves the voice of Tang while age prefers the tone of Song. This change in human mood and interests as one advances in years is quite symbolic of the historical path traversed by China's late feudal society and its leading participants, the secular landlord class and its intellectuals: the path from youth and vigour to senility, from throbbing vitality and recklessness to complacency, decadence, and a wish to avoid reality. The poems of the early, prime, middle, and late Tang are reflections of certain important stages and scenes along this path.

The transition from the imperial style o f the Six Dynasties[8] to the style of the early Tang was expounded eloquently by Wen Yiduo (1899–1946), modern poet and scholar, whose essays on Tang poetry for a long time did not receive due attention from writers of literary history. According to Wen, the early Tang poet Lu Zhaolin's rhythm 'had the power and vitality of living dragons and tigers' (*Random Notes on Tang Poetry: Self-Redemption of the Court Style*) and at the same time Luo Binwang's melody 'which breezes through in one breath and yet is lingering and recurring reveals an optimistic and soaring spirit' (*Random Notes*). Wen also pointed out that 'in the hands of Lu Zhaolin and Luo Binwang, court-style poetry passed out of the imperial court to the common people, and by the same time Wang Bo and Yang Jiong had poems moved from terraces and pavilions to hills, rivers, and deserts' (*Random Notes on Tang Poetry: The Distinguished Four[9]*).

---

[8] The imperial or court style of the Six Dynasties refers to a category of poetry that described life in the imperial palace, not only the pomp and luxury of court life but also the sorrow and bitterness of the court maids.

[9] The Distinguished Four, or the Distinguished Four of the Early Tang, was a title of respect given to the four great men of letters Lu Zhaolin (c.635–689), Wang Bo (650–676), Luo Binwang (c.640–?), and Yang Jiong (650–c.693). These men, especially the first two, were opposed to the poetic style of their day, which they considered excessively rigid and meticulous in its structural considerations.

With changes in the times, poetic themes passed from court life to ordinary life and the decadent songs sung by court maids of the Six Dynasties were replaced by fresh and lively songs of youth in its prime. The principal representatives of this youthful style of the early Tang are Liu Xiyi (c.651–?) and Zhang Ruoxu (c.660–720), two writers whom Wen Yiduo emphasized in his work.

The blossoms of the plum and peach east of Luoyang town.
Are flying hither and thither, where will they come down?
The lovely maids of Luoyang whisper many a sigh,
As pensively they sit and watch the falling flowers fly.
This year the flowers have fallen, their colours have faded too;
Next year when they bloom again, who will admire the view?
We've seen men chop for firewood the pine and cypress trees;
We've heard of fields of mulberry transmuted into seas.
Men of old have left Luoyang to return here never more;
Men today still see the peach as in the days of yore.
Day by day, year by year, the same flowers bloom and blow;
But year by year, day by day, all men must come and go.
(Liu Xiyi: 'Lament for the White-haired Man')

Liu Xiyi was the author of many so-called frontier poems. This poem, however, more aptly expresses the style of the early Tang.

The tide on the river is level with the sea,
The moon on the sea arises with the tide;
It sails with the ripples over a thousand *li*,
On a river in spring there's always moonlight.
The water flows gently round a meadow fair,
As moonbeams like sleet fall on flowers and trees;
Frost floats in the air, it seems to be still,
The sand on the spit is soon seen no more.
Of one hue is the speckless river and sky,
In the glow of the lonely moon on high.
What man on the shore first saw the moon?
What year did the moon first shine on man?

Thus life goes on through ages unending,
And the same moon shines here year after year.
We know not for whom the moon is waiting,
We see only the waters rolling by.
A cloud bank above drifts slowly away,
The maple on the shore is laden with sorrow.
Is someone boating on the river tonight?
Is someone waiting in her chamber alone?
(Zhang Ruoxu: 'Moonlight and Flowers on the River')

Wen Yiduo was lavish in his praise of these poems, especially the second one: 'It is the optimum in its awareness of the universe. Describes a truly profound, spacious, and tranquil realm! Confronting the miraculous infinity, the author was confused and astonished, but he had no grief or longing.' 'It seems he had only a quiet and mysterious smile; he was more perplexed than ever, but was also contented.' 'It was a mysterious but sincere conversation as if in a dream, revealing a strong awareness of the universe.' 'It is poetry within poetry, the peak of peaks' (*Random Notes on Tang Poetry: Self-Redemption of the Court Style*).

Actually, there was some measure of sorrow and longing in the poem, but it was the sorrow and longing of youth, of one who 'standing alone in a high tower sees the end of the road in the horizon.' Thus there is a liveliness in the sorrow and a lightheartedness behind the sighs. This is totally different from the heavy, melancholic songs of the Wei-Jin when human life was cheap as grass, and from the real grief that permeated the works of Du Fu, who had experienced the hardships of life. What this poem reveals is the evanescent and inexplicable gloom often felt by young people when they first take stock of their position in life. Amid the spring flowers and moonlight, the flowing water and infinite universe, youth feels deeply the briefness of his prime and the transiency of life. It is the self-awakening as he approaches manhood and acquires his first awareness of life and the universe. He shows a deep feeling and affectionate regard for the world, for beautiful nature and his own existence, but also a sense of helplessness. Is it not true that young people in their late teens, the stage from puberty to maturity, often experience some form of mental distress when they awaken to the infiniteness of the universe and the finiteness of life? The poem does not show any heavy and specific sorrow founded on reality. While it professes sorrow, its language is brisk, happy, and full of charm, for 'youth does not yet know what it is to worry' (a poem by Xin Qiji, 1140–1207). This is its artistic style and the aesthetic feeling it conveys. What the eternal hills, river, wind, and moon must have given the poet are a youthful human philosophy and joy with a tinge of sadness and languor. And what Wen Yiduo describes as 'mysterious,' 'perplexing,' an 'awareness of the universe,' was actually a reference to this kind of aesthetic psychology and artistic conception.

Zhang Ruoxu's 'Moonlight and Flowers on the River' was the acme of early Tang poetry. But through the influence of the Distinguished Four, especially Wang Bo, poetry soon approached greater heights—the prime Tang. The void felt by youth who had not yet experienced the world was being transformed into high ideals and ambitions:

> There are bosom friends the world over,
> The remote is like a neighbour near;
> When we reach the point of parting,
> What need is there for tears?
> (Wang Bo)
>
> In the morn I heard your parting song,
> In the cold of night you crossed the river.
>   .   .   .   .
> Think not of Chang'an as pleasure ground,
> On which to squander all the years.
> (Li Qi, 690–751)

These are lines to stir and encourage young people when the sentimentality of youth has passed. The message is more solid and mature, the words of people who are truly entering into society and the world.

The mature individual feels that now is the hour for dedicated efforts to prepare to do great things so as not to waste the best years of his life. And so, on the heels of the Distinguished Four came a truly colourful period, the full flowering of Tang art and literature, heralded in a four-line poem by Chen Zi'ang (661–702), when he climbed the peak of a mountain:

> I see no ancients before me,
> No followers behind;
> I think of the vastness of heaven and earth;
> Sad and lonely, the teardrops fall.
> ('Atop the Youzhou Terrace')

Though it was in a moment of grief and indignation that he wrote these lines, nevertheless what is reflected in them is the breadth of vision of a pioneer, a great lonely spirit eager to move forward and sail with the wind. They are lines of heroism, not of despair. Meng Haoran's (689–c.740) poem 'Spring Dawn' is in a similar vein:

> In my spring slumber I felt not the dawn,
> Till I heard birds singing all around;
> There was sound of wind and rain in the night,
> How many petals lie strewn on the ground!

Though the poet showed regret over the fallen flowers, the picture he paints is of a pleasant spring morning, fresh and lively, not gloomy and sad. This is the voice of the prime Tang, of which other examples are:

A thousand *li* of yellow clouds,
    A white sun dim and low;
The north wind drives the wild geese
    Amid the flying snow.
Fear not that on the road ahead
    You meet no bosom friend;
For who is there that knows you not,
    Throughout this spacious land.
(Gao Shi, 706–765)

Fragrant wine in a luminous cup
    Of polished jade stone white;
Fain would drink, the *pipa*[10] calls
    From the saddle out of the night.

Laugh not at my thirst for wine, good sir,
    If drunk on the field I lie;
But think how few from the wars returned
    In the thousand years gone by.
(Wang Han, dates of birth and death unknown)

The poets' words were of courage, daring, ever on the go, undaunted by the hardships of the battlefield, candid and cheerful on the march.

Clear shines the moon of ancient Qin
    Above the pass of Han;
The soldier's marched ten thousand *li*,
    He's still not home again.
If but the Flying Warrior's there
    To guard the Longcheng way,
No alien horseman ever shall
    To south of Yinshan stray.[11]
(Wang Changling, c.698–756)

---

[10] The *pipa* is a plucked string instrument with a pear-shaped body. It originated in the minority nationalities of northwestern China, where it used to be played on horseback.

[11] The Flying Warrior was a name given by the Xiongnu to Li Guang, a famous general of the Western Han who guarded the country's northern frontiers. Longcheng was a town near the border. Yinshan is a mountain range in what is now the Inner Mongolian Autonomous Region. In ancient times, invaders from the north had to cross these mountains to attack China's hinterland.

The grass is torn asunder as the north wind sends its blast;
In Hu land it's only summer, but the snow flies thick and fast.
As if a gust of warm spring wind had risen in the night,
Pear trees in their thousands are clothed in 'blossoms white.'[12]
(Cen Can, c.715–770)

As individuals, nationalities, classes, and country were immersed in a social atmosphere of growing prosperity, poems of the frontier became increasingly popular, forming a basic content and aspect of the voice of the prime Tang. Poetry of this kind had never appeared before in Chinese literary history.

China was a land of charm and beauty, of which frontier poems described the active and heroic side. Its quieter and more picturesque side is mirrored in the works of the 'tender-minded' school, some examples of which are 'Spring Dawn' quoted above and the following lines of Wang Wei (701–761), composed in his villa at Wangchuan:

The osmanthus fades in a world of silence;
The hills are empty in the still of night.
The moon rises and startles the mountain bird;
From the shadows below we hear its cry.

Cottonrose buds on the treetop,
Calyces red in the shade;
In the valley where all is quiet,
The flowers blossom and fade.

Terse, objective, and truthful; profound and philosophical; intensely quiet, yet with stirrings of life; the lines describe the beauty of nature with great clarity and are also typical of the voice of prime Tang. If we compare them with the following poems by Du Mu (803–852) of the late Tang, we will find that the latter, while very similar to the prime Tang style, are more refined but less grand.

(1)
Dim are the grey-green mountains,
    Far the river flows;
Tis the end of southern autumn,
    But fresh the green grass grows.
I see four and twenty bridges,
    Beneath the bright moonlight;
Where will our lovely singers
    Play their tunes tonight?

[12] Hu was a general name for minority nationalities in the north and west in ancient times. The 'blossoms white' are snowflakes.

(2)
He sang for us a melody—
  Who will join his song?
Overgrown with weeds and moss,
  The path he walked along.
A short repose at sunset,
  Beneath the hills I dream—
White as a sheet the moonlight,
  Bright as pearls the stream.

Unquestionably, the voice of the prime Tang when expressed in poetry reached its zenith in form and content in the writings of Li Bai. For in his works there were not only springtime, frontiers, hills, rivers, and landscapes, but mockery of kings and lords, contempt for the vulgar, disatisfaction with the existing order, chastisement of life as it is, wine, poetry, and pleasures indulged to the extreme. 'I will not embark though the emperor commands; I regard myself as a genius in wine' (from the poem of Du Fu describing Li Bai). These lines and the stories of how he made the emperor's brother-in-law grind his ink and Gao Lishi, a eunuch with great power, unlace his shoes, are reflections of the feelings, desires, and aspirations of the intellectuals of his day, who were just beginning to gain prominence. They wanted to break with traditional inhibitions. They were eager to do great things, to win fame, honour, and riches. They longed to enter the highest social echelons. They indulged in pleasures but entertained high ambitions and were arrogant, intractable, and rebellious. Such behaviour could be tolerated only in an era when intellectuals as a class were on the upgrade and society as a whole was prosperous and free.
  Wrote Li Bai:

(1)
I confide in thee and hold thy hand,
Grace or disgrace means naught to me!
The Sage grieved for the phoenix and unicorn;
What chicken or cur is that man Dong Long!
I was proud all my life, but aloof from others;
Toiled with frustration and little reward.
Yan Ling only bowed to the emperor of Han;
What need is there to wear a sword and serve at court![13]

[13] 'The Sage' is a reference to Confucius, who once grieved because the phoenix no longer appeared and the unicorn was in captivity. Li Bai was using this as an allegory to show that in a troubled world his ideals could not be realized. Dong Long was a powerful but unscrupulous official of the Qin, one of the Northern Dynasties. In mentioning him, the poet was chastising some of

(2)

What deserted me was yesterday, a day that would not stay;
What worries me is the present day, a day so full of woe.

. . . .

Draw the sword and smite the water, it flows on faster still;
Raise the glass to banish sorrow, it returns to haunt you more.
So disappointing is this life on earth,
I'll undo the hair and sail away tomorrow.

(3)

I left the rosy clouds of Baidi in the morning,
　　Covered a thousand *li* to Jiangling in a day
While the apes on both banks were still calling.
　　My boat had sailed ten thousand hills away.

Here, in the poems of Li Bai, the art of the prime Tang had struck
a forte. It was delightful, overwhelming, the mark of a genius. There
were virtually no rules or inhibitions; everything was spontaneous,
composed on the spur of the moment, yet always novel and beautiful. It
was an unpredictable outpouring of emotion in inimitable tones.
Though Li Bai lacked the speculative power of Zhuangzi and the
emotional profundity of Qu Yuan, because he lived in a totally different
era, the naturalness of Zhuangzi and beauty of Qu Yuan were
amalgamated in his works, which were the climax of ancient Chinese
romantic literature and symphonic poetry.

This climax, like many another peak of romanticism in literature
and art, lasted only a short time. It quickly passed into a stage of more
durable realism represented by the Sage of Poets Du Fu which, though
still a part of the prime Tang chronologically, no longer represented its
true voice.

Musical Beauty

Poetry and calligraphy are the two oldest branches of Chinese art. Both
reached heights during the Tang that have never been equalled in later
dynasties. They were the most popular and at the same time the most
mature forms of art of this period, as may also be said of the handicrafts
and *fu* literature of the Han, the sculpture and *pianwen* (a kind of
rhythmic prose) of the Six Dynasties, the painting, *ci*-poetry, and *qu*-

the high officials of his day. Yan Ling was a recluse who refused to serve at
the court of the Han; when brought before the emperor, instead of prostrating
himself he merely bowed.

songs of the Song and Yuan, and the dramas, short stories, and novels of the Ming and Qing. All were the focal point of the artistic spirit of their time. Tang calligraphy and poetry paralleled each other, possessing an identical aesthetic quality. Of the different styles of calligraphy, the one that fully accords with the voice of the prime Tang and is expressive of the style and features of this period is the cursive script, especially the ultra-cursive hand in which not only the individual strokes but also the characters are virtually joined to each other.

Like Tang poetry, Tang calligraphy also underwent a process of development. It was already very beautiful in the early Tang, and because of the strong encouragement of the imperial court, for example Emperor Taizong, it acquired a new throbbing vitality somewhat as songs and poems had done after they broke away from the court style of the Qi and Liang. Emperor Taizong ardently loved the handwriting of Wang Xizhi. Although further study should be made of Wang Xizhi the man and the authenticity of extant copies of his famous essay, 'Preface to the Orchid Pavilion Collection,'[14] it is a fact that this essay was highly appreciated for its calligraphic beauty during the early Tang, that prominent calligraphers of the time like Feng Chengsu, Yu Shinan, and Chu Suiliang all made copies of it. This appears to be reason enough to regard the preface, that is, the copies of it that are extant, as representative of the aesthetic style and features of early Tang calligraphy, just as Liu Xiyi and Zhang Ruoxu represent early Tang poetry. The handwritings of Feng Chengsu, Yu Shinan, Chu Suiliang, and Lu Jianzhi and the copies they made of the Preface are specimens of the best calligraphy of this period. They reveal the same youthful spirit as expressed in 'Moonlight and Flowers on the River.' In both quality and spirit, they are comparable to the poetic works of Liu Xiyi, Zhang Ruoxu, and the Distinguished Four, expressing clearly the aesthetic ideals, standards of taste, and artistic requirements of their time.

[14] In the spring of A.D. 353 (ninth year of the reign titled Yonghe of Emperor Mudi of the Eastern Jin), 41 poets gathered at Orchid Pavilion on the outskirts of Shaoxing, Zhejiang Province. They composed poems to mark the occasion, and these were later compiled into a book, for which Wang Xizhi wrote the preface, titled 'Preface to the Orchid Pavilion Collection.' Centuries later, Emperor Taizong of the Tang saw the manuscript of the preface and was so fascinated by the handwriting that he ordered Zhao Mo and other prominent calligraphers of his time to make copies of it. Unfortunately, when the emperor died, Wang Xizhi's manuscript was interred with him and has never been recovered. Only copies made by others have been preserved and their authenticity is questioned by some modern scholars, including Guo Moruo.

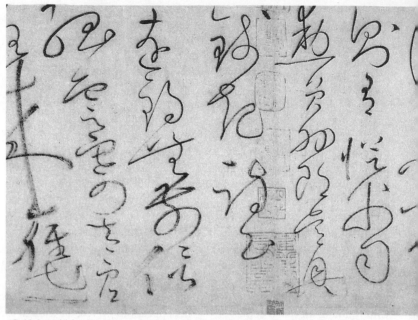

'Self description', calligraphy in cursive hand by Huai Su, Tang Dynasty.

The nature of calligraphy changed when the Tang Dynasty reached its prime. The emphasis shifted from formal beauty to the expression of moods and feelings. Although Sun Guoting, calligrapher and theorist of the prime Tang, in his book *Shupu* (*On Calligraphy*) followed the traditions of the early Tang in extolling Wang Xizhi's handwriting while disparaging Wang Xianzhi's, he put forward some new theses such as 'use substance to indicate mood; beauty changes with custom' and 'changing rapidly is a normal physical law,' and stressed the need to 'express one's temperament and feelings and give form to one's sorrow and joy' and 'let appearances accord with one's nature and desires.' He regarded calligraphy as an artistic way of expressing one's emotion and character, consciously stressed this point and elevated it to a theoretical plane on a par with poetry: 'When the feelings are aroused, they take shape in language; this may be apprehended in the *Book of Songs* and *Songs of Chu*' (*Shupu*). Like Chen Zi'ang, who meditated on the 'vastness of earth and heaven' and with a keen sense of historical responsibility heralded the arrival of prime Tang poetry, Sun Guoting's philosophy of lyricism heralded the climax of romanticism in prime Tang calligraphy.

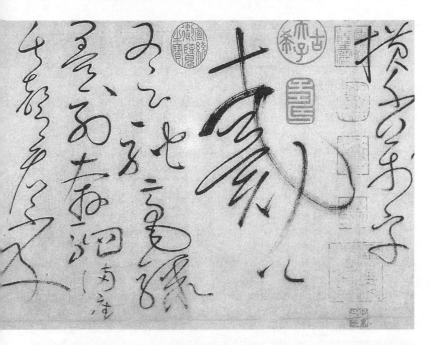

The cursive and ultra-cursive styles represented by Zhang Xu and Huai Su were like Li Bai's poetry, free and uninhibited and yet not without rules. They were fast flowing, with strokes and characters virtually joined, moving at a pace that takes one's breath away. Both sad and joyful feelings were poured into the brushwork in a forceful and impassioned manner. Thus it was not incidental that Zhang Xu, the 'genius of the cursive hand,' should be considered the equal of Li Bai, the 'genius of poets.'

Han Yu (768–824), the great man of letters of the mid-Tang, once wrote:

> Zhang Xu excelled in the cursive hand and did not practise any other skills. Joy, anger, poverty, or predicament; worry, sorrow, pleasure, or comfort; grievance, hatred, envy, or longing; drunkenness or boredom—anything that stirs the heart would find its way into his handwriting. Likewise, the things he sees and hears—hills, rivers, rocks, and ravines; birds, beasts, insects, and fish; flowers, fruit, grass, and trees; sun, moon, and stars; rain, wind, thunder, lightning, fire, and water; singing, dancing, fighting; all changes, happy or frightening, in the universe—would be expressed in his calligraphy, which is therefore as changeful and unpredictable as the gods.
>
> (*Preface to Seeing Off the Monk Gao Xian*)

These words describe not only the cursive writing of Zhang Xu; they are a mirror of the epochal features of all calligraphy in prime Tang. The *Xuanhe*[15] *Book of Calligraphy*, in a reference to He Zhizhang (659–744), another prime Tang poet and calligrapher, says: 'In both cursive and official scripts, it is a case of emulating nature.' Everything was romantic, creative, a matter of genius; all reproductions became originals; every simulation became an expression of emotion; all nature, all material existence was transformed into a stream of changing moods and feelings. Is this not music? It is, indeed. The aesthetic quality and artistic nucleus of prime Tang poetry and calligraphy is a kind of musical beauty.

The prime Tang witnessed a climax in the whole realm of music. Exotic music and musical instruments introduced from the western regions and India amalgamated with China's *yayue* and *guyue*[16] to create many new forms of music.

From the imperial court to the open market, from the central plains to the far frontiers, from Emperor Taizong's favourite dance 'The Prince of Qin Smashes the Enemy's Battle Line' to Emperor Xuanzong's 'Rainbow Skirt and Feather Dress,' from quick and strenuous dancing to quiet singing and slow movements—musical performances reflected the social atmosphere, culture, and psychology of this era. According to historical records: 'All dances since the one that depicted the smashing of an enemy battle line were performed to the accompaniment of large drums intermingled with Qiuci music; they echoed through the mountains and could be heard miles away.' 'During celebrations, only Xiliang[17] music was played, as its mood was leisurely and refined.' Militant or courtly, powerful or refined, music in those days was like frontier poetry and idyllic poetry. It was no longer ritual singing and dancing performed at important ceremonies, but joyful worldly music coming from the heart.

A music-like power of expression pervaded all branches of art during the prime Tang, becoming the very soul of its beauty. Not only the content, but even the form, was controlled and determined by this

[15] Title of the reign (1119–1125) of Emperor Huizong of the Song.

[16] *Yayue* is music and dancing performed on important occasions in ancient China, for example, when emperors and kings offered sacrifices to heaven or their ancestors, or during court ceremonies or banquets. Confucians considered it the highest form of music and dancing. *Guyue* is a general term for ancient music and dances.

[17] Qiuci and Xiliang were the names of regions in western and northeastern China in ancient times.

soul, which is why *jue* poems and the old-style songs with seven-character lines collected in the *Yuefu* were so popular at this time. For they were in forms that could be set to music and turned into popular songs. Songs, poems, and the pipa (music) were indivisible in those days. Sound and music were the form; the *jue* poems and seven-character old-style songs were the content. Or, we can turn it around and say that the *jue* and seven-character line were the form, and music and lyric the content.

Old-style poetry with five-character lines began in the Han and Wei, but by the time of the Tang it had run its course. Five-character *lu* poetry, whose form was established in the early Tang, became the orthodox form and style required in imperial examinations throughout the Tang Dynasty. Seven-character *lu* poetry did not fully mature until Du Fu's time and was not popular until the Song and later. All these forms of poetry, however, were basically literature, not music. In society as a whole, it was the so-called worldly *jue* poems and the seven-character verses whose form had not yet been standardized (that is, verses interspersed with three-, four-, five-, and six-character lines), which could be adapted for singing, that were the most popular and the principal form of poetic art. They were also the principal form of literature of the prime Tang.

Dancing is to calligraphy as music is to poetry. There is a well-known story of a man who improved his handwriting by watching a dancer's postures: 'Zhang Dian saw Madame Gongsun perform a sword dance and it taught him how to give greater power to his brushwork' (*Linquan Gaozhi*, a collection of writings on Chinese painting by Guo Xi of the Northern Song). Chinese dances in those days evolved mainly from a dance of the northern minority nationalities that consisted largely of quick steps and spins (called 'Hu prancing'), described as 'jumping left and right, up and down' and 'spinning like the wind.' The cursive script of the prime Tang, with its vigorous and flexible serpentine lines, its varied, continuous, loose, or compact structure, its sudden and unpredictable changes, its unbridled moods and power, is the representation of violent dancing on paper.

Jue poetry, cursive handwriting, music, and dance—the combination of these arts was the crowning beauty of a kingdom of poetry and calligraphy. They advanced to a new stage China's traditional 'art of line' with its emphasis on rhythm and feeling, and reflected the spirit of an epoch in which intellectuals of the secular landlord class were rising to prominence. They were the true voice of the prime Tang.

Du's Poetry, Yan's Calligraphy, Han's Prose[18]

The voice of the prime Tang is actually a rather vague concept. Li Bai and Du Fu both lived during this period, yet their works represented very different types of beauty. Zhang Xu and Yan Zhenqing also both belonged to the prime Tang and they, too, represented different types of calligraphic beauty. In point of time, the art of Du Fu and Yan Zhenqing did not reach full maturity and their finest works did not appear until after the An-Shi rebellion,[19] which was in the last years of the prime Tang. They were different from their predecessors in style, too, and opened new paths in their spheres. Thus there were two phases of the prime Tang which were aesthetically different in significance and value.

The prime Tang represented by men like Li Bai and Zhang Xu was highlighted by attacks upon and a breakthrough of the old social order and aesthetic standards, by intellectuals of the new secular landlord class. A characteristic of its art was that the content was completely unrestricted by form. It was an inimitable expression of genius, for which there were not yet any fixed forms. But in the prime Tang represented by men like Du Fu and Yan Zhenqing, new artistic patterns and aesthetic standards were conceived in which the stress was on form: on a strict integration and unity of form and content, establishing models for study and imitation. If the first phase reflected primarily the destruction of the old and the breaking of previous forms, the second phase was the creation of new forms.

'There are talented people in all generations; each leads in literary excellence for several hundred years' (Du Fu). But Du Fu, Yan Zhenqing, and Han Yu (in prose) were in the vanguard of literary excellence for a much longer period. They laid down the criteria, established models, and represented the orthodox school for a whole millennium, that is, all of late feudal society. They were far more closely related to the art and society of later generations, and exerted a far

[18] Du Fu (712–770), venerated as the Sage of Poets, is regarded by many as the greatest of the Tang poets. Yan Zhenqing (709–785) was a calligrapher and high official of the Tang Dynasty. His regular and running scripts established a new style called the Yan style, which had a profound influence on the calligraphy of later generations. Han Yu (768–824) was a philosopher and man of letters of the mid-Tang. He was a strong opponent of the *pianwen* prose style of the Six Dynasties, and advocate of a free style without rhyme and parallelism.

[19] This was a rebellion against Emperor Xuanzong led by *An* Lushan and *Shi* Siming. It broke out in 755 and lasted about seven years.

greater influence on them, than did their predecessors Li Bai and Zhang Xu. Even today, Du Fu's poetry, Yan Zhenqing's calligraphy, and Han Yu's prose are still models of art and literature whose influence is both deep and far-reaching. Their work parallels the poetry of Cao Zhi, the calligraphy of Wang Xizhi and the *pianwen* that evolved from the Han Dynasty *fu*, which were models of art in the early feudal society and whose influence as the orthodox style continued until the late Tang and Song. Thus the two genres—the Cao family, Wang Xizhi *pianwen* prose, and figure painting on the one hand, and Du's poetry, Yan's calligraphy, Han's prose, and landscape painting on the other— represented two distinctly different aesthetic trends, artistic tastes, and basic standards in the art and literature of China's feudal society.

According to Su Shi, Du's poetry, Yan's calligraphy, and Han's prose were 'epitomes of the best.' 'Poetry reached its acme in Du Fu; prose, in Han Yu; calligraphy, in Yan Zhenqing; painting, in Wu Daozi' (*Preface and Postscript to the Works of Su Dongpo*).

No original works of Wu Daozi are available at present. But extant copies made by others of his paintings such as 'The King of Heaven Seeing His Son Off,' Su Shi's complimentary remark that in Wu's paintings 'there are new concepts in established methods and subtle laws in the uninhibited style,' and the generalization of art critics that 'Wu's robes blow in the wind' give us some idea of the innovations he made in the laws and methods of Chinese painting. Such innovations are expressed concretely in his superb rendering of lines, which may be the basic reason for the man's lasting influence on the paintings of later periods. Some of the best examples of this influence are the scroll painting, 'Eighty-seven Immortals,' and the Yuan Dynasty frescoes in Yongle Palace. In these paintings, the elegant and stately walking postures of the figures, the continuity of thought, the lively and buoyant atmosphere are all expressed by means of lines—spiraling, twisting, fast-flowing lines that represent a standardized form of musical beauty (as opposed to the unstandardized calligraphy of the prime Tang), whose influence on the brushwork of Chinese painting, especially landscape and flower-and-bird painting, has lasted at least a thousand years. Unfortunately, because of the absence of original works, an in-depth study of the man and his art is impractical. Our present discussions therefore must be confined to Du's poetry, Yan's calligraphy, and Han's prose. What are some of the common characteristics of those models of late feudal art and literature, represented by Du, Yan, and Han, that appeared between the prime and middle Tang?

One common characteristic is that they standardized the powerful moods and momentum of the prime Tang, refining them into fixed forms and styles governed by rules and regulations. Consequently, their beauty was not of the kind created by genius which could never be learnt or imitated, but the creation of man which everybody could learn, master, and re-create. They retained the boundless spirit and the mood and power of the former, imposing tight restrictions and rigid standards only on the form. As later generations put it:

> Du Fu's poetry is like the generalship of Sun Zi and Wu Qi; Li Bai's is like that of Li Guang.
> (Yan Yu: *A Talk on Poetry*)

> In ability, Li Bai and Du Fu are on a par, but Du Fu's form is clear and close-knit with rules that may be followed, while Li Bai composed superbly on the spur of the moment, which is something that cannot be learnt.
> (Hu Yinglin, 1551–1602: *Shi Shu* or *Anthology of Poems*)

> The rules and regulations of writing: the laws of modulation, intonation, opening and closing, expression and response, that were initiated during the Tang and Song were unknown in the Jin, Han, and earlier periods. They were established by the great masters Han Yu, Liu Zongyuan, Ouyang Xiu,[20] and Su Shi. . . . That is why all literature before their time was of a different order.
> (Luo Wanzao: *Collected Works of Ciguan Hall*)

Li Guang was a general who worked wonders but he had no definite military strategy; Sun Zi and Wu Qi had definite and clear strategies that others could follow. Li Bai and Zhang Xu are of the category with no rules or patterns to follow. Du's poetry, Han's prose, and Yan's calligraphy had set patterns, and it was they who provided the models of beauty for later generations to learn, follow, imitate, and emulate.

The whole aspect of beauty was therefore greatly changed. The aristocratic style that had been aloof and above the common run, highly refined, and as unpredictable as a fairy dragon that showed only its head, gave way to a worldly style that was closer to the people, more orderly and easier to understand. It was indeed a more popular style that could be more generally accepted and of course was more widely welcomed. Now everybody could seek, discover, and create beauty along the rules and regulations these men had formulated.

[20] Liu Zongyuan (773–819) was a poet and prose writer of the mid-Tang. Ouyang Xiu (1007–1072) was a scholar and historian of the Northern Song.

Yan Zhenqing's calligraphy is an example. Yan regarded the regular script as the most standard form of handwriting, for it was 'steady, clear, and easy to use' (Bao Shichen, 1775–1855: *The Two Oars of the Art Boat—A Talk on Brushwork Down the Centuries*). It was the kind of script people used when making copies, and in time it became the model for the printed script of the Song Dynasty. It was a form of handwriting that everybody could learn and use, which is of course very different from the ultra-cursive script of the prime Tang, and when compared to the traditionally extolled handwriting of Wang Xizhi and Wang Xianzhi, it was quite different in style. Basically symmetrical, like the frontal view of an object, executed in simple and vigorous strokes, square in shape, solemn, orderly, and impressive, Yan's characters are superior to those of the two Wangs, which lean slightly to one side with the left shoulder tilted, are graceful and varied in appearance, and free and flexible in style. Because of the new artistic criteria and concepts, it is not surprising that remarks and opinions like the following should have appeared: 'Wang Xizhi's vulgar handwriting has a womanish charm' (Han Yu). '[Yan's calligraphy] cleanses what is ugly in the style of the two Wangs and will shine through imperial Song and all ages' (Mi Fei[21]). 'The handwritings of Ouyang Xun, Yu Shinan, Chu Suiliang, and Lu Jianzhi (all were Wang's imitators) are truly of the slave mentality.' 'Wang Xizhi's cursive script shows an effeminate quality, not a masculine style.'

The modern Chinese historian Fan Wenlan, in *A Concise History of China*, sums it up aptly:

> The people of the Song learnt from Yan Zhenqing in the same way as the people of the early Tang regarded Wang Xizhi as their master. The line 'calligraphy values the hard and thin' in one of Du Fu's poems was an old criterion when Yan's calligraphy was not yet known to the world. Su Shi's remark, 'Du Fu says that calligraphy stresses the hard and thin, but I will not abide by this statement for it is unfair,' reflects the new criterion after Yan's calligraphy became popular.

Here we have two different aesthetic tastes and artistic criteria. A specimen of Yan Zhenqing's handwriting is the inscription on a tablet in the Yan family's temple. It possesses grace as well as strength, suppleness as well as rigidity, roundness in the square, curves in the straight. It is indeed exquisitely beautiful, and yet can be learnt and imitated.

---

[21] Mi Fei (1051–1107), Northern Song painter and calligrapher, was a supporter of Yan Zhenqing's style, though he also criticized it at times.

Specimen of Yan Zhenqing's calligraphy, rubbing from a tablet in the Yan family's temple.

The same may be said of Han Yu's prose writings. If we compare them with the *pianwen* four-six style[22] that was regarded as the orthodox literary style for hundreds years, Han Yu's progressive style of colloquial simplicity is obvious. Herein is the true implication of such sayings as 'literature (prose) revived after the Eight Dynasties'[23] (Su Shi) and 'Han Yu's prose is like the mighty Yangtze River' (Su Xun, 1009–1066, Northern Song writer). From the Song Dynasty onward, Han Yu was recognized as the greatest forerunner in prose writing.

From the reign of Zhengguan onwards, all men of letters followed the styles of the Six Dynasties. After the reigns of Kaiyuan and Tianbao[24] there was a change in the style of poetry, but prose writings still followed the old patterns. Yuan Jie and I (Dugu Ji) were the first to

[22] The four-six style was one form of the *pianwen* style. It consisted mainly of alternate four-character and six-character lines.

[23] Eight Dynasties is a popular reference to the Eastern Han, Wei, Jin, Song, Qi, Liang, Chen, and Sui which together lasted from A.D. 25–618.

[24] Zhengguan (627–649) was the title of the reign of Emperor Taizong. Kaiyuan (739–742) and Tianbao (743–755) were titles of the reign of Emperor Xuanzong.

oppose them; we were supported by Xiao Yinshi and Li Hua[25] and later by Han Yu and Liu Zongyuan. As a result, the Tang style of classical prose rose to prominence.

(*Siku Quanshu Zongmu: Pilingji* or *General Catalogue of the Four Complete Libraries of Books: The Piling Collection*)

Thus the classical prose represented by Han Yu was a new form of literature different from the 'old pattern' of the Six Dynasties.

The difference between Du Fu's poetry and earlier poetic works was even more marked. As critics pointed out long ago:

Li Bai was romantic and indulgent, free of all restraint, but Du Fu was elaborate in sound, rhythm and parallelism from beginning to end.
(Yuan Zhen, 779–831, Tang poet)

Only Du Fu could compose like Zhou Gong; nobody in later generations could compare to him.
(Remarks by Ao Qi, quoted from Zhu Dongren's *An Outline History of Chinese Literary Criticism*)

One should learn from Du Fu in poetry; he writes according to rules so is easy to follow.
(*Houshan Notes on Poetry*)

The writings of the prime Tang, like the poems of the two Hans, are unclear in sentence structure so they cannot be interpreted on the basis of single words. It was not until Du Fu and after him that key words serving as guidance appeared in sentences, along with which syntax also appeared.
(Hu Yinglin: *Anthology of Poetry*)

These statements show from different angles the role of Du Fu's poems as standard and model. Therefore, learning from Du Fu became virtually obligatory for poets in later generations who, following his approach, deliberated at length on every word and sentence and sedulously sought after beauty and perfection. This is reflected in such sayings as 'It may take three years to compose two lines, but when they are recited they cause tears to flow' and 'Once a couplet is well done, all troubles are forgotten' (lines from Du Fu's poems). Of course, poets like Li Bai knew nothing of such things and did not care to know. To this day, the seven-character *lu* poem that was Du Fu's forte is still the most favoured and most popular style of classical poetry. With its eight lines and fifty-six characters, its apparently limited sounds and rhythm,

[25] Yuan Jie (719–772), Dugu Ji (725–777), Xiao Yinshi, and Li Hua were men of letters of the Tang Dynasty. Dugu Ji was the author of *The Piling Collection*.

and its rigorous matching of sentences, people have been able to write beautiful verses of infinite variation.

People liked the seven-character *lu* poem because it had form but not rigidity, it had rules and yet was flexible. The orderly matching of sound and sense enhanced the aesthetic quality while the fixed structure of lines still accommodated changes in style. Du Fu mastered this form of poetry to the point of perfection. His numerous poetic works in seven-character *lu* and other styles have always been models for study, imitation, and enjoyment in later generations.

Solemn but stirring, with marked pauses and a sweeping momentum, all strictly patterned in an orderly matching of sound and sense from line to line—this is Du Fu's poetry. Compared to the works of Li Bai, it is different in style, spirit, and artistic conception. Li Bai's poems follow no pattern: they are characterized by a natural, innate beauty that has not been sculpted. Du Fu's poems possess a worldly, man-made beauty, every character and every line carefully weighed and considered. But this deliberation on the part of Du Fu was not the simple seeking of external form, of propriety in tone and rhyme that had been the aim of poets before. The strict demand for form *at any expense* was a feature of the decadent stage of the art and literature of the great families of the Six Dynasties. The standards set by Du Fu were closely related to content. His demand for standard form was an expression, through art, of ideological and political demands. Basically, it augured the reestablishment of Confucian supremacy in the wake of the strong influence of Buddhism and Taoism during the Six Dynasties and the Sui and Tang. Du Fu, Yan Zhenqing, and Han Yu were all worshippers or advocates of Confucian ideology. That the aesthetic standards created by these titans of art and literature embraced both form and content may be seen in the poet's ethical and political principles of loyalty to emperor and country, in the prose writer's semi-philosophical Confucian belief that 'universal love is benevolence, to act with propriety is righteousness; this is the Way' (*Yuan Dao*, or *Origin of the Way*[26]), and in the calligrapher's nobility: 'Loyalty and righteousness as bright as the sun and moon, and as durable as rock and gold' (a tribute to Yan Zhenqing paid by Ouyang Xiu in the *Six-One*[27] *Preface and Postscript*).

As distinguished from the art of the early feudal society, which since the Wei, Jin, and Six Dynasties had been closely associated with

[26] An essay by Han Yu defending Confucianism against the Buddhist and Taoist ideas of his time.

[27] Six-One was a nickname Ouyang Xiu gave to himself.

supernaturalism and Buddhist concepts and often used them as a philosophical basis, the art of the late feudal society pioneered by Du, Han, and Yan was philosophically based on Confucian teachings. Although such teachings afterwards lost their power of control, nonetheless until the end of feudal society they were constantly part of the aesthetic standards of their time, the moral and ethical aspect of those standards. That is why literary scholars of later periods stressed the need to apply such Confucian ethics as loyalty to emperor and country in evaluating and interpreting the works of Du Fu, Yan Zhenqing, and Han Yu.

It is interesting to note that the works of Du, Yan, and Han gained wide popularity and were revered and established as orthodox schools not in the Tang Dynasty but in the Song. From the Tang through the Five Dynasties, it was the *pianwen* that dominated and that style produced quite a few celebrated writers such as Lu Xuangong (754–905), noted for his memorials to the throne, and Li Shangyin (c.813–858), who excelled in writing four-six essays. The prose writings of Han Yu and Liu Zongyuan were not yet popular during this time. In poetry, Du Fu was not as famous as Yuan Zhen and Bai Juyi (772–846), and perhaps was even less known than Wen Tingjun (c.812–866) and Li Shangyin. It was through the praise of men of the Song Dynasty like Ouyang Xiu, who revered Han Yu, and Wang Anshi, who admired Du Fu, that Han and Du became famous. As for Yan Zhenqing's calligraphy, although its quality had already been noted during the Tang, its supremacy was not established until the four great schools of calligraphy of the Song, represented by Su Shi (1037–1101), Huang Tingjian (1045–1105), Mi Fei (1051–1107), and Cai Xiang (1012–1067), all imitated his style.

This confluence of events in the Song Dynasty may appear incidental, but it is not. It reflects clearly from an aesthetic point of view the changes in the basis and superstructure of society. The scholars and officials of the secular landlord class that emerged during the early and prime Tang consolidated their position in the course of the middle and late Tang. By the time of the Song they were in full control in all spheres, economic, political, legal, and cultural. The process by which Du's poetry, Yan's calligraphy, and Han's prose rose to prominence paralleled this historical development. The secular landlords, who rose from the common people, in contrast with the monastic landlords and hereditary great families, had a much broader social basis and numerically were much stronger than the great families and aristocracy of the Six Dynasties. They were large and small landowners scattered all over the country. It is quite understandable that they appreciated and accepted more popular standards of beauty. While this may not have been a conscious and intentional process, the natural and inevitable development of history is very often the result of individual, unintentional acts. The history of literature is no exception.

These titans of literature and art (represented by Du, Han, and Yan) of the new secular landlord class established the standards of beauty for later generations, just as their immediate predecessors (represented by Li Bai) had broken the fetters of tradition for posterity. In both cases, the artists possessed a strength and power born of an uninhibited vitality. Since they all lived during the prime Tang, it is quite in order that they should be regarded collectively as the 'voice of the prime Tang', though it is the earlier artists who truly represented this voice.

8

Beyond the Rhythm

Important Characteristics of the Mid-Tang

As was pointed out in the last two chapters, the mid-Tang was a period of transition from early to late feudal society in Chinese history. A legal landmark of this period was the country's financial reform, spearheaded by the enactment of the two-tax law.[1] The great families and hereditary landlords were gradually replaced by a secular landlord class (that is, non-hereditary landowners) whose social position became increasingly important. This social change was completed and the new order firmly established in the Song Dynasty.

> Taizu (first emperor of the Song) wrote an inscription on stone, which he kept in a secure place in the palace. He instructed that every one of his successors, on being enthroned, was to kneel before this stone and read the inscription, which contained three admonitions: (1) The family and posterity of the House of Chai[2] were to be protected. (2) Officials and scholars must not be executed. (3) Agrarian taxes must not be increased. . . . . Civil servants did not indulge in any sword fighting during the Song.
>
> (Wang Fuzhi: *The Song Dynasty*)

By this time it was no longer a society of great families fighting for power, as during the Wei, Jin, and Six Dynasties when the emperor represented the will of certain factions of these rival noble families. He was now the political centre of landlords of all strata and represented the interests of the whole landlord class. Neither was it a mere change of dynasty in which whoever became emperor mattered little to society and the gentry, or as Xiao Yan[3] put it: 'I ascend the throne in obedience to Heaven and the people; of what concern is this to the scholars and officials?'

[1] A system of taxation of the Tang Dynasty enacted in the year 780. It stipulated that taxes were to be collected on the basis of land and property twice a year, in summer and autumn.

[2] The House of Chai was the imperial family of the Later Zhou, the last of the Five Dynasties that followed the Tang. It was overthrown by the Song.

[3] Xiao Yan was Emperor Wudi of the Liang, the third of the four Southern Dynasties.

The popular saying, 'The common man has a share of responsibility in the fate of his country,' became the call of the new era. Not only the country and the world, but also the rise and fall of the imperial family and even ranks and titles were now of serious concern to the new secular landlord class, whose scholars and officials wrangled long and loud over all matters, even when they were pure family affairs of the imperial household. The 'common man' here, though it seems to indicate the whole people, was in its real class content a reference to members of the landlord class who did not hold official posts and therefore were regarded as 'commoners.'

Studies show that most of the prime ministers of the Tang Dynasty came from great families and the nobility. In the Song things were the exact opposite; more and more 'white garments' became high officials and prime ministers.[4] In the Tang Dynasty, it was the custom to show off one's family status or background. Poor and frustrated men like Du Fu still bragged about their glorious ancestors and even enlightened rulers like Emperor Taizong took a great interest in the family backgrounds of his officials. By the Song, however, this custom was no longer very prevalent, for the position of the whole landlord class and of scholars, officials, and intellectuals in particular had improved greatly. Scholars, civil servants, and literary men, with or without distinguished family backgrounds, had acquired a status they had never enjoyed before. The Song Dynasty boasted numerous civil servants with high salaries and arrogant ministers who received rich rewards and grants. Civil affairs received more attention than military ones and there was a conscious effort to promote culture. From the imperial court and the emperor himself to the public market, social customs and atmosphere had very much changed since the days of early feudalism.

All these changes began in the mid-Tang, after the quelling of the An-Shi rebellion.

Notwithstanding the devastations of the rebellion, Tang society did not decline. On the contrary, because the new relations of production brought about by the social changes were beneficial to the country's productive forces, the national economy as a whole remained in a state of prosperity, even when the country was still divided and fighting had not ceased. Capable ministers like Liu Yan managed the country's finances so well that Guanzhong in the north became just as rich and prosperous as the Yangtze valley, and tax reforms introduced

----

[4] 'White garment,' an old term for a man without rank or title, a commoner, who was usually plainly dressed.

by Yang Yan[5] increased the country's revenue. Because of the material abundance, the lifestyle of the upper classes in mid-Tang society was one of increasing ease and luxury. As Li Zhao, scholar of the late Tang, described it in his *Supplement to the National History of the Tang Dynasty*:

> Since the days of Zhenyuan, banquets and excursions were the vogue in Chang'an city. Later people also indulged in calligraphy and painting, in *weiqi* (the game of go), in food and clothing, and in divination, celebrations, and offerings. . . . For over 30 years, cultivating and enjoying peonies was considered a respectable pastime. In late spring, horses and carriages drove like mad to scenic spots, it being considered a disgrace not to set aside time for pleasure.

Thus frontier life with its bows, arrows, swords, and war chariots gave way to drinking, singing, banquets, outings, and horse-drawn carriages. Said Bai Juyi (772–846): 'An outsider will only laugh if he sees the fashions of the last years of Tianbao,'[6] because wide sleeves and long robes had by that time replaced the tight-fitting sleeves and gowns of Tianbao's time.

All this was related to the large number of intellectuals who entered into or formed a new upper social stratum after successfully passing the imperial examinations. 'The grand imperial examination system of the Tang was initiated in the reign of Emperor Gaozong, institutionalized in the reign of Xuanzong, and reached its acme in the reign of Dezong' (Chen Yinke: *Authenticated Manuscripts of the Poems and Letters of Yuan Zhen and Bai Juyi*). Emperor Xuanzong (reigned 847–850),[7] a devoted follower of Confucianism, attached special importance to the degrees awarded in the examination system. Therefore, *jinshi* (successful candidates in the highest examinations) enjoyed greater honours and privileges than ever before. They had servants and horses, lived in luxury, and dined and travelled extravagantly. This was quite different from the rebellious spirit of scholars of the early and prime Tang, who tried to break with traditions, and from the arrogance and aloofness they had shown as trail-blazers. *Jinshi* scholars, whose

[5] Liu Yan (715–780) was minister of finance under Emperor Suzong (reigned 756–780). Yang Yan (727–781) was minister of finance under Emperor Dezong (reigned 780–805).

[6] Zhenyuan was the title of Emperor Dezong's reign from 785–804. Tianbao was the title of Emperor Xuanzong's reign from 742–756.

[7] Not the Xuanzong of the prime Tang, whose reign was titled Kaiyuan and Tianbao.

numbers increased yearly, with their linguistic eloquence, wit, and discretion, sank deeper and deeper into a prosperous city life of sound and colour, music and singing, phrase-making and word play. There was no more ambition for military glory on the frontier, only rivalry over the ownership of horses and servants and in literary accomplishment; no more angry protests such as 'The Great Way may be wide as the sky, but I alone cannot come out' (Li Bai), only luxury and comfort because 'extravagance and unconventionality had become the vogue by the end of Zhenyuan' (Du Mu).

However, it was also at this time that the country witnessed a full flowering in its garden of literature and art. Though not as brilliant and impressive as the voice of the prime Tang, the garden was far more colourful and varied in form. Different styles, schools, thoughts, and feelings emerged almost simultaneously, all competing for pre-eminence. It may be more correct to say that it was not in the prime but in the middle and late Tang that a truly magnificent spectacle appeared in the arena of art and literature and that prose, poetry, painting, and calligraphy all reached high levels of achievement.

In the realm of poetry, there were such prominent figures as the 'ten talented men of Dali'[8] and Wei Yingwu, Liu Zongyuan, Han Yu, Li He, Bai Juyi, Yuan Zhen, Jia Dao, and Lu Tong, followed by Li Shangyin, Du Mu, Wen Tingjun, and Xu Hun of the late Tang. It was at this time that individuality came to the fore. In the ancient style poetry of the Han and Wei and the poems of the prime Tang, artistic individuality had not been very evident except in the cases of a few of the greatest poets. Epochal differences were sometimes discernible, for example, people speak of the 'vigorous style of Jian'an' and the 'voice of Zhengshi,'[9] but it was hard to distinguish individual or personal differences. In the prime Tang, there were various schools of poetry, but individuality was still not apparent. Poetic individuality in well-developed forms did not appear until the mid-Tang and later, just as individuality in painting did not fully reveal itself until the Ming and Qing (see Chapter 10). Mid-Tang poetic works no longer shared the same basic features; numerous different styles, each with its special characteristics, had appeared. It was this, and only this, that produced

[8] Ten poets of the reign titled Dali (766–780) of Emperor Daizong: Lu Lun, Jizhong Fu, Han Hong, Qian Qi, Sikong Shu, Miao Fa, Cui Dong, Geng Wei, Xiahou Shen, and Li Dun.

[9] Jian'an (196–220) was the title of the reign of Emperor Xiandi of the Eastern Han. Zhengshi (240–249) was the title of the reign of Emperor Cao Fang of the Wei.

the extremely rich and varied scenes of the realms of art and literature, which lasted through the late Tang.

A hundred flowers blooming, hosts of competent writers coming to the fore—this was the unprecedented scene on the poetic tribune. In the world of prose, it was much the same. Here Han Yu and Liu Zongyuan were the two great masters revered highly in later generations. In their time, however, they were not as well known or as popular as their contemporaries Yuan Zhen and Bai Juyi, who were widely acclaimed as much for their essays as for their popular verses. No doubt the thriving state of prose was linked to the classical literature movement that began in the prime Tang and reached a climax in the mid-Tang. But what is of greater significance, and paralleled the new literature movement, was the flowering, in greater splendour, of the traditional *pianwen* four-six style of writing, espoused by writers like Li Shangyin. The whole literary tribune was indeed a garden of hundred flowers rivaling for beauty.

Calligraphy also flourished. The art of Yan Zhenqing had reached maturity by this time, and many other influential schools, such as Liu Gongquan's regular script and Li Yangbin's seal writing, also appeared.

Painting, too, was thriving. Religious art had disintegrated rapidly. Figure, animal, flower-and-bird, and landscape painting all acquired independent status as genres and developed quickly, with some of the best artists becoming masters of specialized subjects. Such celebrated painters as Han Gan, Han Huang, Zhang Xuan, and Zhou Fang exemplify the important transition from the prime to the mid-Tang. Themes like spring excursion, boiling tea, leaning on a balustrade, playing the flute, holding a mirror, and blowing a pipe, and minute delineations of young ladies of the aristocracy, as in 'Flower-wearing Ladies'—plump, leisurely, complacent, and extravagant, in costly robes with low necklines—represented the aesthetic standard and artistic tastes of the upper society. As was pointed out in Chapter 6, worldly life with its diversified realities revealed or reflected in literature and art constituted the artistic style and spirit of the mid-Tang.

If we exclude the Pre-Qin era, the three periods in Chinese history that were relatively free and open in the ideological sphere are the Wei-Jin, mid-Tang, and late Ming. The Wei-Jin, with a society based on the great feudal families and the nobility, was rich in speculative philosophy and noted for its theoretical creations and ideological emancipation. The late Ming saw the beginning of bourgeois ideology, characterized mainly by urban literature and a romantic ideological trend. From the mid-Tang to the Northern Song, the main current was the all-round development and maturation of the secular landlord class in the cultural and ideological realm, which established a solid basis for late feudal society. In terms of artistic form, there was the maturity of the seven-character *lu* poetry, the appearance of *ci*-poems,[10] an increase in prose styles, and the popularization of the regular script in calligraphy. It would have been difficult, however, to preserve and carry on these various artistic and literary forms without the brilliant achievements and consolidation, through the full flowering of art and literature, during the mid-Tang. People often speak only of the prime Tang, or extend it chronologically to include the mid-Tang as well. Actually, in terms of the historical development of art and literature, it was the mid-Tang, which linked the past with the future, that was the more important period.

The aesthetic style of the mid-Tang was different from that of the prime Tang. It had none of the powerful and unconstrained ways of men like Li Bai and Zhang Xu, to whom the sky was the limit, and it also lacked the sincerity, steadfastness, and momentum of Du Fu and Yan Zhenqing. While artists of the mid-Tang were also free, natural, and unconventional, there was a slight tinge of loneliness, sorrow, and anxiety about them that was not present during the early and prime Tang. Such lines as Wei Yingwu's 'Worldly affairs are so boundless, they're hard for one to handle; spring sorrow is so gloomy, I can only sleep alone'; Liu Zongyuan's 'A sudden gust of wind agitates the lotus pond; thick rain blown sidewise wets the climbing fig'; Liu Yuxi's 'In the dreariness of the Ba hills and Chu water, I've lived alone and forsaken three and twenty years'; or Bai Juyi's 'Eternal Sorrow' and 'Song of the Lute Player' and the works of men like Lu Lun, Qian Qi, and Jia Dao were completely different in style, features, charm, and appeal from prime Tang prose and poetry. Relatively speaking, they were closer to Du Fu, not only in thought and content, but also in aesthetic ideals, such as conformity to standards, stress on meaning, strict rules and forms. The new aesthetic concept initiated and established by Du Fu in the last years of the prime Tang, namely the basic requirement of seeking, creating, and expressing beauty within prescribed forms and strict standards, was consolidated and developed during the mid-Tang.

[10] Poems with tonal patterns and rhyme schemes, but with lines of varying lengths; sometimes called 'long and short lines.' *Ci* could be set to music.

Inner Contradictions

It was also during the mid-Tang that a deep contradiction affecting intellectuals began to brew.

As was mentioned in the last chapter, the aesthetic ideals of the great men of letters Du Fu, Yan Zhenqing, and Han Yu, who set the rules and standards for art and literature of late feudalism, were infused with Confucian teachings. They demanded the expression of social ideals and political ethics with a very realistic content by means of relatively simple and standardized forms. This aesthetic concept, which based art on Confucian teachings, belonged not just to these few individuals; it was the general trend of a whole epoch and class. Despite differences in style and taste, the same ideological vein ran through all schools and sects. Bai Juyi and Yuan Zhen were opposed to Han Yu, but they also advocated that 'essays should be written to accord with the times and poetry composed to record events' (Bai Juyi: *Nine Letters to Yuan Zhen*). The free, unconventional, and licentious Du Mu, who was dissatisfied with both Yuan Zhen and Bai Juyi, nonetheless joined them in extolling the ancient poems of Chu for 'speaking about kings and subjects, order and disorder, and being spiritually uplifting at times' (*On the Songs and Poems of Li Changjie*). Their viewpoints, concepts, and theory regarding art and literature were quite different from those of the great families and nobles of the early feudal era.

Zhong Rong writes in *Shipin (On Poets and Poetry)*: 'The wind and bird in spring, the moon and cicada in autumn, clouds and rain in summer, moonlight and cold weather in winter—these are things that inspire poets in the four seasons. At a happy meeting, poetry enhances the cordiality; at parting, it is in poetry that we repose our grief.' And *Wenxin Dialong* tells us: 'Literature has great virtues; it is born with the universe' and 'Literature describes the glory of heaven and earth to open up the eyes and ears of the people.' In these examples from early feudal literature, the point being stressed is that art and literature are the product of what the objective world (nature and society) impresses upon man.

But Han Yu cautioned, 'I dare not read any book not written in the Three Dynasties[11] or the two Hans.' And Bai Juyi (c.772–846) lamented that 'there is very little to learn from since the Jin and Song [of the Southern Dynasties].' Both these men aimed to repudiate and

---

[11] Three Dynasties: the Xia, Shang, and Zhou.

replace the ideology and viewpoints on art and literature of the great noble families of the Wei, Jin, and Six Dynasties down to the early and prime Tang so as to return to the era of Confucian classics of the Han and to gear art and literature to the needs of ethics and politics. Bai Juyi put it most clearly in the following lines: 'To sum up, write about the king and the people, about history and society; do not write for the sake of writing'; and 'When what is written is plain and straightforward, all who are willing to see will apprehend it easily. When what is said is direct and sincere, all who are willing to listen will take warning from it. When what is recorded is the truth, all who take notice will pass the message on. When the style is smooth and uninhibited, it can be set to music to make a great influence on people.'

This is indeed a clear definition, but what a hidebound one! That art and literature should be defined as docile, practical tools of ethics and politics, that the aesthetic and formal laws of art itself should be abandoned, is of no benefit to the development of art and literature. Sooner or later, such a state of affairs must turn against itself. Thus, many of Bai Juyi's political allegories were not a success. His most popular and lasting works were poems like 'Eternal Sorrow,' which has nothing to do with ethics or politics but just tells a tragic love story of Emperor Xuanzong and his favorite concubine Yang Guifei.

As a matter of fact, within the bosom of those who advocated that 'literature is to serve the Confucian way' a deep contradiction was already fomenting. As intellectuals of the secular landlord class, the defenders of Confucianism had hoped that the 'heavenly ruler [the emperor] will be wise,' that imperial power would be consolidated, and that they themselves would become officials, fulfilling their own dreams and saving the nation. But reality is never so ideal and life often goes against one's will. The emperor was not so wise after all, the path to officialdom was not plain sailing, and the world was not as peaceful and good as they had wished. The faith and ideals they had eagerly sought, the path to the future on which they lived and struggled, turned out to be nothing more than officialdom, profit, and emolument, a sea of bureaucracy in which they had to sink or swim, a ceaseless struggle for power and position fraught with intrigues. And so, while they stressed the need for 'literature to serve the way,' they themselves, consciously or unconsciously, were going the other way, avoiding or withdrawing from the strife and struggle to preserve their moral principles in isolation. Thus, on the one hand, there was a concern for politics and an interest in officialdom and, on the other, a compulsion to retire and avoid them. 'The day when you, sirs, were being executed

with white hair was the hour for me to roam the green hills alone'—
these were Bai Juyi's sorrowful words of self-comfort after the
unsuccessful Ganlu coup.[12] It was fortunate for him that he did not
become a victim of the bloody purge that ensued.

The position of men like Bai Juyi differed from that of the great
families and the nobles of early feudal society. Unlike Ruan Ji and Ji
Kang, for whom there was no escape from the political eddies of their
day (see Chapter 5), Bai Juyi and his contemporaries could avoid or
leave politics if they wanted to. So Bai, after writing his allegorical
poems, went on to compose such leisurely verses as:

(1)
Though Heaven knows the ultimate,
Joy or sorrow is man's will;
So one who understands the real way,
Gives up sorrow and chooses joy.

(2)
Long white walls and big vermilion gates,
Where is your master now?

. . . .

Better to be a very small manorial lord,
And come and go freely with a cane.
With this I shall be contented,
I crave not terraces and halls.

Here it was no longer a case of writing about the king and people
so that those in power would look askance, but rather a case of seeking
ease and comfort in body and soul and finding happiness in
contentment.

It is therefore not difficult to understand why the same Han Yu
who wrote militant, provocative, and popular essays should also write
poems that were cold, stern, abstruse, and aloof. Despite his principle
that 'poetry should be like prose,' Han's prose and poetry were
opposites in their aesthetic style and features. For the same reason, it is
not difficult to explain the blending of excitement and indignation with
calmness and aloofness in Liu Zongyuan's prose and poetry, or the
interconnection of leisurely comfort and bleakness in Wei Yingwu's
writings. The beauty of these works often lay in their complex
integration of opposites, very different from the works of Li Bai and Du

[12] The Ganlu coup was an unsuccessful attempt in the year 835 to rid the Tang
court of a gang of despotic eunuchs headed by Chou Shiliang. The plot was
discovered and Prime Minister Li Xun and many others who were involved
were put to death.

Fu. The following is a passage from the very famous 'Eight Sketches of Yongzhou,' essays by Liu Zongyuan (c.773–819):

> Going west about 120 steps from Xiaoqiu, I heard on the other side of a bamboo grove the sound of water like the tinkling of rings and bracelets. My heart throbbed and I cut a path through the grove to find myself standing above a small pool of clear water with a bed entirely of stone. Close to the bank, rising straight from the bottom, were mounds, islets, and crags. Green trees and trailing plants in irregular patterns ornamented the shores on all sides. I counted about a hundred fish in the pool, swimming leisurely as if in thin air. The sunlight shining through the water cast their shadows upon the stone bed, motionless at one instant, vanishing the next, coming and going, gathering and dispersing, as if playing hide-and-seek with the visitor on the shore. Looking to the southwest, I saw a winding, serpentine path that continually disappeared and reappeared as I followed it into the distance. The shores were jagged and irregular, and I could not trace the origin of the water. Sitting there, hemmed in by trees and bamboo, I felt lonely, companionless, dejected, and chilled, overwhelmed by the deathly stillness. The place was too lonely to linger in, so jotting down these notes I left.

Stern, silent, remote, and removed, this is clearly not the voice of the prime Tang, but a typical product of the mid-Tang. The mutually complementary roles of Confucianism and Taoism have been discussed before (see Chapter 3). Actually, in the traditions of ancient Chinese intellectuals there was always a philosophy of two mutually complementary opposites, summed up in the parallel sayings: 'uplift oneself alone' and 'assist others concurrently.' But it was not until late feudalism, which began in the mid-Tang, that this dualistic philosophy developed fully, so that its contradiction acquired a deep, special significance of an epochal nature.

Zhu Xi, philosopher of the Southern Song, once criticized Han Yu for 'writing essays only so that others would praise them.' Su Shi, too, said of Han Yu: 'With regard to Han Yu's concern for the Sage's philosophy, he knew how to revere it in name but took no interest in its substance.' Han Yu flaunted the orthodox teachings of Confucius and solemnly stressed the importance of benevolence, righteousness, and morality. His own life and interests, however, did not conform to these ideals; they were quite different. He craved fame and position, loved wealth and property, indulged in sensual pleasures, and toadied to the rich and powerful. Because of this, true devotees of Confucianism of his day and of later periods were very displeased with him. But he was a true example of the intellectuals (represented by a coterie of *jinshi*) of the secular landlord class who appeared in large numbers during and after the mid-Tang and knew how to live. Although they flaunted the

Confucian coat of arms, they were also concerned with their own interests, which were to enjoy life, to take things easy, to indulge in wine and women, and to dissipate in the countryside. Above all, they connived with each other. As they assumed an increasingly dominant position in all spheres of society, the contradiction described above, characteristic of the mid-Tang, gradually polarized. After passing through the late Tang, Five Dynasties, down to the Song, one aspect of this contradiction—the one which upheld the banner of Confucius and Mencius and claimed that art and literature must serve feudal politics— evolved into the Neo-Confucian school (called *lixue*) of the Song Dynasty and its associated artistic and literary viewpoints. Its opposite, which lamented the existing world order in which it was floundering, turned increasingly to artistic and literary creation. If during the Wei and Jin art and literature on the one hand and philosophy on the other had been parallel, complementary, mixed, and harmonious, by the Tang, Song, and later dynasties things had changed; except in Chan Buddhism, the two had separated, each going its own way. But the philosophy represented by the Neo-Confucianism of the Song and Ming and prose and poetry, including the *ci*-poems and *qu*-song[13] of the Song and Yuan, both brought Chinese aesthetic tastes to a new stage and realm.

Here we are referring to the poems of Han Yu and Li He, the sketches of nature of Liu Zongyuan, and, in particular, the verses of Li Shangyin, Du Mu, Wen Tingjun, and Wei Zhuang, to a new kind of verse, popular for many centuries, that was more personal and sentimental in theme. For example:

> They all tell me that Jiangnan[14] is good,
> Tourists are agreed to stay here even to be old.
> As the blue of spring water touches the sky,
> In a painted boat I slumber and hear raindrops fly.
> (Wei Zhuang)

> Hard it was for us to meet, harder still to part;
> The flowerets have died away, the east wind loses heart.
> Spring silkworms never cease to spin, not until they die;
> And candles flicker into dust before their teardrops[15] dry.
> (Li Shangyin)

---

[13] *Qu*-song is a kind of verse for singing popular in the Yuan Dynasty.

[14] Jiangnan is a geographic term that refers, vaguely, to regions immediately south of the Yangtze River.

[15] In Chinese, melted tallow dripping from a lighted candle is rhetorically called *zhulei*, meaning 'candle tears.' The last two lines imply that lovers who have parted will never cease to think of each other until they die.

Painted screens in the cold of autumn are lit by candlelight;
With silken fan she whisks away a fleeting firefly.
Alone she sits on palace steps in the dimness of the night,
To watch the Cowherd and the Maid high up in the sky.[16]
(Du Mu)

In these verses the aesthetic taste and artistic themes are different from those of the prime Tang. More refined sensory feelings and subtle emotional colours were being sought along a line that had begun in the mid-Tang. Although intellectuals of the day still talked glibly about politics and were still full of ambitions to run the country well and restore peace and prosperity throughout the land, their real interest, as far as aesthetics was concerned, was quite divorced from such things. This point becomes very clear if we compare the works that represent the vogue of the late Tang and Five Dynasties with the works of Li Bai and Du Fu and the frontier poems of the prime Tang. The spirit of the times was no longer to be found on horseback but in the boudoir; not in the world at large but in the internal world within the heart. And so, from the mid-Tang on, the most successful branches of art and literature were landscape painting, love poetry, *ci*-poetry, and pure-colour ceramics; not the critical kind of Song poetry nor the dazzling tricolour pottery of the Tang.

By this time, not only had the religious paintings that taught people how to worship degenerated; even depictions of imposing figures wearing crowns or high buns had been reduced to a secondary role. The pleasure and comfort of the heart were paramount. Thus, it was not the conquest or taking of the world but escape or withdrawal from it, not human figures or character, and still less human activities and adventures, but moods and feelings that became the subjects of art and aesthetics. The art of the Warring States and Qin-Han was a representation of man's awareness and conquest of the world; that of the Wei-Jin and Six Dynasties featured man's manner and deportment and his speculative philosophy; in the prime Tang, art reflected man's will, spirit, and deeds; now, it mirrored his moods and feelings. In strong contrast to the rousing, militant poems of the prime Tang, there emerged the gentle and refined *huajian* style[17]

---

[16] This is a song about lonely courtmaids, young girls forced to leave home to serve the emperor. According to Chinese legend, the stars Altair and Vega were the transfigurations of a cowherd and a weaving maid, two lovers cruelly separated by the queen of heaven.

[17] *Huajian* (among flowers) was a book and also a category of *ci*-poetry that described the pleasures and extravagance of the upper classes in the late Tang and Five Dynasties.

and the Northern Song *ci*, the transition to which began with the late
Tang poets Li Shangyin and Wen Tingjun.

What are the differences in a nutshell? They might be summed up
as follows: the poetry of the prime Tang was marked by a broadness of
vision and powerful momentum born of the desire to win glory on the
battlefield; the works of the mid-Tang were low-key and retiring; those
of the late Tang revealed an interest in the trivialities of life—hence the
transition to *ci*. All this was not a mysterious dispensation of heaven, as
some scholars supposed, but the result of the progress of society and
changes in the times.

The form of a work of literature is connected with its content. The
social psychology of the middle and late Tang and later periods found
its most fitting form of expression in the *ci*:

> Amid falling flowers, the cuckoo sings;[18]
> Behind green-shaded windows, the lone sleeper dreams.
> (Wen Tingjun, c.812–866, *ci*-poet of the late Tang)

> The man is silent, but the wind blows on;
> Fallen petals will be strewn o'er the path at dawn.
> (Zhang Xian, 990–1078, *ci*-poet of the Northern Song)

The concept in these lines of *ci* is entirely different from the
'poetic'[19] concept before. *Ci* may be defined as a more specific, subtle,
detailed, and concentrated expression, through lines of varying lengths,
of a certain frame of mind or train of thoughts. In classical Chinese
poetry, each line usually embodies an idea or concept; thus a whole
verse has wide implications and many images. In *ci*, however, a whole
composition or stanza may contain only one idea, so the image is
described in minute detail and with subtle implications. A *ci* is often a
more complicated presentation of an ordinary everyday scene, not the
impressive, phenomenal scenes and events described in poetry. The
object, event, or circumstance is depicted specifically and ingeniously,
and thickly coated with subjective feelings, unlike the 'poetic concept,'
which is more general, vigorous, and sweeping and broader in scope.
This is why Tan Xian (1830–1901) said of *ci* that 'it affects people
more quickly; the feeling comes readily. The significance of *bi* and
xing, the rise and fall in tone, are more apparent than in poetry' (*A Talk
on Ci*), and Shen Xianglong said that 'poetry uses *fu*, *bi*, and *xing*, but

---

[18] In Chinese poetry, the cuckoo is sometimes a symbol of sadness, for it is
said to have a very mournful call.

[19] *Poetic* here refers to classical Chinese poetry.

ci uses *bi* and *xing* more than *fu*'[20] (*Random Notes on Ci*), for it must express fine, complicated moods and feelings, which can only be presented through scenes and objects by means of subtle *bi* and *xing*. In this respect, *ci* is indeed more effective than orthodox poetry.

> I wake from a dream to find the chamber bare;
> Sober once more, I see the curtains lowered.
> As the sorrow of last spring returns once more,
> I stand alone among fallen flowers,
> And swallows in pairs fly in the rain.[21]
> (Yan Jidao, c.1030–1106)

> I stand in a tower, the wind is low,
>   Grief rises in the sky as I gaze afar.
> I see smoke and grass in the sun's last glow;
>   Speechless, who knows what my feelings are.
> I would drink and sing, all cares forget;
>   A smile constrained is of no avail.
> My belt is loose, there is no regret;
>   For her I'm willing to thin and pale.
> (Liu Yong, dates unknown)

> The cold mist floats into my chamber;
> The grey dawn reminds me of autumn's last days;
> I see light vapour and flowing water on the silent screen.

> Catkins fly freely, light as a dream;
> Fine rain drizzles on, like teardrops thin;
> Loosely hang the curtains from a silver ring.
> (Qin Guan, 1049–1100)

This is a different kind of artistic concept, not found in earlier poetry: catkins ('willow flowers') are light and transient as in a dream, the rain is thin and misty like teardrops. Though the concept of *ci* was smaller and narrower in scope, it was novel, ingenious, and more closely associated with everyday life. Even themes like grief over home and country and the bitterness of the life of a soldier or exile, which hitherto had been described on a grander poetic scale, were now expressed in more moving and sentimental ways:

> Falling leaves flutter to the scented steps;
>   The night is still, the cold air crisp.
> I draw the pearled curtains high,

---

[20] For definitions of *fu*, *bi* and *xing*, see Chapter 3.

[21] This is the song of a man thinking of his lover who had left home in the spring of the year before.

From my empty chamber go;
The Milky Way in the pale blue sky
   Hangs down to earth below.
This night each year the full moon shines,
   As pure and fresh as foam;
As oft the lonely exile pines,
   A thousand *li* from home.
My heart is broke, I crave for drink,
   Ere wine comes teardrops flow;
My arms upon the pillow sink,
   The lamp burns dim and low.
Too much the lonely sleeper's borne
   Of sorrow deep as the sea;
Search high and low, I'm all forlorn,
   There's no way out for me.
(Fan Zhongyan[22])

The differences between the *ci* concept and the poetic concept (one line in poetry might be enough for all these lines) are comparable to the differences between human moods and thoughts versus human deeds and actions; each possesses its special features and excels in its own way. But why is it that over the years many young men and women are drawn to *ci* and associate themselves with it? Is it not because *ci* expresses or describes human emotions and feelings, especially love, in a more intimate and delicate way?

What then are the special features of *ci* that reflect the spirit of the times, of the late Tang to the Song? There is a poem by Li Shangyin that reads:

Feeling uneasy as late evening comes on,
   In a carriage the Plain[23] I ascend;
Lovely indeed is the setting sun,
   But the day is near its end.

Sunset, evening, and rosy clouds, but no more the vitality of the morning sun nor the brilliance of midday. These are only signs that night is approaching and the mind is ill at ease. Though written in the

---

[22] Fan Zhongyan (989–1052) was a *ci*-poet and *jinshi* of the Northern Song. Though not a professional soldier, he was for many years a commander of troops guarding the northern frontiers of the country. His *ci*-poems are a departure from the usual themes of love, flowers, and moonlight; they describe the loneliness of soldiers at the front.

[23] The Plain was an ancient pleasure ground near Xi'an. It was called *Leyou Yuan* (Pleasure Plain).

late Tang, this poem aptly reflects the mood and feelings one generally finds in the *ci* of the Five Dynasties and Northern Song, of which the following verses are examples:

> Life is eternal sorrow, there is little joy or rest;
>   Why value gold and riches, and care not for a smile?
> I bring you wine, and urge the sun that's setting in the west
>   To shine on o'er the flowers for yet another while.
> (Song Qi, 998–1061, Northern Song *ci*-poet)

> Green leaves conceal the oriole,
> Red curtains keep the swallow out;
> Quiet burns the incense as the spider spins its web.
> I wake up sober from a sorrowful dream,
> And see in the courtyard the last rays of the sun.
> (Yan Shu, 991–1055, Northern Song *ci*-poet)

There is a quiet and leisurely beauty in these verses, but also a tone of boredom and sadness, a craving for pleasure, which is so elusive and momentary. It is the leisureliness one feels at sunset, which is often mingled with regret. However lovely the scene may be, the day is near its end. The authors were intellectuals of the landlord class, who had reached the summit by this time and, like all who have passed their prime, thenceforth must go downhill.

One prominent aspect of aesthetic theory that coincided with the development of art from the middle to the late Tang to the Song was the seeking of artistic style and charm. The conception of aesthetics revealed in the truly great works of late feudal society is best represented by Sikong Tu's *Shipin* (*On Poets and Poetry*), not Bai Juyi's essays on poetry. This conception acquired a more complete theoretical form in Yan Yu's *Reflections on Poetry*.

Representative works on aesthetics of early feudalism, such as Zhong Rong's *Shipin* (*On Poets and Poetry*)[24] and Liu Xie's book of literary theory, *Wenxin Diaolong*, focused mainly on certain basic characteristics in artistic and literary creation, for example, 'In regard to things that affect the heart and soul, only poems can fully convey the meaning and only long ballads can give full rein to one's feelings,' and 'The spirit is revealed through an external phenomenon; moods change only when circumstances do; physical objects are described by their physical form; what is in the heart is reflected in one's thoughts and feelings.'

But the works of late feudalism, such as Sikong Tu's *On Poets and Poetry* and Yan Yu's *Reflections on Poetry,* went a step further.

---

[24] Not to be confused with Sikong Tu's work of the same title.

They put greater stress on the aesthetic quality and artistic style and sensibility that a work of art must possess, for example:

'A strong wind blowing in the wilderness'—an expression of strength, power, and nobility;

'The vitality of late spring'—late spring conceived of as a garden of flowers in full bloom;

'Speechless is the fallen flower; pale like the chrysanthemum are men'—used to describe a character that is aloof and disinterested in material gains.

The later works go deeper than their earlier counterparts in stressing the aesthetic characteristics and the laws of creation of literature and art. The earlier works mentioned only that the 'spirit must roam with the objects,' implying identity of form and spirit, subject and object; the later works demanded further that the 'thought must harmonize with the environment,' the unity between heaven (cosmos) and human being. The former stressed the establishment of ideal characters; the latter, the seeking of the right attitude in life. It was not enough, according to the later authors, just to pay attention to the psychological characteristics of artistic and literary creation; certain artistic ideals must be created. To them artistic ideas, styles, sensibilities, lingering charm, and lasting appeal were the centre of aesthetic study. What mattered was not differences in the types of writing and forms of literature, but differences in charm and appeal. As Sikong Tu described it in his book: 'Images close and familiar must not appear trite and insignificant: ideas profound and comprehensive must not end with the language; this is what we mean by "beauty beyond the rhythm."' He mentioned again and again such figurative phrases as 'relish beyond the taste,' 'taste beyond sourness and saltiness,' 'imagery beyond the image,' 'scenery beyond the scene,' and 'visible but not to the eye.' All this was a demand that art and literature should seek, express, and create what could be felt or apprehended but not communicated in words: moods, emotions, charm, and interest that are hard to describe yet stir the heart and soul. This of course was something that could not be achieved through imitation, reproduction, and cognition; it further projected the characteristics of lyricism and expressiveness in the tradition of Chinese aesthetics.

This conception of aesthetic values was adopted in its entirety in Yan Yu's *Reflections on Poetry*, which was strongly opposed to poetry as a 'product of scholarship, discourse, or language' and stressed the need for 'disinterest,' 'atmosphere,' and 'some miraculous inspiration.' This was coming closer to the basic laws of aesthetics in artistic creation, for example, thinking in terms of images. In Zhong Rong's *On Poets and Poetry* and Liu Xie's book of literary theory, aesthetics was dealt with as a part of artistic and literary theory. Sikong Tu's book and Yan Yu's *Reflections on Poetry* describe a purer and more standard form of aesthetics. While Liu Xie's book may be superior to Yan Yu's as a comprehensive study and analysis of literary theory, the latter shows a better grasp of the special features of aesthetics.

Yan Yu was noted for his sensibility to aesthetic values. Naturally, he had a very high respect for Qu Yuan, Tao Qian, Li Bai, and Du Fu, these titans of Chinese poetry, and called on his contemporaries to learn from the poetic works of the Han, Wei, and prime Tang. In his heart, he was unquestionably an admirer and follower of Li Bai and Du Fu. But the weight of circumstances, that is, the historical trends and social vogues of the late Tang and Northern Song, compelled him, in practice, to place greater emphasis on charm and appeal in poetry writing rather than on power and spirit; and to stress the need for ease, mildness, implicitness, and a natural beauty in works of art. Thus, objectively, he was closer to Wang Wei and Meng Haoran. Similarly, Sikong Tu listed 'power and spirit' first in his twenty-four grades of poetry, but in practice favoured 'mildness' and 'implicitness.' The apparent contradiction between theory and practice of these two men is but a manifestation of the inner contradictions that worried intellectuals and a reflection of the ideological trend in art and literature of their time.

A similar trend existed even in ceramics. Although the art of the potter, it was designed for the enjoyment of the upper classes and the literati. In the Song Dynasty, the stress was on fineness, pureness, simple colours, and refined tastes. While this was distinctly different from the brilliance of Tang tricolour figures and from the ornateness of Ming-Qing porcelain, it paralleled the seeking of charm and appeal in prose and poetry and accorded with prevailing aesthetic standards.

The Significance of Su Shi

Su Shi (1037–1101), a famous writer, poet, and painter of the Song Dynasty, was a typical—but paradoxical—representative of the ideological and aesthetic trends described in the last section. A man of multiple talents, he could create prose, poetry, painting, and calligraphy, all at high level. He was much loved by the writers and artists of China's late feudal society. However, his achievements in art and literature were not very remarkable as compared to Qu Yuan, Tao

Qian, Li Bai, Du Fu, Wang Xizhi, and Yan Zhenqing. His calligraphy was inferior to his prose and poetry; his prose and poetry were not as good as his *ci*; few *ci* can even be credited to him; and no authenticated examples of his paintings have survived. Nonetheless, he exerted a greater influence than others on the history of Chinese art and literature and is an important figure in our aesthetic history.

How did he attain such eminence? The reason, as I see it, is that he fully expressed the contradictions felt by scholar officials of the landlord class. Their dualism, which had begun in the middle and late Tang, was developed by Su Shi to a new point of qualitative change. He exemplified a psychology in which a sincere wish to advance in public life came into conflict with the equally sincere wish to retire into seclusion.

Su Shi was a patriot and a loyal supporter of the emperor. He was ambitious, studied hard in order to become a good official, and followed closely the teachings of the Confucian school. All this is revealed in his *Memorial to the Throne*,[25] his moderate-conservative stand on the Xining Reform,[26] and many of his other writings and actions. In this respect, he resembled his predecessors Du Fu, Bai Juyi, and Han Yu, as well as many scholars, officials, and intellectuals of later periods. In fact, at times he supported the existing order with stubbornness, for example, his criticism of Li Bai for joining the insurrection of the Prince of Yong.[27] But this was not the principal aspect of Su Shi's image in the eyes of later generations; it was the other aspect, the wish to retire into seclusion, that was more prominent.

Su Shi never really retired from public life, nor did he ever truly return to the country to live in seclusion. Yet the feelings of emptiness about life he expressed in his poems and essays were more profound and serious than the actual or professed retirement, hermitage, and returning to the country of his predecessors. For Su Shi, 'retirement' meant not withdrawal from politics alone, but from all society. Unlike Ruan Ji's fear of and grief over political persecution ('I grieve for the siskin, can't help shedding tears'), or Tao Qian's specific political

[25] *Memorial to the Throne* was a petition to the emperor, opposing the reforms of Prime Minister Wang Anshi (1021–1086; prime minister 1070–1076).

[26] The Xining Reform was a political reform carried out by Wang Anshi in 1069, second year of the reign titled Xining of Emperor Shenzong of the Northern Song.

[27] The Prince of Yong was a kinsman of the Tang imperial family. Li Bai served under him for a time. When the prince's insurrection failed, Li Bai was sent into exile.

grievances ('wealth and fame may be valued; regrets they bring as well'), Su Shi, though he had such grievances too, expressed skepticism about and weariness over more fundamental issues: the purpose and meaning of life and its flurry, coupled with a desire to abandon or be freed from it all.

This, of course, meant much more than merely retiring from politics. Retiring from politics was possible, but retiring from society was not, unless one took monastic vows. And even monks have their worries; they cannot escape completely from the world. Thus Su Shi's world-weariness was a sorrow from which he wanted to but could not extricate himself.

The awareness of self and life manifested in Su Shi's works is vastly different from that in an early Tang poem like 'Moonlight and Flowers on the River,' quoted in the Chapter 7. That work reflects only the sighs of youth; though melancholy, it does not communicate feelings of being severely oppressed. In Su Shi it is the opposite—little is said, but the weight of sorrow is heavy: 'Now I know too well the taste of bitterness. To speak or not to speak. I'll say only what a cold day in autumn this is!' One can almost see the poet smile tightly, feigning humour, as he tosses off the final line. But the deep sadness, like the hopelessness that sometimes overwhelms us as the day draws near its end, is visible just under the surface.

Although he was probably not aware of it, Su Shi was the first Chinese poet to use literature and art to express feelings of total emptiness towards life and despair about all creation. His famous essays, the first and second 'Song of the Red Cliff,' deal directly with this issue. Regardless of whether he was questioning the value of human life, as in:

> We are only mayflies that live but one day, specks of grain in the ocean. I grieve for the transience of life and envy the long river that flows forever!

or attempting to find an answer:

> If you look at its changing aspect, the whole universe passes in the twinkling of an eye; but if you look at its changeless aspect, all things, like ourselves, are imperishable.

or looking for diversions with which to console himself, such as:

> Only the cool breeze on the river and the bright moon over the hills . . . are the inexhaustible treasures of the creator, for you and me to enjoy.

or depicting Buddhist ideas of illusoriness, such as:

> The priest looked at me and smiled. I woke up with a start, opened
> the door, but he was nowhere to be seen.

his ideas are always enmeshed in feelings of emptiness. Su Shi feels,
ultimately, that he has nothing to sustain him.

The same philosophy is also revealed in his *ci*, but in a more
implicit and profound way:

(1)
The chill of spring wind sobers me,
   I feel the cold;
But sunset greets me from the mountaintop,
I look back at the bleakness whence I came,
   And on I go,
Unmindful of the sun or wind or rain.

(2)
The whole world is but one long dream,
And life but cycles of misery;
A storm whistled through the porch in the night,
As I brooded over the grey on my brow and temples.

(3)
I drank at Dongpo[28] in the night, was not yet sober when I awoke;
It seemed midnight when I returned,
The houseboy was snoring like thunder.
I knocked on the door but all in vain,
So, leaning on my staff I listened to the flowing water.
I often regret this body belongs not to me:
When can we forget the toiling?
It is late, the wind is still, the waves are calm;
In a small boat I take my leave,
To spend my last days on the seas and river.

According to accounts by some Song Dynasty writers, the third
verse led to a rumour that Su Shi had hung his hat and robes by a river
and gone off in a boat. Prefect Xu Junyou of Huangzhou was shocked
when he heard the rumour the next morning, thinking he had let a
convict escape. He ordered his carriage harnessed and drove at once to
Su Shi's house, only to find the poet still asleep and snoring. Su Shi had
not gone away to spend his last days on the seas and river—why should
he? He knew too well that there is no escape from the human world.

[28] Dongpo is a place east of Huangzhou where Su Shi was living in exile at
the time.

Su Shi's feelings of emptiness, regret, and indifference, his impractical wish to escape, and his desire for distraction, sometimes pushed him to turn to Buddhism for explanations. He still believed in Confucianism, but discussed worldly affairs with much abstruse and illusive thinking. And so he vacillated, digressed, satirized, and cursed in his writings. He did not share the real worries and indignation of Qu Yuan and Ruan Ji. He lacked the boldness and frankness of Li Bai and Du Fu. He was not clear and open like Bai Juyi, nor stern and solitary like Liu Zongyuan. Least of all did he display any of Han Yu's domineering arrogance. His attitudes towards life were founded on a world-weariness and a wish to retreat from society; the aesthetic ideal he sought was a charm and appeal that was plain, natural, and unadorned; he was most strongly opposed to any artificiality, affectation, and embellishment. All of this he raised to a philosophical height characterized by some sort of thorough awakening, like the Buddhist concept of enlightenment.

It was therefore not surprising that among all his predecessors, ancient and modern, only Tao Qian (Tao Yuanming) measured up to his criteria. Only the man who 'while gathering chrysanthemums under the eastern fence, sees in the distance the southern hills,' and who 'knows there is real flavour here but forgets the word for it' (lines from Tao's poems that Su Shi admired for their simplicity and naturalness) was the hero before whom Su Shi would prostrate himself. Tao Qian's poetry was little known during the Tang Dynasty: neither Li Bai nor Du Fu paid much attention to him. It was not until Su Shi's time, and because of Su Shi's acclaim, that Tao was elevated to the peerless position he still retains. Su Shi saw in Tao's poems a beauty that emerged from extremely plain, everyday imagery and a simple artistic concept, and he regarded Tao's work as the acme of art because it expressed the true significance of life. It is because of Su Shi's interpretation and appraisal that Tao's poems have been passed on from generation to generation for almost a thousand years.

In his own work, Su Shi showed himself fascinated by people who relinquish wealth and power and refuse to go along with the existing order. For example, in his essay, 'Biography of Fang Shanzi,' he wrote:

> Fang Shanzi . . . slept in a hut and lived on vegetables. He isolated himself from the world, destroyed his hat and robes, gave up his horse and carriage, and went everywhere on foot. Nobody in the mountains recognized him. But he came from a distinguished family, was an official with followers at one time, and was well known in his day. His home was in Luoyang, where he had a magnificent house

and gardens comparable to the mansion of a duke or marquis. He owned land in Hebei from which he received a thousand bolts of silk yearly. So he had quite enough of wealth and pleasure, all of which he gave up to come alone to this barren mountain. Was he not doing all this for nothing? I have heard that there are many strange people who are very dirty and pretend to be mad. I have not been able to meet one, but could they be men of Fang Shanzi's type?

Fang Shanzi may have been Su Shi's idealized *alter ego*. Though Su Shi lived in an era of relative peace and prosperity, his thoughts were of 'strange people' who gave up their official hats and robes to live in hideaways in the mountains. Another manifestation of his unique outlook is expressed in these lines from one of his poems, which communicate both sorrow and a Buddhist-influenced reflection on the uncertainty of life:

> And what should human life be like?
> Like the swan goose treading mud and snow;
> By chance it may leave tracks behind,
> When soaring it cares not east or west.

Though Su Shi constantly tried to console himself and at times showed optimistic contentment with what he had ('Listen not to the patter on forest leaves; why not whistle and sing as we plod along'; 'What matters if my hair is turning grey'), he differed from poets like Tao Yuanming and Bai Juyi in the wish, buried deep within him, to be completely freed of this world. Because of this, it is not surprising that later philosophers like Zhu Xi and Wang Fuzhi, men with the same penetrating insight, should speak more favourably of their political rival Wang Anshi than of the world-weary Su Shi.[29] Actually, both these men perceived clearly that Su Shi's philosophy was potentially more disruptive to the social order.

Su Shi was unfortunate in that he was born before his time and could not become the negator of feudal society, but his aesthetic ideals and interests presaged the trend towards romanticism that began with Yuan painting and Yuan *qu*-songs and lasted until the mid-Ming. Even the thought expressed in lines like 'an aristocratic mansion enveloped in cold mist,' a remark by Lu Xun on the Qing Dynasty novel *Dream of Red Mansions*, was a product of Su Shi's philosophy under new historical conditions (see Chapter 10). Herein lies his far-reaching significance in the aesthetics of late feudalism.

[29] Zhu Xi (1130–1200) was a philosopher and educator of the Southen Song and the chief exponent of Neo-Confucianism. Wang Fuzhi (1619–1692), a philosopher of early Qing, opposed Zhu Xi's philosophy.

9

Landscape Painting of the
Song and Yuan

Beginnings

CHINESE sculpture reached its zenith in the Six Dynasties and the Tang, and Chinese painting in the Song and the Yuan. By painting, we are referring mainly to landscape painting, which outshone many other branches of art in this country. Indeed, paintings of this genre rival the Chinese sacrificial bronze vessels of several thousand years earlier in their importance as rare treasures in the history of world art.

Chinese landscape painting began more than fifteen centuries ago. Depictions of 'hills towering above the woods' (Zong Bin, 375–443: *An Introduction to Landscape Painting*) were allegedly being made as early as the Six Dynasties, though it is hard to ascertain how true this is. Also, early landscape painting was probably inferior to landscape poetry with respect to imagery, technique, and composition, judging by the hills and trees in extant copies of 'The Nymph of the Luo River' and 'Admonitions of the Palace Instructress,' both attributed to Gu Kaizhi (345–403), and by the murals in the Dunhuang caves. The depictions were crude and clumsy, with hills and mountains that resembled mounds of earth and trees that looked like arms and fists. During this period the landscape served only as a setting or backdrop for figures, carriages, horses, gods, demons, and portrayals of human activities.

There was some improvement but no great change in the Sui and the early Tang periods. The landscapes of the early Tang were still executed in a rather clumsy manner, with 'rocks resembling blocks of ice hewn out with an axe and leaves that look like carvings' (Zhang Yanyuan: *Famous Paintings Through the Ages*, compiled in 847).

The great change began in the prime Tang, and by the mid-Tang landscape painting had become a totally independent genre. As social life underwent important changes and the influence of religion waned, the natural world lost its magical quality and began to acquire a realistic character. Just as human figures, horses, and oxen ceased to play subordinate roles in religious art and became independent motifs, so too mountains and rivers, trees and rocks, birds and flowers came to be eulogized as aesthetic objects in their own right.

A maple grows not in a hall;
Mists lend charm to hills and rivers.
(Du Fu)

When Zhang Cao paints pines and rocks,
He grasps their true spirit.
(Yuan Zhen)

In these lines by poets of the prime and mid-Tang, it is clear that natural scenery, trees, and rocks were being appreciated for their own sake and not as a backdrop to human activities.

Wu Daozi, painter of the early eighth century, was one of the great innovators in Chinese landscape painting. Although primarily a painter of religious subjects, he introduced important innovations in landscape painting. His technique of rendering lines in depicting the billowing folds of a long robe apparently opened up new possibilities for landscape artists to come. Some critics of later periods have said that he attached too much importance to line and not enough to colour—'had brushwork but no inking.' And Zhang Yanyuan wrote, in his *Famous Paintings Through the Ages*, that 'When Wu the scholar [Wu Daozi] paints, he does the outlines and then goes away, leaving it to Duo Yan and Zhang Zang to fill in the colours.' This tendency to attach greater importance to lines than to colours exerted a profound influence on later generations of landscape painters.

Landscape painting reached maturity as an independent genre much later than did figure and animal painting. Human beings, oxen (the chief means of production in an agricultural society), and horses (tools of war much prized by the upper classes) were obviously regarded as more important and more immediate; therefore, they were the first subjects to become independent from religious art. If paintings of figures and animals replaced religious paintings as the most popular genres during and after the mid-Tang, then landscape painting must have reached maturity in the Song Dynasty, some 200 years later. As Guo Ruoxu, an official and art critic of the Northern Song, said in his book *Tuhua Jianwenzhi* (*Notes on Painting*), 'The ancient surpasses the modern in [paintings of] religious figures, court ladies, horses, and oxen; the modern surpasses the ancient in hills, water, woods, rocks, flowers, birds, and bamboo.' Similarly, Shao Bo, also of the Northern Song, in his *Wenjian Houlu*, or *Notes After Observations*, asserted, 'In the art of landscape painting, our present dynasty ranks first in history.'

The shift in aesthetic interest and ideals from human life, ladies, horses, and oxen to natural scenery occurred not by chance but as an indirect reaction to historical trends and social changes. Feudalism entered its later stage in the period from the mid-Tang to the Northern Song and with it came a change in the mentality and tastes of China's landlords and scholar-officials. Though these people continued to lead luxurious and even licentious worldly lives, they also discovered and indulged more and more in another world—the world of natural beauty: mountains, rivers, birds, and flowers.

For this huge group of secular landlords and their scholar-officials (not just a few great families and aristocrats), the world of nature in which they lived, rested, and enjoyed themselves was actually part of the network of social relationships that made up their daily lives. Life no longer demanded struggle and constant efforts to forge ahead under pressure from the noble families as it had during the early and prime Tang. Nor had these men to trail-blaze by plunder and exploitation, as the aristocracy of the Six Dynasties had done. In general, they had become a class with vested interests: they were content with what they had and wanted to keep and perpetuate it. Consequently, they idealized feudalistic country life with its pastoral ways, thoughts, and feelings.

The great families and nobles glorified their hereditary class status; the secular landlords took pride in official titles and ranks. These two groups differed in their attitude towards natural scenery, country life, and people of lower social strata (often depicted as fishermen or woodcutters in paintings). For example, each group attached a different meaning to the term 'hermitage.' In the Six Dynasties, an era dominated by the great families, 'hermitage' meant 'withdrawal from politics.' By the Song and Yuan, when the secular landlords and their scholar-officials were supreme, it had taken on the broader connotation of 'withdrawal from society.' These secular landlords and their scholar-officials had a deeper interest in, and appreciation of, idyllic poetry and landscape painting because both were closely related to the idea of a secluded life in the country.

Unlike the urban-based families, the large numbers of scholars of the secular landlord class who had passed the imperial examinations and received official appointments were relatively new city dwellers. Most of them had risen from insignificance to power, from rich peasant or landlord to official, and consequently had moved in from the country-side to the cities, or from the provinces to the capital. But they felt a strong nostalgia for the country which, given their family origin, had a special significance to them. Hills, valleys, and streams, country inns and village houses—psychologically, these became needed supplements and alternatives to the wealth and honour, luxurious buildings, terraces and pavilions that were now a part of their lives, while emotionally they were an endearing memory and cherished dream.

Apart from technical advances, this is perhaps the reason why Chinese landscape painting matured not in the Six Dynasties, a period of manorial economy, but in the Song, when urban life had developed.

Chinese landscape painting was the art of the secular landlords. These landlords were less isolated from the common people than were the great families, or hereditary landlords, in a rigidly stratified feudal society. Thus the ideas and sentiments reflected in the landscapes of the Song and Yuan have more affinity with the common people than do the figure paintings of the Six Dynasties and the Sui and Tang, as exemplified in Yan Liben's (?–673) portraits of emperors or Zhang Xuan's and Zhou Fang's paintings of court ladies.

The philosophical trend represented by Chan Buddhism, which accorded with the class nature and social life of the Song and Yuan, was the subjective factor that led to the formation of the aesthetic tastes of this period. With its carefully formulated doctrines and numerous branches, Chan Buddhism had become increasingly popular after the mid-Tang and by the time of the Northern Song had become the predominant Buddhist sect.

Like the ancient Chinese philosophies of Laozi and Zhuangzi, Chan Buddhism advocated oneness of self and nature and taught that people could free themselves of worldly cares and obtain emancipation of their souls by seeking the truth or enlightenment in nature. It claimed that the lasting world of nature, with its hills and water, was superior to the transient glories of the world of man; that conforming to nature was better than seeking artificial creations; and that hills, streams, rocks, and nature itself were of more enduring value than mansions, gardens, and courtyards. Since it was already a custom in those days to use Chan teachings to explain and evaluate poetry, Chan theories of landscape painting must have existed long before Dong Qichang[1] founded his 'Chan studio of painting' at the end of the Ming Dynasty. An inner connection between the Chan philosophy and landscape painting existed much earlier—and it was the former that provided the ideological background for the development and maturity of landscape painting in China.

[1] Dong Qichang (1555–1636) was a painter, calligrapher, and theoretician on painting of the late Ming.

'Absence of Self'

Chinese landscape painting has not remained unchanged during its 1,500 years of existence. Just in the two dynasties of the Song and Yuan, it passed through three important stages, corresponding roughly to the Northern Song (primarily its early period), the Southern Song, and the Yuan. Each had its distinctive features and artistic concepts.

According to historical records, there were three chief exponents of Northern Song landscape painting: Li Cheng of Yingqiu, Guan Tong of Chang'an, and Fan Kuan of Huayuan.[2] 'They stand like the three legs of a tripod, setting the standards for a hundred generations to come,' wrote the 11th-century art critic Guo Ruoxu in his *Notes on Painting*. The distinctive style of each was described thus by the modern critic Tang Shuye: 'Guan Tong's precipices, Li Cheng's distance and space, Fan Kuan's power and grandeur represent the three different styles of early Song landscape' (*A Talk on Tang and Song Painting*).

These three different styles evolved mainly from the artists' realistic depictions of natural scenery in regions with which they were familiar. Most of their followers, too, specialized in painting their native places. Thus, landscape painters of Shandong tended to be influenced by Li Cheng's style, while those of eastern Shaanxi Province tended to follow Fan Kuan. Though Li Cheng had studied the art of Guan Tong and could paint towering peaks and ridges, his real forte was the vast misty plains of his native Shandong. This is why Guo Ruoxu said that 'the ingenuity of depicting mist-enshrouded woods and plains originated at Yingqiu' (*Notes on Painting*).

Fan Kuan's paintings were the opposite, according to his contemporary Liu Daochun, who wrote in *Famous Paintings of the Imperial Court*: 'Under Li Cheng's brush, what is viewed at close range appears to be a thousand *li* away. Under Fan Kuan's brush, what is viewed at a distance is brought to one's side.' Fan Kuan's style was cultivated through diligent practice in sketching from nature. He chose as his home the Zhongnan Mountains, where he patiently studied the clouds and smoke, mists and shade, wind and moon. His paintings of crags and ravines were described in *Manual of Xuanhe Paintings*[3] as evoking the feeling of actually walking along a cold, dark mountain

[2] Yingqiu is the name of an ancient city in north-central Shandong Province. Chang'an is a historical name of Xi'an in Shaanxi Province. Huayuan refers to the plains near Mount Huashan in eastern Shaanxi.

[3] An anonymous work that describes the paintings in the collection of Emperor Huizong of the Northern Song, whose reign title was Xuanhe.

path: '. . . though it may be the height of summer, there is a chill that makes one reach for a padded gown.'

Guan, Li, and Fan were all influenced by Jing Hao,[4] painter of the Five Dynasties who became a precursor of Northern Song landscape painting because of his penetrating observation and study of the scenes he depicted. *Notes on Brushwork*, a work attributed to him, contains the following passage: 'Astonished at the wonders of Taihang Mountain, I admired it from all sides and the next day returned with brushes to paint the scenery. It was not, however, until after I had made thousands of sketches that I achieved a true likeness.' Jing is said to have been the first to formulate the six essentials of landscape painting: spirit, rhythm, concept, scenery, brushwork, and ink. These supplemented the six principles[5] of figure painting formulated by Xie He of the Six Dynasties.

Jing Hao believed that formal resemblance was not enough; the spirit of a natural object must also be expressed. He described the relationship and difference between 'resemblance' and 'true representation' as follows: 'Resemblance is capturing the physical aspects of an object, but neglecting its spirit. A true representation possesses both spirit and substance' (*Notes on Brushwork*). In other words, resemblance is not true representation, because the latter must reveal the inner spirit, quality, and charm of the subject.

This means that rhythm and spirit, or 'rhythmic vitality,' originally put forward as an aesthetic criterion of figure painting in the Six Dynasties, should be applied to landscape painting as well. Enriched with new content and connotations, it eventually became an aesthetic criterion of all Chinese paintings. Artists must not be content with reproducing only the external form of an object, or just achieving formal resemblance; they must try to capture its spirit and inner quality. This required that the scene or object be observed, grasped, and depicted in a realistic yet generalized way.

Though 'rhythmic vitality' was stressed as the most important criterion in aesthetics, artists were also called upon to make detailed observations of the physical features of a natural scene and to arrange carefully the composition of their paintings. They were asked to pay

[4] The exact dates of Jing Hao's birth and death are not available. He lived during the Later Liang (907–924), the first of the five minor dynasties that followed the Tang.

[5] Xie He's six principles: rhythmic vitality; disciplined brushwork; proper representation of objects; specific colouration; good composition; copying of old masters.

special attention to what mountains and streams looked like; how they appeared from a distance and at close range; how to depict spring, summer, autumn, and winter, clear and cloudy days, hot and cold weather, morning and evening scenes, in a word, the numerous changes in the world of nature along with changes in climate, time, place, and aspect.

While all this required minute and accurate observation, it did not mean there was no room for flexibility. For while there is a general visual difference between morning and evening scenes, artists did not have to be exact to the hour. Similarly, whether skies were depicted as cloudy or clear, variations in the degree of lightness were permissible. Whether a northern or a southern landscape, hilly land or waterside village, there was no need to be so exact as to portray only one particular mountain or stream. Irrespective of the season, climate, day, hour, location, or object, what was required was not only realism but a high degree of generalization. This is one of the most important characteristics of Chinese landscape painting. As Guo Xi, landscape painter of the Northern Song, wrote:

> Real hills and streams are like smoke and vapour; they differ from season to season. In spring the hills are light and seductive as if smiling; in summer they are green and moist as if dripping; in autumn they are clear and bright as if dressed up; in winter they are barren and silent as if slumbering. The painting gives the general idea but does not sharply delineate the details.
>
> (*Linquan Gaozhi*)

This approach might be called 'imaginative realism': the realistic portrayal of images evoked by a scene or object when the general idea is grasped and the artist's feelings infuse his work. It is not just the realistic portrayal of physical form as perceived directly by the senses. This kind of realism does not produce the kind of direct effect on the sensory organs that Western painting does; it allows the viewer greater freedom of the imagination. As such, it might almost be said to resemble a hallucination.

To quote again from Guo Xi: 'Some hills and streams are for passing through; some are to be viewed; some are to tour and enjoy; some to live in. The last two are to be preferred over the others' (*Linquan Gaozhi*). Chinese landscape painters cater to this aesthetic taste by offering a many-pointed perspective: the scene is not meant to be viewed from just one angle, and may be seen equally well from a distance or at close range. Also, the scene is not just for looking, but for touring and living in imaginatively. The stress is not on complexity or variation of light and shade, colours and shadow, but on the emotional effect produced by a relatively lasting and complete artistic concept.

Such an effect lies not in the realism of a scene or object, nor in what can be viewed or passed through, but in what can be toured and enjoyed or lived in. This, of course, implies an object, period, or scene of some durability. 'Looking at the painting, one feels as if one were actually in the mountains. This is what is meant by "significance beyond the painted scene"' (*Linquan Gaozhi*). In other words, the circumstances, ideals, charm, and atmosphere of life as a whole should be expressed in the painting, which should be a relatively broad and lasting representation of life and nature, not an isolated scene with only a momentary effect. This is the aesthetic ideal that landscape paintings of the Northern Song sought to achieve—especially those of the early period of this dynasty.

In terms of basic imagery and artistic conception, Northern Song landscapes represent the first stage of Song-Yuan landscape painting. Dense woods and hills; broad, spacious fields; luxuriant verdure spread over the earth; limitless plains and skies; huge, towering cliffs; streams, rivers, bridges, fishermen; islets in open water or half-concealed—such panoramic views of nature, objectively portrayed, are typical scenes in Northern Song landscape painting.

Their aesthetic effect on the viewer is rich and full, but also rather diffuse, for they do not bring to mind any particular or specific poetic theme, idea, or feeling. Nonetheless, viewers feel the pastoral kinship between humanity and nature, as if here before them lies a scene they could really tour, enjoy, and live in. A certain way of life is indeed reflected in these seemingly objective depictions of nature. But because there is no specific poetic or picturesque theme, no precise mood or concept, the viewer's imagination, feeling, and comprehension, unrestricted by any preconditions, possess greater freedom and breadth. The vistas and objects offered in a complete, panoramic scene give viewers more room for discovery and expression by means of their own aesthetic sensibility. The painting is richer and more diversified in meaning, which makes for more lasting pleasure and enjoyment.

Northern Song landscape painting is characterized by an 'absence of self' in a highly developed state. In fact, in all branches of art and literature—prose, poetry, painting, etc.—we can find examples of this kind of beauty and artistic conception characterized by an 'absence of self.' This does not mean the artist's own thoughts and feelings are truly absent, only that these have not been revealed directly. The following lines by Tao Yuanming are examples:

Dim is the distant village,
Light is the hamlet's smoke;
Dogs bark deep in the village lane,
Cocks crow on the mulberry tree.

and

Drinking under the eastern fence,
Dimly we see the southern hill,
Its colours soft in the setting sun,
And birds flying to and fro.

These lines offer no direct expression of thought or emotion, but the impersonal description of natural scenery reveals the writer's life, environment, thoughts, and feelings. In fact, artists are not always fully aware of how they are thinking and feeling when they are doing a piece of creative work. Rather, it is in the very process of objectively depicting something—whether it be a natural scene, or a human action—that their thoughts and feelings, as well as the principal theme, eventually become clear. And, not infrequently, thoughts, feelings, and themes become richer, broader in scope, and more diverse in significance in the process.

'Absence of self' is even more apparent in Northern Song landscape paintings than in Tao's poetry because paintings are non-verbal. Still, they clearly convey the aesthetic ideals and feelings cherished by feudal scholars and officials for country scenes or landscapes, the same ideals and feelings as are expressed in pastoral songs.

Viewing such paintings is like viewing a vast landscape of the imagination. And that is exactly what they are, in another sense: the idealized and thus imaginary landscapes of landlords, scholars, and officials living under a feudal mode of production. Large numbers of works of the Five Dynasties as well as the Northern Song belong to this category, for example, Guan Tong's 'Clouds on a Ridge After Rain,' Fan Kuan's 'Travelling Amid Hills and Streams' and 'Winter Forest in the Snow,' Dong Yuan's 'The Xiao-Xiang River' and 'Proud People in Dragon Sleeves,' and the paintings of Ju Ran, Yan Wengui, and Xu Daoning.[6] All portray nature wholly and objectively, presenting a realm without self and without any definite concept, implication, or feeling.

[6] Dong Yuan and Ju Ran were painters of the Five Dynasties. Yan Wengui and Xu Daoning were painters of the Northern Song.

'Travelling Amid Hills and Streams', painting by Fan Kuan, Song Dynasty. Fan used a dense raindrop texture to enhance the reality of the scene. The peaks in the background that loom so large and close to the observer are a typical example of his style, in which what is far away is brought to one's side.

Faithfulness to Detail and the Search for Poetic Flavor

Aesthetic standards in poetry and painting changed with the times. As the Northern Song passed through its early and later stages into the Southern Song, the concept of 'absence of self' gradually moved towards its opposite, 'presence of self.'

This change was associated with and strongly influenced by the so-called academy style that dominated the realm of painting. This was the style practised by the Imperial Academy of Painting of the Northern Song, whose members sought only to please the emperor. As a matter of fact, the emperor took an active and personal part in the academy's creative activities. With excellent facilities at their disposal and ample leisure time, the academy painters developed to the optimum the practice of being faithful to details. Such sayings as 'When the peacock soars it must raise its left foot first' and discussions on how the flowers, stamens, and leaves of the China rose change from season to season and from morning to night[7] typify this search for fidelity to the smallest of details. Initiated by the emperor himself, this became one of the academy's most important aesthetic criteria.

Gongbi[8] birds and flowers were the most appropriate subjects to which this aesthetic criterion could be applied and consequently were acclaimed as the best works of the day. This, of course, influenced landscape painting. The opposing 'ink-play' style[9] of the literati, represented by Su Shi, could not prevail against the academy style at that time. As often happens, the ideology of the governing class becomes the ideology that governs society. And so, the search for faithfulness to details became an important tenet of painting outside as well as inside the imperial academy.

Another aspect of the aesthetics of academy painting, one that paralleled fidelity to details and perhaps deserves even more attention, was a heightened demand for poetic flavour. Actually, incorporating poetic sentiments in painting had begun long before this, for it is said that there was poetry in the paintings of Wang Wei (701–761), poet-

---

[7] See *Hua Ji* (literally *Painting Continued*) by Deng Zhuang, often referred to in histories of Chinese fine arts.

[8] *Gongbi* painting is one of the two major schools of traditional Chinese painting. Akin to Western realism, it is characterized by meticulous brushwork and close attention to details. The other is the *xieyi* school, which is more free in brushwork and may be compared to Western impressionism.

[9] 'Ink-play' is painting in a few simple strokes. It was a style advocated by the literati of the Song.

painter of the Tang Dynasty. But the conscious demand for poetic flavour in painting as an aesthetic standard of the highest order appeared only in the Song. Just as famous as the reference to the peacock quoted earlier in this section are the stories of how the imperial academy used lines from poetry as themes in its examinations—all are poem lines: 'A tender green shoot tipped in red; no need for many colours in a spring scene'; 'Home ten thousand *li* away reappears in a dream'; and, 'Scented are the horse's hooves, treading flowers as it returns' (see *New Talks on Killing Louse* and *Painting Continued*).

Painters were required to express the idea of a poem in their paintings. But because Chinese poetry is often very vague, with much meaning implied beyond the written word, master painters had to ponder and create ways to express these meanings. Thus poetic flavour became an important, consciously sought-after goal in Chinese landscape painting. The following passages, which refer to examinations conducted by the imperial academy, illustrate this point:

> Poetic theme: 'Water flowing through the wild, no one crossing; lone boat lying idle, morning and night.' All but one of the candidates depicted an empty boat moored by the shore, with an egret standing in it or some crows perched on the awning. The best painter in the group, however, did something different. He painted a boatman taking a nap in the stern; beside him is a short flute. The idea was that the boatman was there but he had no passengers.
> (*Painting Continued*)

The total absence of people implies a sense of forlorn and absolute loneliness. A boatman with no passengers more aptly, implicitly reflects the lyrical quality of ease, leisure, and tranquillity in this pastoral scene and accords with the poetic theme.

> Poetic theme: 'The wineshop shaded by bamboo beside a bridge.' Most painters, given this theme, find it easier to depict a busy wineshop. The master painter, however, merely painted a sign with the character 'wine' in front of a bamboo grove at the head of the bridge to signify that the shop lay behind it.
> (Yu Cheng: *Firefly and Snow*)

This rendering had a more poetic flavour: it was a subtly beautiful landscape painting.

The Song Dynasty may have been the most culturally developed in Chinese history. It produced an upper class that was larger and culturally more enlightened than even the Tang. This class comprised the emperor himself, his ministers and their families, lower-level officials, and the whole landed gentry. Fidelity to detail and the search for poetic flavour conformed to their aesthetic interests, which were cultivated in an era of relative peace and prosperity; it was a most refined and delicate expression of aesthetic interest.

Though these aesthetic interests had begun to crystallize in the late Northern Song, they reached their acme in the academy style of the Southern Song, creating a new conception of landscape painting which differed greatly from that of the early Northern Song.

If we look at some exemplary works of the Southern Song, by Ma Yuan, Xia Gui, and others, such as 'Lotus,' 'Music of the Lute in an Inner Chamber,' 'Moored on an Autumn River,' 'Returning from Pasture Along a Willow Creek,' 'Lone Angler on a Cold River,' 'Returning Sails in the Wind and Rain,' 'Selling Fish in the Snow,' 'Snowy Inn at Cloud Pass,' and 'Full Sails on a Spring River,' the characteristics we have just described are obvious. Most of these paintings communicate a picturesque poetic sentiment in a richly lyrical way by means of a limited scene or object that is carefully selected and meticulously described.

The general practice at this time was to use deliberate manipulation, careful positioning, and painstaking arrangement to focus on a particular view or spot, a single object, or even a part of an object. The faithful and detailed presentation of a delimited scene or isolated object was used to communicate poetic charm, thoughts, and feelings. This was very different from the more inclusive but less specific depictions of the early Northern Song. Gone were the impressive, complicated, panoramic, and distant views of that earlier period—expressed verbally in such lines as 'The spring hills are enshrouded in clouds and mist, and people are happy; the summer hills are shaded by luxuriant woods, and people are tranquil.' They were replaced by more specific and concentrated treatments. Even when the theme remained the same, the poetic flavour and emotional appeal had changed. Ma Yuan and Xia Gui were typical representatives of this school—witness the fact that they were often referred to as 'painters of fragmentary hills and streams.'[10]

A typical Southern Song painting might feature only a section of a crag, or half of a branch. But these would occupy prominent positions in the painting and would be depicted in minute detail and with lyrical richness. Ma Yuan's landscapes, though small, convey a strong feeling of spaciousness. He would leave most of a picture blank, or give it over

[10] Though they also painted large, panoramic scenes, they were generally recognized as exemplars of the approach being discussed here.

to distant fields and water, while painting a distinct object only in one corner. But this creates an impression of infinite space and imparts a sense of relaxation and happiness to viewers. Such paintings of fragments of hills and streams by Ma Yuan, Xia Gui, and other Southern Song artists evoke light, pleasant thoughts in their beholders.

'Singing on the Road', painting by Ma Yuan, Song Dynasty.

Southern Song landscape painting turned its audience's imagination, emotions, and understanding towards more definite themes and concepts in contrast to the comprehensive landscapes of the Northern Song. This then is the second kind of artistic conception, or the second stage in the development of Song-Yuan landscape painting.

Compared to the artistic conception that prevailed during the Northern Song, artists of the Southern Song expressed their personal feelings and concepts more directly. But compared to the next stage,[11] the artists still maintained a relatively objective, or impersonal, stand in their depictions of subjects and expressions of concepts and feelings. In other words, faithful representation of natural scenes and objects remained the basic principle, even though this was coupled with a much more conscious and obvious seeking of poetic flavour and expression of feelings than in Northern Song landscape painting. Paintings of this category and period should best be considered as representing an intermediate stage in the transition from 'absence of self' to 'presence of self.' They were still in an institutionalized academy style and were definitely not the sentimental works of literary men. Basically, they still belonged to the 'absence of self' category.

This intermediate stage was an important development in Song painting. Two tendencies were briefly in balance at this point: the search for poetic flavour prevented faithful depiction of detail from becoming stereotyped, like mechanical drawing, while the search for visual fidelity prevented the poetic flavour from turning vague, abstract, and insubstantial. Like the trend in prose and poetry, seeking spiritual resemblance through formal resemblance and expressing the infinite (poetic sentiments) by means of the finite (the limits of a painting) increasingly became the aesthetic criteria of all Chinese art. Symmetry being replaced by balance and proportion, space acquiring greater significance, few being preferred over many—these increasingly became the most developed forms, means, and techniques used in all branches of the arts. The vogue was for 'the abstract and the concrete to generate each other, ingenious concepts to exist where there is no painting' (Da Zhongguang: *The Means of Painting*). This is analogous to such sayings as 'the meaning lies beyond the written word' (poetry) and 'here soundlessness is more effective than sound' (music) in Chinese aesthetics.

Because these Southern Song landscapes focused on one aspect or object set within a delimited natural scene, the regional geographic

[11] See next section, 'Presence of Self.'

features that distinguished Northern Song landscapes disappeared—obviously, subjects like a corner of a hill or lake, half a branch, a small bridge, flowing water, a lone boat, a solitary angler, a spring river, autumn moonlight, or a sailboat returning in the rain could be found everywhere. So while the scenes or objects became smaller and more fragmented, they also became more universal; and while emotions and concepts became more specific, they also became richer and clearer. Indeed, such paintings give shape to scenes and objects that would be hard to portray in a more comprehensive picture and they cause hidden ideas and meanings to reveal themselves. In sum, the panoramic views of the Northern Song—vigorous, spacious, and majestic—had evolved into exquisite close-ups—delicate, meticulous, and rich in poetic flavour—by the time of the Southern Song. In form and content, both enriched the aesthetic traditions of the Chinese nation.

'Presence of Self'

The radical differences between paintings of the Song and Yuan can be attributed to changes in aesthetic standards caused by major changes in Chinese society during this period. The Mongolians, who founded the Yuan Dynasty, seriously disrupted the country's productive forces as they advanced southward to occupy the central plains and the south and southwest. Landowning intellectuals of the Han nationality, especially scholars in the south, suffered much oppression and exploitation, and many of them either chose or were compelled to give up the tradition of studying hard to prepare for becoming officials. Instead they turned to creative work in art and literature, and landscape painting became one of their preoccupations. The fall of the Song Dynasty brought with it the decline of the court, or academy, style of painting. Under the new social conditions, the arbiters of aesthetic values in landscape painting were no longer the imperial academy but displaced scholars and intellectuals—men of letters with no official status. Thus there appeared what is known as *wenrenhua* or 'literati painting.'

Some historians place the origin of literati painting at an earlier date, tracing it back to the Song, in the persons of Su Shi and Mi Fei (1051–1107). It may be that some paintings, now lost, by literary men of the Southern Song differed in style from the academy paintings. But to judge by paintings still extant, it is more appropriate to assume that literati painting. as a trend expressive of the spirit of its time, began in the Yuan, or, to be more exact, with the four great Yuan artists Huang Gongwang, Wu Zhen, Ni Yunlin, and Wang Meng.[12]

As might be expected, literati painting was characterized by a literary flavour. If Southern Song painting represented a fusion of formal and spiritual resemblance and of realism and poetic flavour, the two pairs of opposites existing in harmony, the influence of the social atmosphere and the psychology of the Yuan literati tilted the balance heavily towards the spiritual and the subjective. In fact, the situation two stages earlier in the Northern Song was now completely reversed: formal resemblance and realism became secondary to personal moods and sentiments. The basic aesthetic principle of 'rhythmic vitality' that had always been advocated in Chinese painting no longer applied to objects but only and entirely to the subjective. Originally a principle of figure painting, which should show the spirit of the subject, it now became a principle of landscape painting, in which the artist's moods and feelings must also be reflected (very few of the literati artists did figure paintings).

In *Yiyuan Zhiyan* (*Random Talks in the Garden of Art*) compiled by Wang Shizhen in the Ming Dynasty, there is the following passage: 'In figure painting, the form comes first, the spirit transcends the external appearance. In landscape painting, the spirit is primary, the form implicit.' These lines not only ignore the origins of painting but relegate the role and significance of formal resemblance in landscape painting to a secondary position, in clear contrast to the stress on realism that prevailed during the Northern Song.

As the Yuan painter Ni Yunlin once said, 'My painting consists only of a few cursory strokes of the brush; I seek no formal resemblance, only my personal pleasure'; and, 'I paint bamboo only to show that my heart is there; why should I care whether or not it resembles [real bamboo]?' Wu Zhen held similar views: 'Ink-play is a recreation indulged in by scholars and officials after composing serious verses and letters; it caters to the whims of the moment.' Such statements never appeared in the Northern or Southern Song.

Another feature of Yuan painting, which paralleled its literary flavour and gave concrete expression to it, was the emphasis on brushwork and inking. This was another creative development in Chinese painting, through which Yuan painting acquired its unique aesthetic values. For the literati painters, a work's beauty mainly lay

[12] Huang Gongwang (1269–1354), Wang Meng (1309–1358), Ni Yunlin (1301–1374), Wu Zhen (1285–1354) are called the four great painters of the Yuan.

not in its depiction of nature but in its lines and colours, its brushwork and ink. The literati painters saw these as possessing a beauty independent of the subject or scene portrayed. Brushwork and inking were seen not only as having formal and structural beauty, but also as communicating a painter's spirit or emotional concerns. In this way, the traditional Chinese emphasis on the art of line was elevated to its highest stage in the Yuan. Line had been a principal aesthetic element in Chinese visual arts since the earliest appearance of primitive pottery designs, bronze ritual vessels, and seal inscriptions on metal. Such expressions in figure painting as 'iron-line drawing,' 'water-shield drawing,' 'Cao's clothes have just been taken out of water,' and 'Wu's robes blow in the wind'[13] all referred to the beauty of lines.

China's unique calligraphic art, an example of highly developed linear beauty (see Chapters 2 and 7), became closely associated with painting in the Yuan, and this union of calligraphy and painting has remained a prominent feature of Chinese painting ever since. However, emphasizing brushwork, inking, and calligraphic values should not be regarded as emphasizing formal beauty. It represents a pure aesthetic interest and ideal. The flow and turn of lines, the shades of ink and their placement, the emotion, strength, power, interest, and temporal and spatial effects they produce are all important aesthetically. This is why photography, however true to life, can never replace painting. The latter, which possesses the aesthetic values of brush and ink, produces a beauty that does not exist in nature but was created by man after centuries of experimentation, refinement, and generalization. The union of calligraphy and painting is an obvious and important national characteristic of Chinese art, and it deserves further study. Zhao Mengfu, famous painter and calligrapher of the Yuan Dynasty, once wrote:

Rocks are like the 'flying white,' trees are like the *zhou*;[14]

[13] 'Iron-line drawing': use of thin, clear, and sturdy ink lines to paint creases and contours, especially in *gongbi* painting. 'Water-shield drawing': method of painting in which lines are indistinct and often merge into the surrounding colour. It is generally used in *xieyi* painting. 'Cao's clothes have just been taken out of water'; 'Wu's robes blow in the wind': art critics do not agree on who Cao and Wu were. Most say that Cao was Cao Zhongda, a painter of the Northern Dynasties whose use of compact and overlapping brushstrokes gave the clothes he painted so many creases that they seemed to have been just taken out of water. Wu is generally belived to be Wu Daozi of the Tang. His smooth, easy strokes gave the robes in his figure paintings a soft, blowing quality, as if stirred by a puff of wind.

[14] 'Flying white' and *zhou* are styles of Chinese handwriting. The former

Those who paint the bamboo, the eight kinds of strokes[15]
    should know.
For they must understand this truth, which experts rightly claim:
Calligraphy and painting in their basics are the same.

Painting, calligraphy, and poetry, three arts in one, became the ideal of Chinese landscape painting in the Yuan and remain so to this day.

A parallel phenomenon reaching its culmination in the Yuan was the incorporation of messages and poems in landscape painting. These inscriptions, intended to complement or supplement the painting, had been used in embryonic form in the Tang and Song. In the Tang, painters who wanted to add inscriptions usually put them in obscure places, concealing them in the crevice of a rock or among tree roots (much the same as in other countries). In the Song, the inscriptions became more conspicuous but at first tended to be only one line, and often in small script; the words were not allowed to occupy much space, lest they detract from the enjoyment of the painting itself.

Yuan inscriptions were very different. They might contain as many as 100 characters, or more than ten lines. They therefore took up much of the paper and were deliberately incorporated into the overall composition. On the one hand, calligraphy and painting matched each other well because both possessed linear beauty. On the other, the content of the inscription, whether explicit or implied, enhanced the literary charm and poetic flavour of the painting. This is why critics say of Yuan artists, 'Although by adding calligraphy they have encroached upon the painting, they have also added to its meaning and elegance.' This use of calligraphy, together with the vermilion seal, has become a tradition peculiar to Chinese art. The single square red seal mark amid the expanse of ink and water heightens the solemnity, clarity, and vitality of the overall mood. Both calligraphy and seal can be used to balance a composition, remedy a sparse layout, and increase a painting's visual interest. In other words, both enrich the aesthetic quality of the painting.

It was during this time that ink washes gradually replaced blue-green landscapes, although Zhang Yanyuan[16] had said much earlier:

The luxuriance of trees and grass may be depicted without the use of

originated in the Eastern Han when workmen painting a palace gate wrote characters with a white paintbrush. *Zhou* is similar to what is commonly called the great seal script.

[15] This refers to the eight basic strokes used to write Chinese characters.

[16] Zhang Yanyuan was an art critic of the Tang Dynasty. He lived in the ninth century, but the exact dates of his birth and death are unavailable.

red and green. Clouds and snow fly just as well without being painted white. The freshness of mountains may be felt though there is no emerald green. And the beauty of the phoenix can be perceived without gorgeous colouring. Thus, all colours may be present if you use the ink well. This is what is meant by capturing the essence of an object.

(*Famous Paintings Through the Ages*)

But it was not until the Yuan that painters really turned these ideas into reality by stressing brush and ink techniques. They found that it was possible to describe an object, create atmosphere, and express their meaning, concepts, interests, and feelings through the use of rising or falling, open or closed lines; dry or wet, dark or light ink; dense or sparse, vertical or horizontal dots; and a variety of strokes, such as those that resembled hemp or axe-cuts, which imparted differing textures. They no longer saw any need to recreate the exact shapes and colours of the original object or scene. As Wu Zhen put it: 'When the essence is there, there is no need to seek an exact correspondence in colour. Jiufang Gao's judgement of horses set a precedent.'[17] Jiufang Gao judged a horse only by its temperament, ignoring such details as form, sex, and colour.

Because the Yuan no longer stressed faithful reproduction of objects or natural scenes, but rather refined brushwork and inking characterized by an enduring charm, there was no longer any need for the comprehensiveness that prevailed in the Northern Song or the meticulousness of the Southern Song. Instead, artists aimed at communicating their moods and thoughts, and the means were the techniques of brush and ink and the subject matter, an evocative natural scene.

Yuan paintings provided clear examples of human aesthetic sensibility—elements such as imagination, sentiment, and understanding. A painted scene could be extremely simple and commonplace, but its charm and interest exceedingly strong. The theme of power in simplicity has been much commented on by critics, for example:

Song artists painted trees with hundreds of twists and turns. . . . But

---

[17] Wu Zhen was quoting the Southern Song poet Chen Yuyi (1090–1139). He was suggesting that the beauty of colours could be felt in a good painting done in ink only. Jiufang Gao was a well-known judge of horses who lived in the Spring and Autumn period.

the Yuan artists Huang Gongwang and Wu Zhen went to the other
extreme: the simpler, the better.
(Qian Du: *Reminiscences of Paintings of Pots and Pines*)

Mountain ranges and endless greenery are like a long epic; hills
distant and scattered are like a five-character or seven-character poem
of just four lines. The simpler, the more enduring.
(Shen Hao: *The World of Painting*)

The beauty of hills and water is perceived by the eye and lives in the
heart. What is shaped by the brush and ink is only a matter of *xing*.[18]
(Shen Zhou)

Distant mountains that rise and fall possess power; sparse woods,
high or low, have feeling.
(Dong Qichang)

In other words, all of nature had become the forum for expressing
subjective moods and interests. The works of Ni Yunlin are a typical
example. His paintings generally included only a few trees, a humble
pavilion, some low hills in the distance, or perhaps half a tree branch in
the cold. There were no signs of life or motion. Yet the ingenuity of his
brushwork imparts powerful emotions to these commonplace scenes—
ease and leisure, sorrow, or silence and loneliness, as if the whole
world were barren and ageing. These thoughts and feelings are clearly
evoked by his simple, masterly brushwork. Again, critics have
commented:

The quiet pavilions and beautiful trees created by Yuan artists
possess a quality that goes beyond nature. Its mysticism may be
likened to a swan goose far away on the horizon. The brush in motion
is as effective as a lament played on strings or a presto on winds,
when sound and sentiment arise simultaneously—something that
cannot be found in the great world of nature.
(Yun Shouping, 1633–1690)

Plain, commonplace, without meaning, yet possessing something that
cannot but reveal itself.
(Yun Xiang: *Calligraphy and Paintings of Baoyu Studio*)

Of course, this mysterious 'quality,' this 'something that cannot but
reveal itself,' does not refer to the physical features of a scene or object,
but to the artist's moods, feelings, and concepts. As has already been
mentioned, nature was only the subject matter through which such
subjective qualities were transmitted by the medium of brush and ink.

[18] *Xing*: to conjure up by association (see Chapter 3).

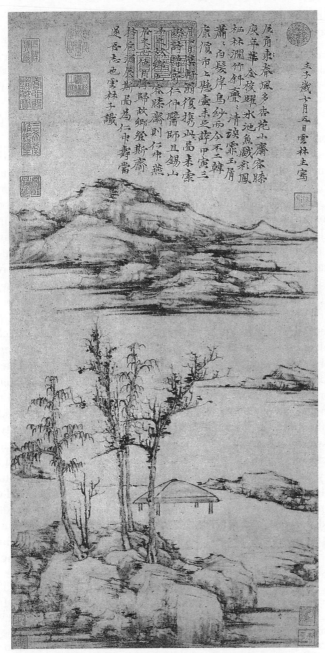

'Rongqi Studio', painting by Ni Yunlin, Yuan Dynasty.

This is what is meant by 'presence of self.' Back in the Song Dynasty, Ouyang Xiu had said:

> Dreariness and indifference are feelings that are hard to portray in a painting. . . . Flying, walking, speed, slowness, things with little depth of meaning, are easy to perceive; but leisure, harmony, solemnity, tranquillity, ideas that are more profound, are hard to give shape to.

Wang Anshi meant much the same when he said: 'There can be no good painting of barrenness and cold.'

Dreariness, indifference, leisure, solemnity, tranquillity, barrenness, cold—all of these are primarily states of mind or ways of thinking or feeling; they have no objective existence in the world of nature, not in the hills and streams themselves. This is why it took so long for artists to learn how to express such subjective states by means of landscapes. This difficulty was creatively resolved in Yuan painting, which consequently established a third model of artistic conception in landscape painting. These three different artistic conceptions, of the Northern Song, Southern Song, and Yuan, stand each in its own right and excel each in its own way.

In the Yuan, it made little difference whether the painting was a complete view or a detail, a general or regional depiction, a sketchy or meticulous work—the aesthetic quality and artistic conception were the same. Huang Gongwang and Wang Meng, for example, were noted for their long scroll landscapes such as 'Hermit of the Fuchun Mountains' and for their portrayals of continuous and overlapping hills and crags ('Hermitage at Qingbian'). Their depictions of nature, though broader in scope than the works of Ni Yunlin, were still typical of Yuan style in their stress on brushwork, charm, and interest. Their sparseness, simplicity, elegance, and grace served to communicate 'presence of self.'

By the time of the Ming and Qing, 'presence of self' had turned into a torrent of romanticism. While the works of Ni Yunlin and other Yuan painters were still true representations of nature—the saying quoted earlier, 'what matters if it resembles or not,' was an overstatement—the works of Shi Tao (1642–1718), Zhu Da (1626–1705), and the eight Yangzhou eccentrics[19] of the Ming and Qing show an almost total disregard for formal resemblance. The

[19] The eight eccentrics were painters of the Qing Dynasty who sold their paintings at Yangzhou. According to most historians, the eight were Wang Shishen, Huang Shen, Jin Nong, Gao Xiang, Li Shan, Zheng Xie, Li Fangying, and Luo Ping, but other names have also been mentioned. Most of them were flower painters. They were called 'deviants' or 'eccentrics' because their style

subjective moods, interests, and characteristics of the artist became paramount. In Song painting such individuality was all but absent; in the Yuan, it was in a budding stage. Its complete flowering took place in the Ming and Qing and continued into the modern era.

Song painters had stressed objectivity: learning from nature, rationality, laws, and careful attention to composition. These concerns were expressed in the following mottoes, from *Collection of Pure Landscapes*[20]: 'When there are rules, there is order'; 'when there is sequence, there is no mixing'; and, 'seek the subtleties of an object through its inherent quality.'

In the Yuan, the stress was on subjectivity, on 'laws that originated in the heart,' on interests, enthusiasm, and what Tang Gou, in *Mirror of Painting*, called 'the writing of ideas' ('painters should write their ideas'; 'master painters are those who express their interests and write their ideas; they should be careful not to seek resemblance only').

These differences between Song and Yuan paintings were also the subjects of the following passage from Dong Qichang's *The Aims of Painting*:

> Su Dongpo says in a poem that
>
> 'To judge a painting by form alone is but a child's way:
> How a poem should be composed is for the poet to say'
>
> This, I believe is an endorsement of the Yuan style of painting. But Chao Yidao[21] says
>
> 'Painting depicts the outer form, this form it must not change;
> Poetry transmits what lies beyond, the spirit must remain.'
>
> This, I think, refers to Song painting.

In Song painting, to quote Liu Daochun's[22] *Critique of Famous Paintings of the Imperial Court*, the proper order was to 'examine the atmosphere [of the scene or object] first; decide what is to be retained and what rejected; establish the basic meaning; and finally seek the laws.'

was different from what was regarded as the orthodox style of their time. Their brushwork had a strong influence on modern Chinese *xieyi* painting.

[20] By Han Zhuo, painter and art critic of the Northern Song.

[21] Chao Yidao (1054–1129) was a landscape painter and a contemporary of Su Dongpo. He was versed in the Six Classics, especially the *Book of Changes*.

[22] Art critic of the Northern Song. The dates of his birth and death are unavailable.

But in Yuan painting, according to Tang Gou, one should 'first observe the true nature [of a scene or object], then the brushwork. Flavour and interest are achieved only when little attention is paid to what is traced out by the brush and ink [i.e., the form]' (*Mirror of Painting*).

In both theory and practice, the differences between Song and Yuan paintings are obvious. Aesthetically, the difference is between 'absence of self' and 'presence of self.'

In the last chapter we discussed the differences between the concepts of classical poetry and *ci*. To these should now be added a third, the concept of *qu*.[23] It will be recalled that the poetic concept is grandiose and profound, while *ci* is meticulous and detailed. In both, however, the stress is on allusion rather than direct revelation. The spirit that lay beyond and behind the actual written word gave readers unlimited pleasure, causing them to sigh again and again as they chanted the verses. The concept of *qu* is different, for it is characterized by ease, clarity, and forthrightness. If classical poems were characterized by 'absence of self,' and *ci* included an appreciable element of 'presence of self,' then *qu* could be said to be dominated by 'presence of self.' The three concepts bear some parallels to the three kinds of artistic conception in Song-Yuan landscape painting: absence of self, faithfulness to detail and search for poetic flavour, presence of self.

> Late at night, by a lighted candle.
> We sat facing as in a dream.
> (poetic)

> I light the silver lamp this whole night through,
> Still fearing that our meeting is a dream.
> (*ci*)

> In a small chamber all night long,
>   I hearken to the spring rain;
> Apricot blossoms they sell in the morn,
>   Down on a quiet lane.
> (poetic)

> 'Mid the thin shadows of the apricot,
> I play the flute until dawn.
> (*ci*)

> I wake to see the red sun on the window screen,

---

[23] *Qu* is a kind of verse written for singing, especially on the stage, from the Yuan Dynasty.

I hear them selling apricots in the streets below.
(*qu*)

Like a thousand specks are the winter crows;
Round a lonely village the water flows.
(poetic, but with a tinge of *ci*)

Beyond the setting sun, a few specks of winter crows;
Round a lonely village the water flows.
(*ci*)

Withered vines, old trees, shadowy crows in their midst;
Little bridges, flowing water, somebody's home nearby;
An ancient path, a westerly wind, horses thin and gaunt.
(*qu*)

Despite the similarities in imagery and subject matter, the artistic conception is different in each of the above examples. The poetic is dignified and serious; the *ci*, novel and acute; the *qu*, clear and forthright. Each is beautiful in its own way and cannot be replaced by the others. There are certain general laws governing them that are similar and related to the laws that govern the three types of sculpture (see Chapter 6) and the three kinds of artistic conception in landscape painting. Of course, not every piece of writing, not every author, can be clearly categorized; some are transitional and others intermediate, sharing the characteristics of two different categories.

As in sculpture and literature, there are good and bad, successful and unsuccessful examples in all three categories of Song-Yuan landscape painting. Moreover, since art is in the eyes of the beholder, people will have different preferences according to their tastes.

10

Main Trends in Art and Literature of the Ming and Qing

Vernacular Literature and Art

The previous chapters may be summed up as follows: The art and literature of the Han Dynasty were reflections of deeds and action; the Wei-Jin style and the sculpture of the Northern Dynasties were expressions of spirit and speculation; Tang poetry, Song *ci*, and Song-Yuan landscape painting were revelations of moods and feelings.

Coming now to the Ming and Qing dynasties, an era noted for its fiction and drama, we find art and literature devoted to more commonplace things. They focus on a world of some dimension, but do not describe the conquest of nature as in Han art, nor flaunt the triumph of ancient brute force. Rather, they depict the everyday life of city dwellers over the past few hundred years, and social customs that were commonplace, yet varied and colourful.

Chinese cities were already prosperous in the Song Dynasty, as can be seen in the famous painting 'Going Up the River during the Qingming Festival,' by the Northern Song painter Zhang Zeduan. A network of commerce and transportation had been formed with Bianliang (present-day Kaifeng), then the nation's capital, as the centre and embracing the various provincial towns that had been the capital cities of the Ten Kingdoms of the Five Dynasties. A class of mercantile landlords and townspeople was in the making. Despite the economic deterioration caused by the Mongolian invasion during the Yuan, elements of capitalism (or post-feudalism) were fairly well established by the mid-Ming, especially in the ideological sphere.

From the mid-sixteenth century to the late eighteenth century, Chinese philosophy, art, literature, and social and political thinking all went through steps during which many schools and sects emerged, developed, and declined in close succession.

Philosophy is the soul of the epoch, a pulse that beats in unison with the times. Among the most prominent philosophers of the period from the Song to the Qing were Chen Liang (1143–1194) and Ye Shi (1150–1223) of the Southern Song, activists who opposed making

peace with the Nuzhen tribes[1] that had invaded China; Huang Zongxi
(1610–1695) of the late Ming and early Qing, one of the first to declare
that industry and commerce were just as vital as agriculture to the
country's economy; and Dai Zhen (1723–1777) of the Qing, who was
noted for his opposition to what he called 'killing by principle.'[2] These
and many other progressive thinkers such as Li Zhi (1527–1602) and
Tang Zhen (1630–1704) represented a trend that they and others
labelled 'heterodox Confucianism,'[3] a kind of democratic thinking that
had elements of modern emancipation.

Another trend was represented by Zhang Zai (1020–1077) of the
Northern Song, Luo Qingshun (1465–1547) of the Ming, and Wang
Fuzhi of the early Qing, who called themselves Confucianists and
espoused a philosophical school that was more speculative in nature.

Although there were differences and even contradictions between
the two schools, both repudiated or tried to destroy the traditions of
feudal rule. Together, they constituted a powerful trend towards
ideological enlightenment during the Ming and Qing. Adherents of the
orthodox school were mainly landlords who opposed existing
administrations. In this they resembled opposition parties in modern
politics. The orthodox school's teachings were a summing up of
historical experience. The heterodox school was more clearly urban and
bourgeois—quite obviously in the ideological sphere and perhaps in the
economic sphere as well. Its disruptive effect on the old feudal system

---

[1] The Nuzhens were a minority nationality that once inhabited parts of
northeastern China. Their leader, Aguda, founded the Jin, or Nuzhen, Dynasty
(1115–1234), which overthrew the Northern Song and occupied large parts of
north and central China. They were later assimilated into the Manchu
nationality and gradually lost their own identity.

[2] 'Principle of Heaven' is a main category of Neo-Confucianism. According
to this 'principle', for example, a woman should never get married again after
her husband's death.

[3] Heterodox Confucianists did not discredit Confucianism entirely, but they
disagreed that it was the supreme authority. As Li Zhi put it: 'Not everything
Confucius favoured was right, and not everything he opposed was wrong.' He
asserted that such famous Confucian classics as the *Confucian Analects*,
Mencius and *Six Classics* were merely collections of study notes taken by
Confucius's disciples and could not be regarded as eternal truths. The
heterodox Confucianists were generally opposed to the system of absolute
monarchy. Extremists such as Huang Zongxi even called the monarch the
'greatest evil on earth,' and declared that 'whether a country was prosperous or
not must not be measured by the rise or fall of a single family but by the
welfare of the whole people.'

was greater, especially in the field of art and literature, where it had a more direct and important influence.

A new type of literature that became popular at this time was the *pinghua* which evolved from the monastic teachings of the Tang (see Chapter 6) and was used mainly for singing and storytelling. By the Song Dynasty, it already comprised such genres as love, ghosts, legends, adventures, and historical romances. But it bears little resemblance to the stories of uncanny beings of the Six Dynasties or the short stories of the Tang. *Pinghua* tales were not pure adventures couched in flowery language and written to be read and enjoyed by a handful of nobles, but descriptions of the realities of life offered for the enjoyment of a much wider audience, the broad masses of city dwellers. Though they offer little in the way of rhetoric, their artistic effects are impressive and exceed those of any type of aristocratic art and literature of earlier periods.

Obviously there is a great difference in aesthetic quality between popular literature like the *pinghua* and traditional-style songs and poems. In *pinghua* artistic beauty is less important than the sense of everyday life, and refinement has given way to crude reality. By the mid-Ming, this new trend in art and literature attained sizable proportions, as when tiny streams join to form rivers, lakes, and seas. Instead of only being sung or verbally narrated, *pinghua* stories now appeared in written forms as well, in collections such as *Yushi Mingyan* (*Wise Sayings to Instruct the World*), *Jingshi Tongyan* (*General Sayings to Warn the World*), *Xingshi Hengyan* (*Common Sayings to Alert the World*), and *Pai'an Jingqi* (*Tales of Wonder and Surprise*).[4]

These collections showed that vernacular literature had reached its zenith and now possessed its own qualities and characteristics. They exerted a great influence on modern literature. For example, a selection of tales from the above-mentioned works, compiled into a volume called *Jingu Qiguan* (*Strange Tales Ancient and Modern*) has remained popular for over three centuries. Its preface notes that the tales 'thoroughly describe the diversity of world affairs and human relations, and fully record human joys, sorrows, meetings, and partings.' The stories offer broad, multidimensional views of people of all classes and strata in a society where commercial prosperity had made inroads into the old social order. What they reveal is not the ancient world, in which men had to prostrate themselves in worship and men and gods were

---

[4] All these are collections of *huaben*, scripts used by storytellers. The first three were compiled by Feng Menglong. The last, consisting of two collections, was compiled by Ling Mengchu of the late Ming.

one, but ordinary, everyday life with a realistic human touch—pleasure in worldly things, longing for wealth and honour, desire for sexual emancipation, and a fascination with adventure, fairies, and monsters.

Though vulgar, low-class, shallow, and philistine, compared to the refined and elegant tastes of the scholar-officials and literati, the new vernacular literature represented not only a new awareness that was full of vitality but also an attack on and disruption of the centuries-old feudal monarchy and Confucian orthodoxy. Its appearance could be compared to the appearance of works like *The Decameron* by Giovanni Boccaccio (1313–1375) during the European Renaissance.

One of the most popular and prominent themes of the vernacular literature was love between ordinary men and women. This theme had not been important in Tang poetry, nor indeed in the literature of earlier periods. In *ci* poetry of the Song Dynasty amorous works largely concerned prostitutes, but writings about true love, especially stories that lauded the zeal, devotion, and faithfulness of young women in love, began to appear at this time. That suggests that society had changed greatly from the feudal days, and especially that women were no longer playthings of the rich but had acquired a true human status.

Along with the growth of bourgeois elements in the social system and the growing prosperity of city life, the theme of sexual love, resting as it does on a natural and universal physiological basis, acquired a different social significance, and the dawning acceptance of equal, mutual, and voluntary love between men and women contributed significantly to breaking feudal yokes and achieving freedom for the individual.

Many colourful tales appeared, among which were such popular ones as 'The Oil-Buyer Wins a Famous Prostitute,' 'Du Shiniang Throws a Chest of Jewels Overboard in Her Rage,' 'Prefect Zhao Picks Girls at Random,' 'Yutangchun Meets Her Husband in a Moment of Distress,' and 'Ren Junyong Seduces in the Ladies' Chamber.' Some of these were descriptions of love at first sight, which nonetheless proved true and lasting; some told of lovers united after many trials; some were tragic tales of unscrupulous affairs and forsaken women; others were tales of outright lust and debauchery. There were eulogies of true love, satires on feudal marriages, stories of how unfaithful lovers were chastised, and even unabashed accounts of sexual pleasure. The thoughts, ideas, characters, images, and themes expressed in these works were clearly different from the highbrow, aristocratic content of orthodox feudal literature and the works of the literati and scholar-officials.

Vernacular literature originated in ballads and oral storytelling and catered to the interests of ordinary city dwellers, the middle and lower classes. In mirroring everyday life and customs, it did not, of course, centre on the theme of love alone but presented a many-sided view of the world at large. Chivalrous warriors, just officials, cruel, avaricious magistrates, and treacherous, double-dealing lords and nobles all had their place.

Since in the womb of feudalism the foetus of a new society was already struggling to be born, men's fortunes and misfortunes gradually lost their monolithic feudal cast and became more varied. People of all types and descriptions were now fighting for a place. Merchants tried to accumulate wealth through trade; scholars sought advancement by taking the civil service examinations. Some gained nothing and remained poor to the end of their days; others, through a stroke of fortune, became rich overnight. Ambition was crucial—but so was chance. As the feudal order weakened and the class structure changed, something new was growing and with it a more complex social order that benefited the development of individualism. The contingencies and inevitabilities in life were now much more complicated. Although it was still too early to speak of individual freedom, there was a growing concern for the fate of individuals.

This concern can be seen in the vernacular stories, in which evil was censured and the good praised. But the stories also preached fatalism, retribution in this life or the next, and resignation to adversity. Thus, the basic feature of this new literary genre was a blending of democratic elements of modern capitalism and the corrupt, backward ideology of feudalism. There were no high ideals, no depth of content, no heroes with really high ambitions, no outstanding characters aflame with enthusiasm—only commonplace but realistic and comprehensive stories of the world, either real or imaginary.

Because it evolved from singing and oral storytelling, vernacular literature shared with these forms the intricate plots and abundant details needed to hold the interest of an audience. On this depended the success or failure of the artist or author and the work. Authors faced these tasks: to conceive, select, and arrange plots so as to produce dramatic effects; to achieve what is unexpected and yet logical if not plausible; to offer descriptions that are real but not long-winded; to create a realistic story, not just one or two typical characters or events; in short, to captivate audiences with a plot that was both reasonable and dramatic, set in a world of joys and sorrows, partings and reunions. It was this genre that established the national style and artistic characteristics of Chinese fiction.

Developing alongside the *huaben* and *ni huaben*,[5] two forms of vernacular literature, was the *xiqu* or traditional Chinese drama. The Mongolian occupation of the central plains, the country's heartland, in the Yuan Dynasty resulted in both economic and cultural decline, but it also created the conditions for the integration of the literati and scholar-official class[6] with folk writers. The Yuan poetic drama, famous for its flowery language, was a product of this integration. Four great dramatists emerged as representatives of the orthodox school of literature of this period: Guan Hanqing, Wang Shifu,[7] Bai Pu (1226–?), and Ma Zhiyuan (?–1321). Their dramatic works, *The Wrongs of Dou E* (Guan Hanqing), *The Western Chamber* (Wang Shifu), and *Wall Top and Horseback* (Bai Pu), are specimens of traditional Chinese drama that are popular even today.

After the mid-Ming, the emergence of large numbers of legends and anecdotes pushed traditional drama to a new stage. Apart from its literary values, it had by this time developed into a comprehensive form of art that combined talking, singing, acting, dancing, and music into an aesthetic whole—an opera form with an artistic beauty that is uniquely Chinese.

This beauty reached new heights in *kunqu*[8] and Peking opera. *Kunqu* in particular, which featured talented, liberal, tender, and sentimental young heroes and heroines, exquisite singing and dancing that described delicate psychological and emotional states, and beautifully written scripts, quite prominently reflected its time.

In traditional Chinese drama, music and singing are polished and arranged to perfection; every move of the hand and foot is as stylized as a dance; poses are sculptural; settings, symbolic and suggestive; plots, clear and simple; and the drama often centres around intense ethical conflicts that produce strong psychological responses. The result is a complete merging of form and content, and the projection of a formal beauty that gives expression to the content; not the simple formal

---

[5] *Huaben* (story copy) was the script used by an oral storyteller. *Ni huaben* (imitation of story copy) was a story written in the form of a *huaben*; it was a style of writing used by Ming scholars.

[6] This class, deprived of its high social position by the ethnic minority that ruled the country, which permitted only the propagation of its own culture, was compelled to fall back on the masses.

[7] Guan Hanqing and Wang Shifu lived in the early Yuan. The dates of their birth and death are not available.

[8] *Kunqu* was a form of Chinese opera that had its roots in the folk dramas of Kunshan, Jiangsu Province. It gradually spread to other parts of the country in the late Ming.

beauty of a dancer's symmetric or balanced pose, nor that of his or her harmonious movements, but beauty interwoven with the drama's content and plot. The arias and declamations in Peking opera, for example, are more than formal beauty; they are a way of expressing the content and meaning of the opera.

Beauty of form is, however, a crucial element in traditional Chinese drama, for it is through the music, singing, dancing, and acting that lyric quality and the art of line—the essence of Chinese art and literature—are developed to the optimum. In the final analysis, traditional Chinese drama achieves its success not through the literary excellence of its libretto but through its significant form of beauty.

The graceful entries and exits, the delicate S-shaped walks, the exquisite music and singing, these features of *kunqu* and Peking opera are enough to captivate any audience. It is art that is highly refined and generalized, yet richly specific, stylized but still individual, not ordinary formal beauty but truly 'significant form' (see Chapter 1). Although these opera forms became more esoteric when they were adopted by the higher echelons of society, including the imperial court, they still rested on their original broad basis, the masses of city dwellers, and remained part of vernacular art and literature.

Woodcuts, which were produced in prodigious numbers after the mid-Ming, were a purely visual form of vernacular art. As illustrations for fiction and dramatic literature, they were much in demand. Their popularity peaked at the end of the Ming. Typical examples are the engravings made from paintings by Chen Hongshou (1598–1652) and those made in the Huike Studio of Anhui.

Like dramatists of the period, woodcut artists usually depicted scenes that were dramatic and not bound by space and time. On a piece of wood of the size of an ordinary woodcut, they carved pictures showing a whole course of events, events that took place at different times and under different circumstances; yet everything is presented clearly, causing no confusion in the viewer while demonstrating the rationalism in Chinese art. Like the novelist and dramatist, the woodcut artist did not try to create what was pure imagination; he did his best to make his creations conform to reality. He did not allow himself to be restricted by the three unities[9] of dramatic structure, but submitted to the realities of life and the logic of reason. In theme, content, mode of expression, and aesthetic awareness, Chinese drama, fiction, and

[9] Unity of time, unity of place, unity of action, three principles governing the structure of drama derived from Aristotle's *Poetics*. They require that a play be confined to one action, occurring in one place and lasting only one day.

'Setting fire to the Green-Cloud Mansion', woodcut illustration of *Outlaws of the Marsh.* This woodcut is an example of the many-pointed perspective in Chinese graphic arts and the presentation of a series of events in a single picture. The story begins at the east gate of the mansion, moves on to the west gate, and ends at the south gate. The events portrayed occurred at different times and in different places.

woodcuts may be traced to the same origin, for they possess similar or interrelated artistic characteristics and aesthetic qualities.

From the mid-Tang onward, drama, fiction, and woodcuts constituted the real basis of Chinese art and literature. On this basis, and in the wake of the demand for freedom of thought, there emerged in the art and literature of the upper-class scholar-officials a torrent of romanticism that was directed against orthodox classicism. This torrent entered into all spheres of art and literature.

The Torrent of Romanticism

The great social changes that began in the mid-Tang were reflected in art and literature as ideological trends. If the trend in novels, woodcuts, and other forms of vernacular art and literature was towards secular realism, in traditional art and literature a trend towards romanticism developed in opposition to bogus classicism.[10] The two trends, realism of the lower social strata and romanticism of the upper strata, intermingled and complemented each other.

The central figure in the romantic trend was Li Zhi, brilliant successor to Wang Yangming,[11] who consciously and creatively developed Wang's philosophy. Li Zhi repudiated the teachings of Confucius and Mencius, lectured on the need for childlike innocence, openly flaunted heterodoxy, and exposed what he regarded as fallacies of pseudo-Confucianism (bogus Confucianism). His teachings were received with enthusiasm because they accorded with the general trend of the times. In his biography[12] we read that 'scholars willingly worshipped at his door'; 'scholars in the southern capital (Nanjing) flocked to him as if driven by the wind'; and 'both along the great Yangtze River and in the north, people listened attentively and were moved by his teachings.' Although on occasion his writings were banned and destroyed, nonetheless his fame and influence spread far and wide.

Li Zhi preached that people should speak the truth. He was opposed to all hypocrisy and affectation, asserting that private thoughts and selfish interests should be revealed honestly. 'For there is selfishness in every man's heart' (*Li Zhi's Archives: Postscript to 'Good Confucian Ministers'*) and 'even sages are not without selfish motives' (*Comments on the Ancients*). He praised novels like *The Western Chamber* and *Outlaws of the Marsh*, placed them on a par with the classics of old, and argued that both literary content and style must change with time and circumstances, asking:

> Why must good poetry always be chosen from the ancients and prose from the Pre-Qin? They [old-style prose and poetry] have already evolved into the style of the Six Dynasties, into new-style literature, into legendary tales, librettos, and poetic dramas like *The Western Chamber* and novels like *Outlaws of the Marsh*. All are good

[10] Bogus classicism was a derogatory term used in reference to the attitudes of certain writers of the Ming-Qing who argued for a full return to ancient forms and styles in art and literature. An example of this is the demand put forward by the earlier and later seven scholars, of the mid- and late Ming, respectively, that 'all prose follow the style of the Qin-Han and all poetry be patterned on that of the prime Tang.'

[11] Wang Yangming (1472–1528) was a philosopher of the mid-Ming. He was an idealist noted for his opposition to the Song philosopher Zhu Xi.

[12] *Biography of Li Zhi, Central Figure of Ming Literature*, from *Emperor Qianlong's Records of the Quanzhou Prefecture*.

literature. Date and dynasty cannot be used as criteria. I feel that good literature comes only from a childlike innocence, so why insist on following the Six Classics, the *Confucian Analects*, and *Mencius*? (*Books for the Fire: On Childlike Innocence*)

Because of these principles, he rejected the often hypocritical practice, much in vogue at the time, of learning and imitating the ancient classics. Instead, he praised novels and dramas that were popular among the masses, and reviewed and annotated some fifteen librettos, plus a number of well-known novels, to counteract the hypocrisy of orthodox thinking. As he explained it:

In our daily life, everybody thinks for himself and his family. Yet when we scholars open our mouths to talk about philosophy, it's 'You are for yourself, I am for others; you are selfish, I am altruistic.' When I think of this, I feel we are not even as good as the ordinary man in the market. At least his words and deeds are consistent: a merchant will talk about trade, a tiller about plowing. This is truly virtuous talk, reliable and interesting, and it does not bore the listener. (*A Reply to Justice Geng*)

It was his opposition to pseudo-Confucianists and hypocrisy that caused him to attach special importance to vernacular art and literature, which he raised to a theoretical plane he called 'childlike innocence.' 'Childlike innocence is sincerity,' he wrote. 'It has no pretensions: it is pure and true, the instinctive idea that arises from the heart' (*On Childlike Innocence*). His argument that 'childlike innocence,' or sincerity, was the basis of creation paved the way for the transformation of vernacular art and literature, based on contemporary worldly life, into romantic art and literature, based on the emancipation of the individual character and spirit.

On Childlike Innocence and its author were catalysts by which the vernacular art and literature of the masses blended with the romantic art and literature of the elite. With childlike innocence as his criterion, Li Zhi rejected all traditional restrictions on thinking, including the supreme authority of Confucius: 'When heaven gives birth to a man, it will make him useful in some way on his own, without the need to learn from Confucius first. If a man had to learn from Confucius before becoming useful, what about those who lived in the centuries before Confucius's time? Were they not fit to be called men?' (*A Reply to Geng Zhongcheng*).

In Li Zhi's view, all humans are useful in their own way and can formulate their own truths without relying on the sage; still less should they make pretensions to understanding Confucianism. Art and literature are valuable because they are media through which people can express what they believe to be true; they are not just for recording what the sage said or for imitating our ancestors. Principles such as these, which were based on the awakening of the soul, on a sincere belief that one's own innate knowledge is more trustworthy than any external dogma or received morality, may be regarded as expressions of freedom for the individual. They had a very enlightening effect on the art and literature of their time.

It was no accident that Li Zhi became the voice of emancipation in art and literature. The chief artistic and literary reformers and progressives of his day were his friends, disciples, or admirers and they all had direct or indirect relations with him. Among them were the man of letters Yuan Zhonglang (1568–1610), the dramatist Tang Xianzu (1550–1616), and the novelist Feng Menglong (1574–1646).

These people also extolled, commended, and formed friendships with each other. For example, Yuan Zhonglang was friends with Xu Wei (1521–1593), a painter, calligrapher, and man of letters; Tang Xianzu with the three Yuan brothers;[13] and Xu Wei with Tang Xianzu. Though they were all conscious promoters of romanticism, we should begin with a discussion of the Gong'an School founded by the three Yuan brothers and named for their birthplace in southern Hubei Province. For this is one of the most influential schools of literature of the late Ming.

The three brothers' thinking, theory, and literary practice were strongly influenced by Li Zhi. Their works were descriptions of everyday affairs, direct expressions of their thoughts and feelings. They opposed affectation and strongly disapproved of the views of bogus classicism. As Yuan Zhonglang wrote in his *Complete Works*:

> I express what is in my heart, without regard for style or pattern. I will not write down what does not come from the heart. . . . As it is the work of an honest man, it generally rings true. It does not imitate the Han and Wei, nor follow in the footsteps of the prime Tang. Give free rein to your nature: it is gratifying to be able to vent your joy, anger, grief, happiness, desires, and passions.

One of their best-known and most characteristic works is *Manjing Youli* (*A Visit to Manjing*), which includes the following simple, vivid sketch of late winter and early spring in Beijing:

[13] Yuan Zongdao (1560–1600), Yuan Zhonglang (also called Yuan Hongdao), and Yuan Zhongdao (1570–1623).

It is cold in the land of Yan.[14] Even after the Huazhao Festival[15] there is still a lingering chill. Freezing blasts rise from time to time, whipping up sand and gravel. Confined to a small room, I long to go out but cannot. Each time I venture into the wind, I go no more than a hundred steps then hurry back.

On the 22nd it was a little warmer, so with a few friends I went out the Dongzhimen[16] to Manjing. Tall willows lined the dikes, on which the earth was just beginning to thaw. Looking up at the sky, I felt like a bird freed from a cage. The ice had just melted, the surface of the lake rippled in the sun, and the water was so clear that one could see to the bottom; it was as if a box with a mirror inside had been opened, releasing a flash of cold light. Hills drenched in light vapour were so fresh and beautiful as if newly cleansed. . . . Willow strands were just beginning to green, their soft tips swaying in the breeze. In the wheat fields, the seedlings were barely an inch tall . . .

In this passage there is no affected tone, no deep symbolism, no grandiose scene or event, and no impressive atmosphere—yet the narrative rolls on and holds the reader's interest. Writing of this kind continued to be influential up to the time of the modern New Literature Movement,[17] for it heralded the birth of modern literary style. A comparison of this description of everyday life and natural scenery with Liu Zongyuan's descriptions of nature—though also well written (see 'Inner Contradictions,' in Chapter 8)—makes the fresh, plain style of the more modern works quite apparent.

The Yuan brothers' style was much more than the style of a single school. It was a powerful ideological trend and a general literary approach that began long before their time and remained influential for an entire century. Famous writers like Tang Yin (1470–1523), Mao Kun (1512–1601), Tang Shunzhi (1507–1560), and Gui Youguang (1507–1571), who lived several decades before the Yuans and may have been very different from them in other ways, showed the same inclination. As Tang Shunzhi once wrote: 'The finest poetry in the world is composed impromptu. Today, men of letters and scholarship have spoken of nothing except moral cultivation, filling up

[14] Yan is a historical name for Hebei Province.

[15] Huazhao Festival, literally Morning-of-Flowers Festival, is a day in the second month of the lunar calendar. Formerly, it was observed as the 'birthday' of flowers.

[16] Dongzhimen was one of the northeastern city gates of Beijing in the old days.

[17] A part of the May 4th Student Movement of 1919, which heralded the so-called New Democratic Revolution in China.

whole sheets with such writing and referring everything to Confucianism. . . . It is extreme affectation, with all its ugliness exposed.' His stance is clearly in line with the thinking of the Gong' an school.

Gui Youguang's lyrical prose is orthodox in form and content, but it impresses people with its plain and unadorned descriptions of ordinary family life. In this, it heralded the Gong'an style. His well-known essay, 'The Xiangjixuan Study,' is a good example:

> Xiangjixuan was an old study on the southern side of the courtyard. It was only about ten feet square, barely enough for one person to live in. It was at least a hundred years old and was covered with mud and dust. When it rained, water leaked through the roof, so time and again I had to move my desk until finally there was no place left to put it. Because the room faced north, it could get no sunlight and became dark soon after midday.
>
> I had some small repairs made so that the roof no longer leaked, installed four windows, and built a wall around the courtyard to keep out the southern sun, whose diffused light now made the room bright and clear.
>
> In the courtyard, I planted orchids, osmanthus, bamboo, and trees, and had the old fences restored and renovated. Then I borrowed books to fill up the shelves and would lie among them, humming or singing, or sit in a trance listening to the drone of nature. The courtyard was quiet; little birds flying in to pick up food were unperturbed by the sight of a human. On the fifteenth of the month, when half the garden wall was bathed in moonlight, the shadows of the osmanthus, cast in mottled patterns and swaying in the breeze, presented a charming picture.
>
> When I married five years later, my wife would come to the study to ask me questions about history or to lean on the desk and read. Returning from a visit with her parents, she told me what her little sister had asked her: 'They say there's a study in your house—what's a study?' My wife died six years later and the study again fell into disrepair. During the next two years I was often ill and, having nothing to do, had the place repaired again. It looked a little different from before. In the years that followed, however, I was often away from home and spent very little time in my old study. There is a loquat tree in the yard that was planted by my wife in the year she died. It has since grown very tall and spreads out into a vast canopy.

Although this is a pure description of scenes and narration of events, it has rich, lyrical undertones. The appearance of such writings heralded the end of orthodox classical literature. Prose writings of this kind, whether descriptions of nature, as in the writings of the Yuan brothers, or lyric-narratives, as in the works of Gui Youguang, are quite different from those of the Eight Masters of the Tang and Song,[18] from Liu Zongyuan's *Eight Sketches of Yongzhou* and Su Shi's first and second *Song of the Red Cliff*. In sentiment, mode of expression, and subject matter, the new prose possesses a more modern everyday flavour. It is closer to daily life and ordinary human feelings.

Of course, these changes manifested themselves in different ways among different writers, depending on their circumstances. For example, Tang Yin, who lived half a century before Li Zhi and was also an exemplar of the change of literary style, differed from Gui Youguang in many ways. Gui was a poor Confucian scholar, Tang, a gay, dashing man of talent. Gui wrote seriously in an orthodox style; Tang wandered about and sang of moonlight and flowers. This is why Wang Shizhen (1526–1590), a staunch advocate of a return to the style of the Qin-Han and prime Tang, admired Gui Youguang's writings but said of Tang Yin's prose and poems, 'They're like the cheap songs of a beggar seeking alms.' Nonetheless, Tang's all-around talent gave clear expression to the thoughts and feelings of the romantic era — to the modern voice that demanded freedom to express oneself and describe everyday life, and demanded reform of literary style and thematic emancipation as well. This was not an issue for just a few persons or a small group, nor was it a fleeting current. Rather, the incorporation of a modern sense of individual freedom was truly an epochal ideological shift.

Other examples of this ideological trend are the famous, now-classic novel *Journey to the West* by Wu Cheng'en and the drama *Peony Pavilion* by Tang Xianzu, both of the Ming Dynasty. *Journey to the West* was based on folk tales but under Wu Cheng'en's brush became an immortal work of romanticism. The great Monkey King—with his wit, dexterity, and indefatigable fighting spirit, his ability to create storms at sea and havoc in heaven, his humour, optimism, and sanguine disposition, and his power to change into any of 72 forms—became a unique artistic image which summed up all the characteristics of our folk heroes. Another unique character created by the novel is the stupid, good-natured, greedy, but lovable Pigsy, who is both ridiculed and liked by readers. *Journey to the West* has become a lasting model of Chinese children's literature and may well influence children's literature of other countries in the future. It is an anthology of wit, fun,

[18] Eight Masters of the Tang and Song: Han Yu and Liu Zongyuan of the Tang; Ouyang Xiu, Su Xun, Su Shi, Su Zhe, Wang Anshi, and Zeng Gong of the Song. All were first-rate prose writers.

and humour that resembles the art of 'comic dialogues' (Xiangsheng) of today, which entertain by their wordplay appealing to the understanding, rather than by exaggerated physical comedy. In this respect, Chinese romanticism retains vestiges of the tradition of classical rationalism.

Peony Pavilion is completely different from Journey to the West in form and content but similar to it in spirit and tone. Both are typical examples of Ming romantic literature. The author of Peony Pavilion was an admirer of Li Zhi, a friend of Xu Wei, and a supporter of the Yuan brothers.

In Peony Pavilion, the plot is based on human emotion, which is deliberately treated as the antithesis of reason. 'What does not accord with human reason may fully accord with human emotion,' writes the author in his preface to the book. This emotion is not confined to the love between a man and a woman. Although it tells of the fantastic return of a soul from the grave, Peony Pavilion took a further step than The Western Chamber: it echoes profoundly the voice of the times calling for changes. It is not a pure love story and Du Liniang, the heroine, was not restored to life just to be reunited with her lover. The message conveyed, unintentionally perhaps, was the spontaneous longing of a whole society for the dawn of a new epoch with joys and reunions instead of tragedies and separation.

The drama's language is flowery and full of vitality. That a story like this should become the strongest voice in the romantic trend of its day is because it called for the arrival of a modern world with individual freedom. But the call was so vehement that it went beyond the bounds of traditional realism and made the absurd death and resurrection of a human being the main thread of the plot, which in all other respects was normal and reasonable. The crudity of vernacular literature and the ways of the world as described in the previous section are here sublimated into refined but uninhibited romanticism. Thus, although different in form, both vernacular and romantic literature were reflections of social trends, moods, and atmosphere with their great upheavals that began in the mid-Ming.

From Sentimental Literature to A Dream of Red Mansions

Both vernacular literature and romanticism reached their prime in the last years of the Ming Dynasty. At this point, however, the budding of capitalism met with an unfortunate setback with the defeat of Li

Zicheng, leader of a peasant uprising at the end of the Ming. This resulted in the establishment of the Qing empire under the rule of the Manchus, a backward minority nationality that accepted and enforced conservative and reactionary political, economic, and cultural policies.

The modern elements were crushed at the very beginning of the new dynasty. Under the long rule of Manchu emperors, orthodox Confucian teachings that called for the consolidation of the small-scale, feudal peasant economy, suppression of commodity production, and a closed-door foreign policy again became the country's guidelines. Serious reversals occurred in the ideological, conceptual, and psychological domains, in art and literature, and in the whole social atmosphere.

In clear contrast to the break with tradition and the current of emancipation that had characterized the Ming, what now prevailed was a full-scale return to the ancients, accompanied by asceticism and bogus classicism. This affected the theme, style, and content of literary works. Vernacular literature not only ceased to develop but quite abruptly died away, and upper-class romanticism changed almost overnight into sentimental literature. Important and representative masterpieces of this new kind of literature are the dramas *Peach Blossom Fan* and *Palace of Eternal Youth* and the short story collection *Strange Tales from a Chinese Studio*.

Peach Blossom Fan,[19] by Kong Shangren, is a first-class drama from a literary point of view. The plot, arrangement of scenes, characterization, in-depth descriptions of life, and language are all superb. Although the love between the hero and heroine is the main thread of the story, the content and theme are not related only to love. Extreme grief over the loss of home and country also permeates the whole drama, but it goes even further. By telling the love story and describing the change of dynasty, the play reveals a feeling of emptiness that matches what we saw in Su Shi (see Chapter 8). This

[19] *Peach Blossom Fan* is a historical drama set in Nanjing, the southern capital of the Ming Dynasty, where remnants of the Ming imperial family fled when the Manchus overran north China. Though the plot centres on the love between Hou Fangyu, a scholar who later became a Qing official, and Li Xiangjun, a singsong girl of the Qinhuai region, it is a realistic portrayal of the sufferings of the people and the corruption of the Ming rulers as the dynasty neared its end. In the drama, Li Xiangjun is portrayed as a staunch patriot who refuses to entertain a tyrannical official and chastises her lover when she finds that he is serving the Qing invaders.

sentiment became latent after Su Shi, perhaps because of the material energy devoted to resisting the invasion of minority nationalities as in the time of the Southern Song poets Lu You and Xin Qiji, or because of hopes and longings for better times as in the romantic Ming. It is only when social progress meets with a serious setback, or when hopes already seen as capable of attainment are suddenly shattered, as in the Yuan Dynasty and early Qing, that pessimistic views of life acquire a truly deep and bitter meaning. With its focus on defeat and loss, *Peach Blossom Fan* reflects just such pessimism. Its theme is revealed in the epilogue, 'South of the River Lament':

> Peach blossoms in the grass of a mountain village;
> I raise my head and there's Moling[20] again:
> Forts deserted by a fleeing army,
> Horses dying in the empty moat,
> City walls in desolation,
> The city turned towards a sunset road.
>
> Wild fires continue to burn and smoke.
> Half-scorched catalpas shelter the graves;
> Mountain goats wander about in herds,
> When did the tomb guardians run away?
>
> Dove feathers and bat droppings are scattered all over,
> Dry leaves and withered branches cover the steps;
> Who will come to worship and sweep them away?
> The shepherd boy cracks the dragon slab.[21]
>
> . . . .
>
> Remember the half-*li* bridge that spanned the creek?
> Not a piece is left of the old red planks.
> Few care to cross the autumn waters neath the open sky;
> They shimmer there cold and lonely,
> A single willow bowing from the shore.
>
> I arrive at the old courtyard gate;
> No need to knock softly,
> No fear of barking dogs;
> Nothing but dried wells and empty nests,
> Nothing but moss on stone and grass on the steps.
> The flowers and willows I planted with my own hands
> Have been plucked and felled at random by others.
> The black soot here—whose kitchen stove is it?

[20] Moling, an ancient town, is now part of Nanjing.

[21] Shepherd boys come and go among the unguarded Ming emperors' tombs and try their knives on the stones—a sign of neglect.

I have heard the oriole greet the dawn in the jade palace of Jinling;
I have seen the waterside flowers bloom early at Qinhuai;[22]
But I never dreamed they would vanish like melted ice.
I have seen them[23] build vermilion palaces,
I have seen them feasting their guests,
And I have seen those same palaces crumble.
Where green moss and blue tiles in heaps now lie,
I once lived and enjoyed the pleasures of life,
And witnessed half a century of rise and fall.
The black-robe lane is no longer called Wang;[24]
Ghosts weep at night in Mochou Lake,
While owls roost in the phoenix tower.
But dreams of the past are ever real,
And scenes of old are hard to forget;
I cannot believe the face of this land will change.
Composing this lament to the southern country,
I shall sing in sorrow to the end of my days.

This is not only grief over home and country, but sorrow over life itself. Seas and mulberry fields will change into each other,[25] like a dream or an illusion, and towers and palaces sooner or later will crumble into dust. Remembering this, the author wonders what man's future will be and what the meaning of life is. He sees all these as mysteries that have no answers. And so, in the end, he seeks the life of a hermit, fisherman, or woodcutter, and the haven of the hills, streams, birds, and flowers.[26]

---

[22] Jinling is a historical name for Nanjing. Qinhuai is the Qinhuai River, a tributary of the Yangtze that flows through Nanjing city.

[23] 'Them' refers to former members of the Ming aristocracy in Nanjing, whose homes had been destroyed by war.

[24] 'Black-robe lane' was a wealthy district where the rich and powerful once lived. The line implies that the district now belongs to others.

[25] This is an old Chinese saying that means worldly things are subject to great changes.

[26] Kong Shangren (1648–1718), author of *Peach Blossom Fan*, was a 64th generation descendant of Confucius. He lived as a recluse on Stone Gate Hill in his native Qufu until Emperor Kangxi of the Qing, while on an inspection tour, summoned him from his retreat to teach the Confucian classics. He was made *aboshi* (the equivalent of a modern doctor) of the Guozijian, the highest institute of learning in the land from the Sui to the Qing Dynasty. This title was seldom conferred on a Han national in those days. For the next ten years or so, he served in various official posts of the Qing government. Eventually, he was dismissed on some pretext and retired again to the seclusion of his hometown.

Palace of Eternal Youth, also a drama and written at about the same time as *Peach Blossom Fan*, conveys a similar message, though its main theme has been subject to debate and dispute. Some say it is the love between Yang and Li, the hero and heroine; others assert that it tells mainly of the destiny of a family and dynasty; still others see it as a clandestine attack on the Qing regime. But the true theme—the drama's keynote and the core of its aesthetic appeal—is the same emptiness in life we find in *Peach Blossom Fan*. This feeling, which represents the ideological trend and sentiment of a whole epoch, manifests itself clearly in the drama, even though it may not be consciously stressed.

Because of its social and historical content, this general feeling of emptiness in life appeared even in the songs of Nalan Xingde (1655–1685), a man who seemed to have every reason to be content with life. He was a Manchu national by birth, a scion of the ruling imperial family, a member of the aristocracy, and a poet who had achieved fame, wealth, and honour early in life. He certainly had no cause to mourn the loss of home and country, or to rue the day he was born, yet his writings are very bitter and sorrowful:

A spell of wind, a spell of snow;
My thoughts of home are shattered,
    I cannot dream;
There were never such sounds in the old garden,
    Never, it seems.

. . . .

Returning home in my dreams, I am stopped by a river,
Whose roars shatter my dream.
Sleep again, sleep again—
It's dull to be awake.

Who cares to read the mournful songs of *Yuefu*?
The wind soughs and the rain sighs,
The candle burns out and another night passes.
Don't know what it is that obsesses the mind;
Cannot sleep, cannot drink,
Cannot come to the lonely bridge even in a dream.

Perhaps no *ci*-poet since the Northern Song was Nalan Xingde's equal in artistic achievement. His sorrow, weariness of life, and boredom with the world, though expressed lightly, weighed heavily on him. 'Don't know what it is that obsesses the mind.' It may be more correct, in his case, to say that although he had no real troubles or worries, he could not help feeling the chill of an oncoming storm and sought to escape in sleep from gloom, boredom, and anxiety. Wealth and honour could offer no relief to his dreadful world-weariness and mental void. His was the mood of a person living in an era and society where there was no apparent struggle or agitation—but no prospects either, a person whose destiny was linked to a society that appeared prosperous but was actually in decline. Just as the fall of leaves signals the approach of autumn and winter, so do the despairing sighs of sensitive artists and writers, while still living in peace, plenty, and even extravagance, herald the storm long before it arrives. In a certain sense, Wang Shizhen's[27] theory of 'spirit' in poetry, widely accepted as an aesthetic theory in his day, was also a reflection of the undercurrent of pessimism of this historical period.

The aesthetic quality of Pu Songling's[28] collection of short stories of the fantastic, *Strange Tales from a Chinese Studio*, not to mention the lyric songs of Gui Zhuang (1613–1673), should also be studied in the context of the sentimental literature of the period. *Strange Tales* was written in a refined and classic style, the opposite of the vernacular literature of the Ming. The contents and features of the stories also differ from the depiction of worldly life in vernacular literature. What is worth noting in these fantastic accounts of ghosts and fox spirits is their sentimental strain. As we read in the second postscript to the book: 'Examining the stories and their implied meaning, why is it that eight or nine out of every ten are so deeply immersed in sorrow?' The author himself says of his book, 'Written while drunk, it is only an account of solitary resentment. Sad enough if such feelings can only be vented in this way' (*Author's Notes on the Strange Tales*).

The stories of life and death and fox spirits in *Strange Tales* did not have the comic aura of *Peony Pavilion*; they were tragedies whose beauty lay in their profound but unconsciously wrought sentimentality. But it was not merely a personal hatred of the world and its ways that

---

[27] Wang Shizhen (1634–1711) was a poet and literary critic of the early Qing. His theory of poetry, called *shenyun* (spirit-rhythm), stressed a plain, simple, and leisurely style. In effect, it diverted the attention of poets from social problems to the trivialities of life and the carefree ways of the scholar-officials. His own writings were mostly descriptions of ideal landscapes, the wind and moon, everyday life, and human passions.

[28] Pu Songling (1640–1751) was a native of Zichuan, Shandong Province. He failed to pass the provincial civil service examinations and, except for a short period as secretary to an official in Baoying, spent almost his whole life as a private tutor in his hometown.

caused the author to write in this way. While the sorrow he displayed may have been linked to his own failings—failure to pass the civil service examinations and win fame and honour—which condemned him to live and die in poverty, objectively his sentimentality echoed the mood of the times. His hopes and feelings could only repose in imaginary things because life was so empty and its goals so chimerical: his fantasies seemed all the more wonderful because reality was so dreary and uneventful.

Sentimental dramas and fiction like *Peach Blossom Fan*, *Palace of Eternal Youth*, and *Strange Tales from a Chinese Studio* differ from *Peony Pavilion* and *The Western Chamber* in another respect: they possess elements of criticism of real history, which is often far more distressing than fiction. Presumably this is because the authors were recalling their own painful experiences or, dissatisfied with reality, wanted to expose and satirize the social life they knew. This led inevitably to critical realism, the next stage of the ideological trend in Ming-Qing literature.

Romanticism, sentimentality, and critical realism, the three stages of this ideological trend, represent a complete and logical process. The third stage appeared during the reign of Emperor Qianlong, who ruled from 1736 to 1796, and was already far removed from the era of romanticism. Chinese society was at this time in the throes of the disorderly death-struggle of feudal rule. The 'return to the ancients' doctrine had been a disaster; the great ideals of democracy and nationalism of the late Ming and early Qing had disappeared. *Kaoju*,[29] a kind of muddled textual research, became the dominant branch of learning. The state of mind of the literati at this time can be seen in the following lines by Gong Zizhen (1792–1841):

They vacated their seats for fear of literary persecution;[30]
They wrote books only so that they might live.

[29] *Kaoju* was a method of studying ancient writings. It consisted of textual criticism and collation, exposition of the ancient meanings of words, and the accumulation and presentation of data and materials for research. It began in the Qing Dynasty and was most popular during the reigns of Emperors Qianlong and Jiaqing.

[30] The implied meaning of this line is that people gave up their posts and went into hiding for fear of being persecuted for something they had written. This kind of persecution, which was very common during the early Qing Dynasty and was directed towards intellectuals, was called *wenzi yu* (literally, 'literature jail'). It refers to the practice of jailing or executing people on the pretext that they had used literature to make veiled attacks on the emperor or the imperial court.

It was indeed an era of darkness, in which even an independent thinker like Dai Zhen (1724–1777) was known only for his *kaoju* and was not understood or appreciated for his real worth. What he regarded as his most important philosophical work, *A Commentary on the Textual Meaning of 'Mencius'*, in which he strongly condemned Neo-Confucianism, was misunderstood and rejected even by his own son.

Those were the last days of feudalism, a long period of darkness that enshrouded eighteenth-century China, during which Chinese civilization fell far behind that of Europe. In the realm of literature, however, it gave birth to China's most prized novel, *A Dream of Red Mansions*, which may well be regarded as a summary of social conditions in China as feudalism neared its end. However much has already been said about this novel by both critics and readers, much more may still be said. It is therefore unnecessary and impractical in a book like this to discuss at length this most beautiful flower of Chinese literature. Suffice it to say that no other Chinese novel can compare to it in making sublime the trend of sentimentality that was so deeply entrenched in the society of its day. It is this sentimentality that makes *A Dream of Red Mansions* so brilliant. Was it not sorrow and despair, often misty like dreams but at times agitated like strings and winds played presto, that loomed over the tragic love of Jia Baoyu and Lin Daiyu, the hero and heroine? Was it not sorrow and despair that clouded the extravagant visit to her relatives of the emperor's concubine Yuanchun, Jia Baoyu's elder sister, and prophesied political misfortune accompanied by great suffering?

This novel was a clear depiction of the illusoriness of life and its goals. Though the reigns of Emperors Kangxi and Qianlong have been extolled as eras of prosperity, they were little more than the embers of a dying system that was collapsing beyond recovery, passing quietly and unknowingly but in the midst of splendour, songs and laughter, bells and tripods, gold and jade. The system was gold and jade without, corruption and debauchery within. Conditions were therefore ripe for the emergence of critical realism with all the severity that could be mustered:

> In sharp contrast to the envious longing for fame, riches, and honour that characterized the realism of vernacular art and literature, what prevailed now was a strong repudiation and condemnation of such things. This came from members of one's own class, who had fully experienced the hardships of the world and knew well its ways. As a result, creative writing at this point attained a brilliance that rivaled the

critical realism of 19th century Western bourgeoisie. But it was also
mournful, like an elegy, without hopes, without revolutionary ideals. . . .
(Li Zehou: 'Aesthetic Awareness and Creative Writing',
Scholastic Studies, No. 6, 1963).

In *The Scholars*,[31] hopes and ideals were reposed in a few pale-
faced scholars and hermits. But in *A Dream of Red Mansions* the
author's only recourse was to have his hero, Jia Baoyu, enter a
monastery, where he finds solace in pondering the illusoriness of
worldly things. This is only a continuation and development of what
has been summed up in *Peach Blossom Fan* as the fisherman and
woodcutter's[32] illusory views of life. Jia Baoyu's grief, anguish, and
groping are those of a man who has awakened from a dream to find all
his hopes and ambitions gone. The aesthetic value of the novel,
however, lies not only in its expressions of sorrow but also in its
realistic descriptions, exposure, and criticism of social life. It is this that
has made *A Dream of Red Mansions* an encyclopedic record of the last
days of feudalism and a novel of lasting enjoyment. In the words of one
critic of vernacular literature, 'The divergencies in human relations and
world affairs are described minutely; the joys and sorrows, meetings
and partings of life are narrated in full.' It differs from the vernacular
literature of the Ming in that it was a novel of upper-class scholar-
officials, yet its description of worldly life and human relations far
surpasses that of Ming writings.

Painting and the Arts and Crafts

In the preceding sections we discussed literature and drama. A similar
ideological trend, though it manifested itself differently, appeared as
well in painting, a realm dominated by scholar-officials and the
literati.

Coinciding with the literary trend of the mid-Ming was a trend in
painting represented by Qiu Ying, an illustrious exponent of the
academy style of blue-green landscape, and by Shen Zhou
(1426–1509), Wen Zhengming (1470–1559), and Tang Yin

---

[31] *The Scholars*, by Wu Jingzi (1701–1754), another famous novel of the Qing
Dynasty, describes the greed and hypocrisy of various types of learned men
and ridicules feudal ethics and the civil service examinations.

[32] Fisherman and woodcutter were representations of the common people in
traditional Chinese painting (see Chapter 9).

(1465–1523), leading figures of the Wu school.[33] The trend was towards greater proximity with worldly life through depicting everyday subjects; the style was characterized by free, uninhibited brushwork, fine lines, and delicate figures. This trend paralleled the vernacular and romantic stages in literature.

Qiu Ying (?–1510), a man of humble beginnings, was a leading painter south of the Yangtze for some 20 years. He excelled in figures and landscapes, but is best known for his depictions of historical tales. Some examples are 'Feasting in the Peach and Plum Garden on a Spring Night' and 'Emperor Gaozu of the Han Entering the Pass.' His paintings are orderly in appearance and delicate in style, and while he was not frugal in his use of colours, there is no garishness in his works. Even Dong Qichang, an unsparing critic of the academy style and blue-green landscape, had to acknowledge his superiority as a painter. Qiu Ying represents a style of painting that corresponded to vernacular literature.

Shen Zhou, Wen Zhengming, and Tang Yin were active around the city of Suzhou, on the lower reaches of the Yangtze. As scholars and men of letters without official posts, they were free and easy in their ways, showing little restraint in their conduct, thinking, and feelings. They had ties with people from many social strata and freely expressed their outlook on the world. Their ideal in art was the seeking of spirit, rhythm, and vitality with brush and ink.

The late Ming and early Qing during the seventeenth century, periods of much suffering because of invasion and conquests by ethnic minorities from the northeast, saw painting enter a new stage represented by artists like Zhu Da (also known as the Bada Shanren, or the Bada Hermit) and Shi Tao (alias Dao Ji). Their style was in marked contrast to the orderliness and subtlety that characterized the earlier Wu school; it was a revival and development of Xu Wei's style of simple composition, prominent images, peculiar scenes, and vigorous brushwork. The works of these painters had a strong impact in their day because they were clear expressions of sorrow and indignation. They corresponded to the sentimental stage in literature.

Most typical are Zhu Da's paintings, with their distinctive signature made up of the four characters that mean 'the Bada Hermit' but purposely written to resemble both the character for smiling and that for weeping. Zhu Da's proud, aloof, and exaggerated images, wide-eyed peacocks and

---

[33] This is a famous school of painting of the mid- and late Ming. Its chief exponents were active in the lower reaches of the Yangtze, a region historically called Wu.

'Lotus and Water Bird',
painting by Zhu Da, late
Ming or early Qing Dynasty.

kingfishers, strange-looking plantains, grotesque rocks, ducks on a spit, wild geese among reeds, and calligraphy that breaks with established patterns attract attention because of their fantastic appearance and reveal a violent passion and agitation. But they cannot disguise the deep-seated isolation, loneliness, sorrow, and regret just under the surface. Trees, flowers, birds, and beasts were but symbols or transmutations of the artist's feelings. On the whole, what was expressed was a human character defiant but weighed down with sorrow.

Shi Tao's paintings reflect the same spirit. His book *Hua Yulu* (*Quotes on Painting*) is perhaps the standard work on aesthetics of this period. He writes: 'The painter is guided by his heart [feelings]' and 'the mountains and rivers ask me to speak for them. . . . They have given me ideas that I must turn into form.' And so he stresses that the objective must be subordinated to the subjective and, emotionally, the artist must be one with the world. Like Zhu Da's, his paintings express loneliness, sorrow, and indignation.

In painting, what corresponded roughly to the third stage, critical realism, in literature was rather an upgraded sentimentalism represented by the flower-and-bird paintings of the Eight Eccentrics of Yangzhou. This southern school of painting, which appeared during the so-called 'golden age of Emperors Qianlong and Jiaqing', during the eighteenth and early nineteenth centuries, inherited the traditions of Zhu Da and Shi Tao. In fact, its style could be traced further back to Xu Wei, the greatest romantic painter of the Ming.

Regret and indignation over the times had gradually died away or at least diminished in intensity, but individuality had come to the fore. Artists began to cultivate their own unique brushwork, composition, colouring, and imagery, rough or refined, bold or constrained, which helped push Chinese painting towards modern styles. This development was associated with a vogue in calligraphy that abandoned the copybook but revered the northern stele.[34] What artists stressed was aggressiveness, vigour, primitive crudeness, and the expression of inordinately violent individual feelings through extremely simple imagery. Brush and ink skills became the core of painting, and while realistic imagery was not totally abandoned, it was transcended, giving brush and ink and the way

[34] The 'copybook' and the 'northern stele' represented two styles of handwriting of the Qing Dynasty. The handwriting in copybooks, also called model handwriting, was in an elegant and leisurely style. It was practised mostly by scholars in the south. Inscriptions on steles were characterized by simplicity, vigour, and a primitive crudeness. As exponents of this style were largely northerners, it was called the northern stele style. At the stage of history we are discussing, the northern stele style was more popular.

these are used an independent aesthetic value. The qualities of brush and ink, not the object depicted, became the 'significant form' that evoked aesthetic emotion.

Flower-and-bird paintings of the third stage possessed a strong flavour of modern abstractionism. This is why they have become so popular among Chinese in the modern era and have continued to develop. Exponents of this style of painting, like Zheng Banqiao, Jin Dongxin, Li Xian, and Luo Pin, blazed the trail for the modern greats Ren Bonian, Wu Changshuo, Qi Baishi, Pan Tianshou, and Liu Haisu,[35] just as *The Scholars* and *A Dream of Red Mansions* were the torchbearers of late Qing fiction. The use of theme, subject, brush, and ink to express moods and feelings in painting is similar to critical realism in literature in that it was, consciously or unconsciously, an exposure and repudiation of the dark reactionary rule and a voice of individuality in this historical period. On the one hand, paintings of this genre, of which Zheng Banqiao's 'Ink Bamboo' is a typical example, may be regarded as expressions of Ming romanticism and Ming-Qing sentimentalism; on the other, they reflect the spirit of resistance—the refusal to accept dark social realities—which characterized critical realism.

These trends in art and literature were not merely the result of coincidence or the doings of one or two individuals. There was a social and ideological logic in them, which should be grasped as a whole because it is crucial to understanding and appreciating the art and literature of the Ming-Qing. Even Yuan Mei's[36] attitude towards the orthodox literature of his day—his emphasis on free emotional expression, opposition to inhibitions and traditions, repudiation of Neo-Confucianism, and ridicule of pseudo-Confucianists—showed certain signs of ideological emancipation and accorded with this same logic in history. Thus, art and literature as a whole mirrored the existing state of feudalism, which was by then only a shell. They echoed the voices of this dying system and showed that modern hopes for freedom, individuality, and emancipation were already visible on the horizon. Such hopes appeared, gradually but distinctly, during and after the

[35] Zheng Banqiao (1693–1765), Jin Dongxin (1687–1764), Li Xian (1686–1762), Luo Pin (1733–1799), painters of the early and mid-Qing. Ren Bonian (1840–1896), painter of the late Qing. Wu Changshuo (1844–1927), Qi Baishi (1863–1957), Pan Tianshou (1898–1971), Liu Haisu (1896–   ), modern painters.

[36] Yuan Mei (1716–1798), poet of the Qing Dynasty, was noted for his opposition to the so-called 'Teachings of the Book of Songs' espoused by the Confucian school. In some of his works, he attacked both Han and Ming-Qing Confucianism, even calling the Six Classics 'rubbish.'

Opium War, notably in the philosophies of men like Gong Zizhen and Su Manshu.[37]

Unlike literature, drama, and painting, architecture saw little development during the Ming and Qing except in landscape architecture and interior design. Sculpture, too, had passed its zenith and was on the decline, as is shown when stone lions sculpted in different dynasties are compared: the sculptures of the Han are heavy and bulky, those of the Six Dynasties are light and gay, and those of the Tang are round and detailed—but those of the Ming and Qing are tame, like domestic cats. Music and dancing had been incorporated into drama and were no longer independent genres.

Only the arts and crafts still deserve mention. Ming-Qing minor arts and crafts, because they were directly related to large-scale commodity production (for example, production for export) and to manual skill, saw some development as capitalist elements appeared in society. But influenced and to some extent manipulated by commodity production and market values, their aesthetic quality, designed both for the enjoyment of the upper classes and to serve the needs of the merchants and townspeople, did not follow the ideological trend of painting and literature. Rather, it developed in the opposite direction.

Nevertheless, because of improved skills and techniques, the minor arts and crafts of the Ming-Qing, especially coloured porcelain, copper enamelware, furniture, embroidery, and textiles, possessed a fineness, richness, delicacy, and sophistication comparable to the European rococo style. Ceramics reached their zenith in the Ming-Qing. The new 'blue-flowered,' dou-coloured,'[38] and 'multi-coloured' products of the mid-Ming and the enamelled and opaque articles of the Qing were increasingly refined and ornate. This was very different from the luxurious, exotic style of Tang porcelain and the monochromatic products of the Song. Ming-Qing arts and crafts were similar in style to the vernacular literature of the Ming, but there were no three stages of development.

---

[37] Gong Zizhen (1792–1841) was a brave thinker of the Qing Dynasty. He maintained that all things on earth are in a process of change, denying that any law, custom, system, or institution can be permanent. Su Manshu (1884–1918) was a man of letters of the late Qing. He was a member of the progressive literary organization called Southern Society that was formed before the Xinhai Revolution of 1911. Besides writing poems and stories, he translated into Chinese the works of Byron, Hugo, and other Western authors.

[38] Dou-coloured refers to a kind of porcelain decoration, of which there are two varieties: one consists of an underglaze of blue flowers and a multicoloured overglaze; the other, of a design of blue flowers, pea green and underglaze red.

Afterword

We have come to the end of our examination of China's classical art and literature. So quickly have we gone through the subject, it was hardly possible to examine any part in detail. We hope, however, that impressions gained from this bird's-eye view, though necessarily general, are not vague.

The unbalanced development of different branches of art may cause one to wonder if examinations like this one are practical or worthwhile. Apparent inconsistencies in their development when compared to that of a country's economy and politics also make one question if there is any connection between art and social conditions. Is it possible to find any general or universal laws governing the development of art and literature—fields of endeavour that can flourish in times of human suffering and social difficulties and deteriorate amid political and economic prosperity? Distinctly different and mutually opposed artistic styles and aesthetic schools can exist in the same historical period and within the same society and social class—indeed, such phenomena are common. What then is the likelihood of an objective law?

Some critics object to the search for laws in art and literature, but we do not concur. As we see it, the apparent inconsistencies mentioned above suggest only that the question is a difficult one and, to deal with it, a thorough study must be made of all related historical and social conditions. But if we believe that humanity and material civilization, as a whole, are moving forward rather than backward and that in the final analysis ideology and culture are determined—though not directly—by economic life, then there must be some law independent of people's will that acts upon art, literature, and the whole realm of culture. It may act in an intricate way and through diverse channels, but it does not act haphazardly.

To quote a few examples, arts and crafts, architecture, and other branches of the arts that are directly related to material production will flourish in times of political stability and economic prosperity, just as science and technology generally do. On the other hand, some branches of art, such as literature and Chinese painting, may prosper in a turbulent society when life is hard, for they are less dependent on material wealth and often are excellent weapons for combating social injustices. In this respect they are like speculative philosophy, which also develops more rapidly in times of adversity because its task is to explore and study the future, a subject of little general interest in times of peace and plenty, when people are too engrossed in material pleasures to seek spiritual comfort and enlightenment in things to come. Thus, if we believe in cause and effect, if we explore the question historically and realistically, we must conclude that there is some innate logic in the existence and development of art and literature. And, consequently, a general survey over the historical path of beauty may be a task worth doing.

A question that may be of still greater interest is why the art and literature of eras so remote from ours should continue to influence and stimulate the world of today, and even tomorrow. Why do people already on the threshold of the twenty-first century constantly reflect upon and find pleasure in relics worn with age? If the question about the law of development of art and literature is a difficult one, having to do with the sociology of art, this second question is an even more difficult one of the psychology of aesthetics. What is the key to understanding the mystery of the eternal nature of art?

On the one hand, every historical period should have its own creations. As N.G. Chernyshevski (1828–1889), the Russian literary and social critic put it, even Shakespeare cannot be a substitute for modern works. The constant creation of new works is the only way in which art can move forward, like a stream of many colours with an ever-changing appearance. On the other hand, this gives rise to the question of the unity and perpetuation of art. Why is it that the aesthetic value and artistic style of works of long ago still accord with the sentiments and interests of people of our time? Why do they still evoke such intimate feelings in us? Is it that the sentiments accumulated and condensed in them are related to and act upon the psychological structure of people today? Is the human psychological structure a product of the accumulation and condensation of historical experience? If so, the secret of the eternal nature of art may reside therein. Or, it may be the other way round—that is, the universal human psychology resides in and is promoted by the eternal nature of art. Just as production promotes consumption and consumption, in turn, promotes production, so may humanity's psychological structure create the eternity of art and the eternity of art, in turn, create and give expression to a common psychological structure that is of a social character and is passed down through the ages.

However, human psychology and art are not immutable; neither are they transitory and elusive. They cannot be mysterious collective prototypes, nor should they be 'superegos' and 'ids.' Psychological structure is a product of the sedimentation of human history and civilization; art is the psychology that reveals the soul of the times. Maybe this can explain human nature as related to art.

In other words, human nature is not a dispensation of the gods, nor is it bestiality seeking only gratification of sensory needs. It blends emotion with rationality, individuality with social conscience, awareness and feeling with imagination and understanding. We might say it is the sedimentation of rationality in emotion, of imagination and understanding in awareness and feeling, of content in form. It is a very complicated mathematical formula in aesthetic psychology that has yet to be worked out. Its objectivized product, manifested in works of art, is what we discussed in Chapter 1 on primitive art—*significant* form, or form in which spiritual freedom and beauty are crystallized.

'All are past and gone' (as one line from the poem 'Snow', by Mao Zedong, reads), but the path of beauty is looking forward to the future.

Index